INTERMEDIATE WORKBOOK

THE OXFORD
Picture
Dictionary

Canadian Edition

MARJORIE FUCHS AND MARGARET BONNER

Canadian Adaptation by Maggie Grennan

OXFORD
UNIVERSITY PRESS

OXFORD

UNIVERSITY PRESS

70 Wynford Drive, Don Mills, Ontario, M3C 1J9 Canada
198 Madison Avenue, New York, NY 10016 USA
Great Clarendon Street, Oxford OX2 6DP England

Oxford New York
Athens Auckland Bangkok Bogota Buenos Aires
Calcutta Cape Town Chennai Dar es Salaam Delhi
Florence Hong Kong Istanbul Karachi Kuala Lumpur
Madrid Melbourne Mexico City Mumbai Nairobi Paris
São Paulo Singapore Taipei Tokyo Toronto Warsaw

and associated companies in
Berlin Ibadan

OXFORD is a trademark of Oxford University Press.

ISBN 0-19-541469-1

Copyright © 1999 Oxford University Press

No unauthorized photocopying.

Canadian Cataloguing in Publication Data

Fuchs, Marjorie, 1949-
  The Oxford picture dictionary, Canadian edition. Intermediate workbook

ISBN 0-19-541469-1

1. Picture dictionaries, English – Problems, exercises, etc.
2. English language – Textbooks for second language learners.*
I. Bonner, Margaret. II. Grennan, Maggie, 1956- . III. Shapiro, Norma. Oxford picture dictionary: monolingual. IV. Title.

PE1629.S49 1999 Suppl. 2   423'.1   C98-933045-1

Editorial Manager: Susan Lanzano
Editors: Lynne Barsky/Julie Landau/P. O'Neill
Associate Production Editor: Tareth Mitch
Art Director: Lynn Luchetti
Design Project Manager: Susan Brorein
Design and Page Makeup: Keithley and Associates
Art Buyer: Tracy Hammond
Cover Design Production: Brett Sonnenschein
Picture Researcher: Clare Maxwell
Production Manager: Abram Hall
Production Controller: Georgiann Baran
Cover design by Silver Editions

Printing (last digit): 10 9 8 7 6 5 4 3 2 1

Printed in Canada.

Illustrations, realia, and handwriting by: Gary Antonetti/Ortelius Design, Craig Attebery, Eliot Bergman, Annie Bissett, Daniel J. Brown/Artworks NY, Rob Burman, Carlos Castellanos, Mary Chandler, Jack Crane/Averil Smith, Dominick D'Andrea, Jim DeLapine, Maj-Britt Hagsted, Pamela Johnson, Claudia C. Kehrhahn, Keithley and Associates, Mohammad Mansoor, Karen Minot, Kristin Mount, Conrad Represents/Max Seabaugh, Stacey Schuett, Carol L. Strebel, Anna Veltfort, Nina Wallace/ Averil Smith, Wendy Wassink Ackison

The publishers would like to thank the following for their permission to reproduce photographs: M. Angelo/Westlight; Bruce Ayres/Tony Stone Images; Sandra Baker/Liaison International; Bie Bostrom; Rick Brady/Uniphoto; Mark Burnett/Photo Researchers; Ken Cavanagh/Photo Researchers; Junebug Clark/Photo Researchers; W. Cody/Westlight; Laima Druskis/Photo Researchers; Michael Goldman/FPG; Mark E. Harris © *Life* Magazine © Time Warner, Inc.; Jeff Hunter/The Image Bank; Helen Marcus/Photo Researchers; Patti McConnville/The Image Bank; Kunio Owaki/The Stock Market; Juan Manuel Renjifo/Animals Animals; Jon Reily/Tony Stone Images; Don Smetzer/Tony Stone Images; Vince Streano/Tony Stone Images; Superstock; Telegraph Color Library/FPG; Camille Tokerud/Photo Researchers

The publishers would also like to thank the following for their help:
p. 121: Microsoft® Word and Microsoft® Excel are either registered trademarks or trademarks of Microsoft Corporation in the United States and/or other countries.

Acknowledgements

The publisher and authors would like to thank the following people for reviewing the manuscript as the book was being developed:

Glenda Adamson, Lubie G. Alatriste, Leor Alcalay, Fiona Armstrong, Jean Barlow, Margrajean Bonilla, Susan Burke, Becky Carle, Analee Doney, Michele Epstein, Christine Evans, Lynn A. Freeland, Carole Goodman, Joyce Grabowski, Kelly Gutierrez, Christine Hill, Leann Howard, Hilary Jarvis, Nanette Kafka, Cliff Ker, Margaret Lombard, Carol S. McLain, Monica Miele, Patsy Mills, Debra L. Mullins, Barbara Jane Pers, Marianne Riggiola, Virginia Robbins, Linda Susan Robinson, Michele Rodgers-Amini, Maria Salinas, Jimmy E. Sandifer, Jeffrey Scofield, Ann Silverman, Susan A. Slavin, Peggy Stubbs, Lynn Sweeden, Christine Tierney.

In addition, the authors would like to thank the following people:

Susan Lanzano, Editorial Manager, for overseeing a huge and complex project of which the *Workbooks* were just a part. She orchestrated the entire project without losing sight of the individual components.

Our editors for their hard work and dedication. Lynne Barsky carried out the important initial research and helped develop the manuscript. Julie Landau took over and made further refinements. Patricia O'Neill carefully and thoughtfully examined the pages and art, checking each comma, space, word, and fact for accuracy. Tareth Mitch scrutinized pages and art, making insightful queries and suggestions. We appreciate the unique contributions of all of these people.

Norma Shapiro and Jayme Adelson-Goldstein, authors of the *Dictionary*, and Shirley Brod, editor of the *Teacher's Book*, for meticulously reviewing the manuscript and offering particularly helpful feedback and enthusiastic support.

Eliza Jensen and Amy Cooper, Senior Editors, for looking at the manuscript at important junctures and offering sage advice.

The design team for making us feel welcome at their meetings, and for giving us the chance to see the huge amount of work and creativity they put into the project long after the manuscript had been submitted.

Luke Frances for always being himself. His honesty, spontaneity, and humour make creativity happen.

Rick Smith, as always, for his unswerving support and for his insightful comments on all aspects of the project. Once again, he proved himself to be equally at home in the world of numbers and the world of words.

To the Teacher

The *Intermediate Workbook* and *Beginning Workbook* that accompany *The Oxford Picture Dictionary, Canadian Edition,* have been designed to provide meaningful and enjoyable practice of the vocabulary that students are learning. At the same time, the workbooks supply high-interest contexts and real information for enrichment and self-expression.

Both *Workbooks* conveniently correspond page-for-page to the 140 topics of the *Picture Dictionary*. For example, if you are working on page 22 in the *Dictionary*, the activities for this topic, Age and Physical Description, will be found on page 22 in the *Workbook*.

All topics in the *Intermediate Workbook* follow the same easy-to-use format. Exercise 1 is always a "look in your dictionary" activity where students are asked to complete a task while looking in their *Picture Dictionary*. The tasks include judging statements true or false, correcting false statements, completing charts and forms, speculating about who said what, categorizing, odd one out, and pronoun reference activities where students replace pronouns with the vocabulary items they refer to.

Following this activity are one or more content-rich contextualized exercises, including multiple choice, quizzes and tests, describing picture differences, and the completion of forms, reports, letters, articles, and stories. These exercises often feature graphs and charts with real data for students to work with as they practise the new vocabulary. Many topics include a personalization exercise that asks "What about you?" where students can use the vocabulary to give information about their own lives or to express their opinions.

The final exercise for each topic is a "Challenge" which can be assigned to students for additional work in class or as homework. Challenge activities provide higher level speaking and writing practice, and for some topics will require students to interview classmates, conduct surveys, or find information outside of class. For example on pages 28–29, the Challenge for the topic Life Events asks students to look up biographical information about a famous person, draw a timeline, and write a paragraph about that person's life.

Each of the 12 units ends with "Another Look," a review which allows students to practise vocabulary from all of the topics of a unit in activities such as picture comparisons, "What's wrong with this picture?" activities, photo essays, word maps, word searches, and crossword puzzles. These activities are at the back of the *Intermediate Workbook,* on pages 170–181.

Throughout both the *Intermediate* and *Beginning Workbooks,* vocabulary is carefully controlled and recycled. Students should, however, be encouraged to use their *Picture Dictionaries* to look up words they do not recall, or, if they are doing topics out of sequence, may not yet have learned.

The *Oxford Picture Dictionary Workbooks* can be used in the classroom or at home for self-study. An *Answer Key* is included at the back of both *Workbooks*.

We hope you and your students enjoy using these workbooks as much as we have enjoyed writing them.

M.F. and M.B.

To the Student

The *Oxford Picture Dictionary, Canadian Edition,* has more than 3700 words. This workbook will help you use them in your daily life.

• It's easy to use! The *Workbook* pages match the pages in your *Picture Dictionary*. For example, to practise the words on page 22 in your *Picture Dictionary*, go to page 22 in your *Workbook*.

• It has exercises you will enjoy. Some exercises show real information; for example, a chart showing the top ten fast foods; a bar graph comparing how long different animals live. Another exercise, "What about you?," gives you a chance to use your own information. You'll find stories, puzzles, and conversations, too.

At the end of each topic there is a Challenge, a chance to use your new vocabulary more independently. And finally, every unit has a one-page summary, called Another Look, in a section at the back of the book. This is a puzzle activity or a picture composition that practises the vocabulary from an entire unit.

Learning new words is both challenging and fun. We had a lot of fun writing this workbook. We hope you enjoy using it!

M.F. and M.B.

Contents

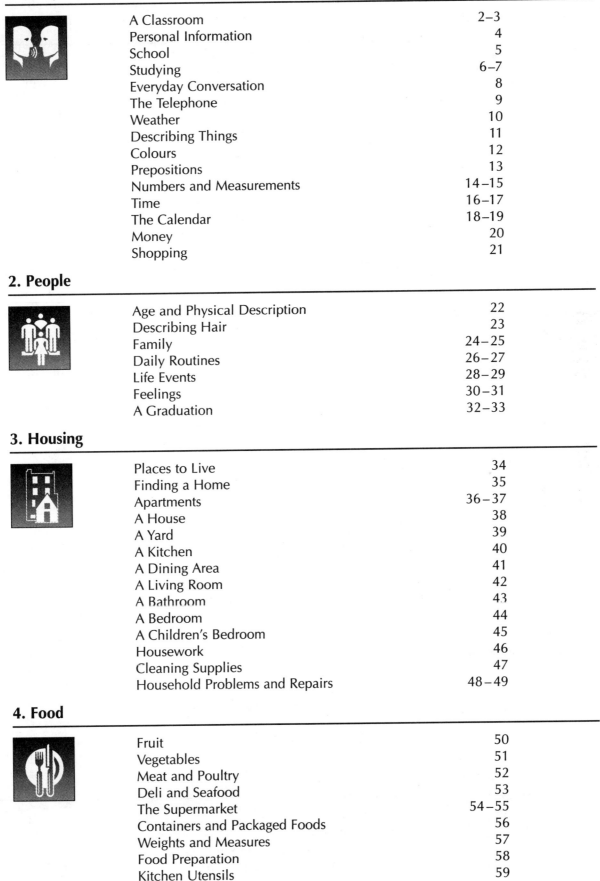

Contents

Contents

A Classroom

1. Look in your dictionary. **True** or **False**? Correct the underlined words in the false sentences.

       talking
   a. **Picture B:** The student is ~~listening~~ to the teacher.   _____False_____

   b. **Picture C:** The student is <u>pointing</u> to a cassette.   _____

   c. **Picture E:** The student is <u>sitting down</u>.   _____

   d. **Picture H:** The woman is <u>writing on</u> the board.   _____

   e. **Picture I:** The man is <u>closing</u> his book.   _____

   f. **Picture L:** The student is <u>putting away</u> a pencil.   _____

2. Complete the instruction sheets. Use your own information and the words in the box.

close	pencil	listen	notebook	erase	~~open~~	write	point

   Name: _____   Date: _____

                                                             Class: _____

   Instructions:

   1. _____*Open*_____ your picture dictionary to page 91. _____ to the cassette. When
              a.   **b.**

      you hear a word, _____ to the picture.
                                    c.

   2. _____ your book. Listen again and _____ each word in your _____.
              d.   **e.**   **f.**

      Use a _____. Do not use a pen. If you make a mistake, _____ it.
             g.   **h.**

   ---

look at	screen	stand up	talk to

   Directions:

   1. _____ and find a partner.
      i.

   2. _____ the picture on the _____.
      j.   **k.**

   3. _____ your partner about the picture.
      l.

3. Complete the classroom inventory. Write how many of each item. (*Hint:* The items are in alphabetical order.) Add another item for **l.**

Classroom Inventory—Room 304

NUMBER	ITEM	NUMBER	ITEM
a. 1	bookcase	**g.**	computers
b. 0	bulletin boards	**h.** 2	
c.	cassette players	**i.**	markers
d. 1		**j.**	overhead projectors
e.	chalkboard erasers	**k.** 2	
f.	clocks	**l.**	

4. Write about the items that are in Room 304 and the items that are not. Use your own paper.

Examples: *There's one bookcase. There aren't any bulletin boards. There are three cassette players.*

5. What about you? Do an inventory of your classroom or office. Use your own paper.

Challenge Describe the ideal classroom. What does it have? How many of each item?

Personal Information

1. Look in your dictionary. Match the information with the line on the form.

   a. January 15, 1980   __16__   **d.** Zakarovsky   _____

   b. John Zakarovsky   _____   **e.** 210 Parker Road   _____

   c. 432 109 876   _____   **f.** 555-4851   _____

2. Circle four more mistakes on this form.

1. TODAY'S DATE: _(12 June) 2004_ MONTH DAY YEAR	2. SOCIAL INSURANCE #: _432 098 765_

   3. NAME (Please Print): _Ann Brown_
   LAST NAME   FIRST NAME   MIDDLE INITIAL

   4. TELEPHONE: _555-4872_   5. SEX: ☐ Male ☑ Female
   (AREA CODE)

   6. DATE OF BIRTH: _March 1 1981_   7. JOB: _Stoodent_
   MONTH DAY YEAR

   8. ADDRESS (Please Print): _92 Adams Street_   _4_
   STREET   APT. #

   Victoria   _BC_   _V6X 4N6_
   CITY   PROVINCE   POSTAL CODE

   9. PLACE OF BIRTH: _Germany_   10. SIGNATURE: _Ann Brown_
   CITY   COUNTRY

3. What about you? Fill out the form with your own information.

   1. TODAY'S DATE: _____
   MONTH DAY YEAR   2. SOCIAL INSURANCE #: _____

   3. NAME (Please Print): _____
   LAST NAME   FIRST NAME   MIDDLE INITIAL

   4. TELEPHONE: _____   5. SEX: ☐ Male ☐ Female
   (AREA CODE)

   6. DATE OF BIRTH: _____   7. JOB: _____
   MONTH DAY YEAR

   8. ADDRESS (Please Print): _____
   STREET   APT. #

   _____
   CITY   PROVINCE   POSTAL CODE

   9. PLACE OF BIRTH: _____   10. SIGNATURE: _____
   CITY   COUNTRY

Challenge   Describe the mistakes in Exercise 2. **Example:** _In number 1, she wrote the day first, not the month._

1. Look in your dictionary. Complete the notes with the job titles.

S u n n y d a l e   S c h o o l   N e w s l e t t e r SEPTEMBER/ OCTOBER·2001

Sunnydale Staff Notes...

a. Welcome, all. It's going to be a great year! *Rita Riggs,* ———— Principal ————

b. Seniors—Let's talk about college soon. *Ana Thomas,* ————————————

c. If you're late, come to the office to sign in! *Thelma Black,* ————————

d. Our class will visit historic places around the province. *Dan Rivers,* ————————

2. Look at the list of events. Write the names of the places. Use the words in the box.

field	~~library~~	gym	main office	cafeteria	auditorium

Date and time	Event	Place
a. Sept. 24, 2:00	Reading Club	library
b. Oct. 1, 11:00–1:00	Sandwich and Cookie Sale	
c. Oct. 15, 7:00 P.M.	Concert: Sunnydale Choir	
d. Oct. 23, 2:30	Football Game, Home	
e. Oct. 25, all day	Registration for Senior Class Trip	
f. Oct. 30, 4:30	Girls Basketball Practice	

3. Make words with the scrambled letters.

S C H O O L   S C R A M B L E

a. rcakt   t r a (c) k

b. lacsmoors   __ ◯ __ ◯ __ __ __ __ __

c. hswa moro   __ __ __ __ ◯ ◯ __

d. chleabers   __ __ __ __ ◯ __ __ __

Make a new word with the circled letters: __ __ __ __ __ __

Challenge   Draw a map of your school. Label the places.

1. Look at the pictures in your dictionary. **True** or **False**? Correct the <u>underlined</u> words in the false sentences.

   repeating
   a. **Picture D:** The woman is ~~looking up~~ the word.   ___False___

   b. **Picture K:** The students are <u>brainstorming</u> a list.   _____

   c. **Picture O:** A student is <u>collecting</u> the papers.   _____

   d. **Picture P:** The students are <u>talking</u>.   _____

   e. **Picture T:** The student is <u>checking</u> the answer sheet.   _____

   f. **Picture X:** The student is <u>underlining</u> the items.   _____

2. Fill in the blanks to complete the instructions for the test. Then take the test.

   Review Test

   ---

   1. ___Circle___ the correct words to complete the questions.

      a. (What) / Who is your name?

      b. When / Where do you live?

      c. How much / How many brothers and sisters do you have?

   ---

   2. _____ the word in each group that does not belong.

      a. small   cold   fast   ~~hello~~

      b. pen   marker   coach   pencil

      c. greet   province city   country

   ---

   3. _____ the words in alphabetical _____.

      | talk | collect | say | discuss | spell | copy |
      | draw | dictate | ~~answer~~ | help | ~~ask~~ | share |

      answer   _____   _____   _____

      ask   _____   _____   _____

      _____   _____   _____   _____

3. Circle the correct words to complete the article.

There are many different ways to learn.
Which of these match yours?

- "Word-smart" students like to (read) / tell books, listen to a teacher, and talk / copy
  a.   b.

  information into their notebooks.

- "Body-smart" learners like to move around. They're often the ones who

  collect / dictate the homework from classmates and circle / pass out papers for the teacher.
  c.   d.

- "Picture-smart" people draw / repeat pictures to understand new ideas.
  e.

- "Music-smart" students tap their feet while they learn. They love to repeat / look up
  f.

  information again and again in songs or rhythm.

- "People-smart" students need to dictate / talk with others, working in a group to
  g.

  brainstorm / point to a list, for example. They often share / help others in the class.
  h.   i.

- "Feelings-smart" learners like to discuss / check stories and share / correct their feelings.
  j.   k.

In which ways are you smart? Find your style, and make learning fun!

Based on information from: Kennedy, M.: "Finding the Smart Part in Every Child." *Good Housekeeping* (October 1995).

4. What about you? What helps you learn? Check (✓) the columns that are true for you.

ACTIVITY	HELPS ME A LOT	HELPS ME SOME	HELPS ME A LITTLE	DOESN'T HELP ME
Looking up words				
Copying words				
Repeating words				
Helping other students				
Asking questions				
Discussing stories				
Reading books				
Learning songs				
Doing dictations				
Talking with students				
Talking with my teacher				
Drawing pictures				
Filling in blanks				

Challenge Interview someone about the way he or she learns. Use the ideas in the questionnaire. Write a paragraph about what you learn.

Everyday Conversation

1. Look in your dictionary. Circle the correct answer. What can you say to…?

   a. make sure you understand   "How are things?" / "Did you say *Tuan*?"

   b. introduce your friend   "Beth, this is Mary." / "Hi, I'm Bud."

   c. apologize   "Excuse me." / "How are you?"

   d. end a conversation   "Good evening." / "Good night."

   e. begin a conversation   "How are you?" / "I'm sorry."

2. Read the start of a romance novel. Match each numbered sentence with its description below.

❦ 1 ❦

"Ouch!" Nikki cried, as something heavy fell on her foot.

"I'm really sorry.¹ My science book fell out of my locker," said a deep voice next to her. He picked up the book and stood up. He was tall, and Nikki didn't recognize the handsome face that matched the deep voice.

"Oh, I'm OK," Nikki said. They walked toward the classrooms.

"My name's Ben Ives, by the way.² What's yours?"

"I'm Nikki. Nikki Lewis."³

Ben stopped and stared. "Did you say *Nikki Lewis*?"⁴ he asked.

"That's right. Why?" asked Nikki.

"I heard your piano concert last week. You were great."⁵

"Thanks."⁶ Now what? Nikki felt her face turning red. She never knew how to begin a conversation.

"So, how are your classes this year?" Ben asked.

"They're OK. My English class is fun."

"Uh-oh, I hear the bell. See you later, Nikki."

"Nice meeting you, Ben."⁷

"Hi, Nikki.⁸ Why are you just standing there? Let's get to class!"

It was Nikki's best friend, Lori.

---

a. _____ Nikki and Ben ended the conversation.

b. _____ Ben made sure he understood.

c. _____ Lori greeted Nikki.

d. _____ Nikki thanked Ben.

e. _____ Ben introduced himself to Nikki.

f. _____ Nikki introduced herself to Ben.

g. __1__ Ben apologized.

h. _____ Ben complimented Nikki.

Challenge Choose two items from page 8 in your dictionary (for example, beginning and ending a conversation). Make a list of the different ways people do them.

The Telephone

1. Look in your dictionary. What do you need to...?

   a. call from a pay phone without coins   _phone card_

   b. make calls from your car   _____

   c. take messages when you're not home   _____

   d. walk from room to room when calling someone   _____

   e. know if someone is trying to call you   _____

2. Complete this information from a phone book. Use the words in the box.

dial	directory assistance	~~emergency~~	hang up
international	local	long-distance	operator pay phone
911	0	phone book	wrong number

For Fire, Police, or Ambulance

• **The number to call in an** _emergency_ : _____ .
                       a.   **b.**

• **Look it up!** You can avoid calls to _____ by looking up numbers
                                         c.

   in the _____ .
         d.

• **Dial direct and save.** Calling another city or province? It costs less when you make a

   _____ call yourself. If possible, try not to use the _____ .
     e.   **f.**

• **Ask for credit.** If you reach a _____ , you should _____
                              g.   **h.**

   and _____ "0" immediately. Explain what happened so you can get credit.
      i.

• **Ask for a refund.** If a _____ takes your money but you don't speak to anyone,
                       j.

   report it by dialing _____ (operator) from another phone. We'll see that the phone
                k.

   gets repaired and mail you a refund.

   To place an _____ call you will need:
           l.

• The country code   • The city code   • The _____ number.
                                      m.

Challenge Look at **page 182** in this book. Answer the questions.

Weather

1. Label the weather symbols.

Legend

a. ☀ _____sunny_____   d. ⟩ _____   g. ⋮⋮ _____

b. ▼▼▼ _____   e. ☁⚡ _____   h. ☁ _____

c. ☁ _____   f. ❄ _____

2. Look at the weather map. Write reports for six cities. Use your own paper.

   Example: *It's raining and cool in St. John's with temperatures in the teens.*

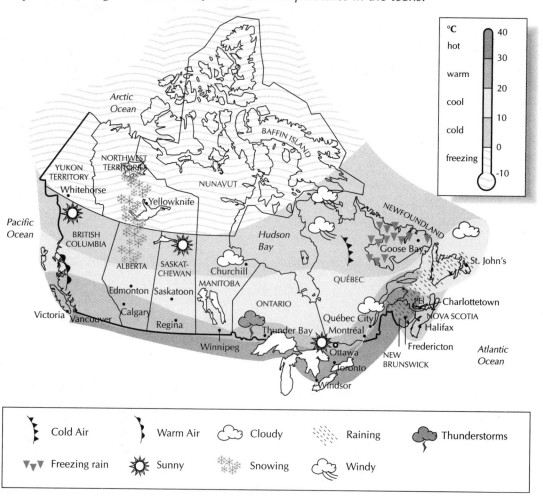

Legend:

⟩ Cold Air   ⟩ Warm Air   ☁ Cloudy   ⋮⋮ Raining   ☁⚡ Thunderstorms

▼▼▼ Freezing rain   ☀ Sunny   ❄ Snowing   ☁ Windy

3. What about you? Write today's weather report for your city. Use Exercise 2 as an example.

_____

_____

Challenge Look at **page 182** in this book. Follow the instructions.

1. Look in your dictionary. Write all the words that end in *-y*. Then write their opposites.

a. ___empty___ ___full___   d. _____ _____

b. _____ _____   e. _____ _____

c. _____ _____   f. _____ _____ or _____

2. Look at the classrooms. Find and describe six more differences. Use your own paper.

Example: *Classroom A has a little clock, but the clock in Classroom B is big.*

Classroom A

Classroom B

3. What about you? How does your classroom compare to Classroom A? Write about the differences. Use your own paper.

Challenge Write six sentences that describe this workbook. Use words from page 11 of your dictionary.

11

Colours

1. Look at **page 65** in your dictionary. What colour is the…?

    a. coveralls _orange_   **b.** jumper _____   **c.** uniform _____   **d.** tunic _____

2. Many colours have a special meaning in Canada. Some are used in idioms. Others are used at holiday times. Read the sentences. Circle the correct word to complete each sentence.

    a. He was so sad that he was feeling ⟨blue⟩ / in the pink.

    b. She was so angry that she was red / purple in the face.

    c. He felt sick. His face was orange / green.

    d. She loved the gift. She was tickled pink / brown.

    e. He was truly a king. He was born to the black / purple.

    f. She was so frightened that her face was as white / green as a ghost.

    g. He was jealous of his rich neighbour. He was green / blue with envy.

    h. He was always afraid. He had a brown / yellow streak up his back.

    i. She wore a black / red dress to the funeral.

    j. The Christmas elves were dressed in yellow and purple / red and green.

    k. The Halloween costumes were red and white / orange and black.

3. Survey your classmates. Find and write the name of a person who is wearing an article of clothing in the following colours.

    a. black _____   **b.** brown _____

    c. white _____   **d.** red _____

    d. green _____   **e.** blue _____

Challenge Survey your classmates. What colours do they or don't they like to wear?

1. Look at **page 12** in your dictionary. Complete the sentences. Write the locations.

   a. The purple box is ___*above*___ the pink box.

   b. The grey box is _____ the orange box, on the _____.

   c. The green box is _____ the same shelf as the brown box.

   d. The black box is _____ the white box.

2. Look at the checklist and the picture of the school supply room. Check (✓) the items that are in the correct place.

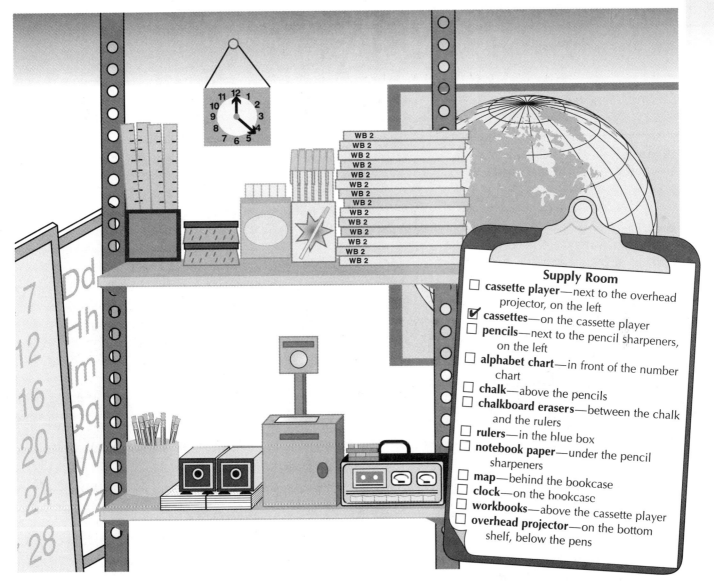

3. Look at Exercise 2. Write about the items that are in the wrong place. Use your own paper.

   Example: *The cassette player is next to the overhead projector, on the right. It isn't on the left.*

   Challenge Write a description of your classroom.

13

Numbers and Measurements

1. Look at the top picture on **pages 2 and 3** in your dictionary.

   a. How many people are male?   _____7_____

   b. How many are female?   _____

   c. What per cent of the people are male?   _____

   d. What fraction of the people are female? _____

2. Look at the math test. Circle all the mistakes. Then give the test a per cent grade (each question = five points).

Baker High School   **Math 101**

Student's Name: _Ryan Miller_____   _____ %

1. What's next?   **2. Write the numbers.**

a. eleven, twelve, thirteen, ____fourteen____   a. XX ___twenty_____

b. one, three, five, _____seven_____   b. IX ___nine_____

c. two, four, six, _____(ten)_____   c. LI ___fifty-one_____

d. ten, twenty, thirty, _____forty_____   d. IV ___six_____

e. ten, one hundred, one thousand, _ten thousand_   e. CX ___a hundred and ten___

3. Match the numbers with the words.   **4. Write the numbers.**

__1__ a. 12   1. ordinal number   a. one hundred _100_____

__6__ b. DL   2. fraction   b. one million __1 000 000 000__

__5__ c. 2nd   3. per cent   c. ten thousand _10 000_____

__4__ d. 10 cm   4. measurement   d. one hundred thousand _100 000_

__2__ e. 2/3   5. cardinal number

__3__ f. 98%   6. Roman numeral

---

3. Explain the mistakes on the test in Exercise 2. Use your own paper.

   Example: *Question 1c.—The next number is eight, not ten.*

4. Forty-two per cent of the students at Baker High School are female. Which pie chart is correct? Circle the correct letter.

a.
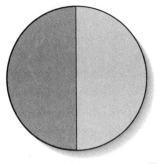

b.
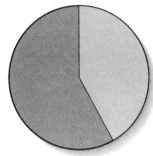

c.
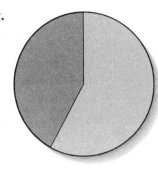

Female = ▨   Male = ▢

5. The pie graph below shows "Enrolment in Canadian Elementary and Secondary Schools." What per cent of students attend public schools?

    a. forty-eight

    b. ninety-five

    c. twenty-three

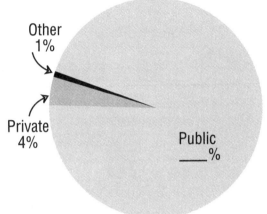

Adapted from Statistics Canada Catalogue 81-229-XPB

6. Look at the graph below. Rank the degrees (first, second, third, etc.) according to the number granted per subject area. (First = Greatest number of degrees granted)

    a. Engineering   _____

    b. Health Studies   _____

    c. Education   _____

    d. Social Sciences   _first_

    e. Agriculture   _____

    f. Math   _____

    g. Fine Arts   _____

    h. Humanities   _____

    i. Arts and Sciences _____

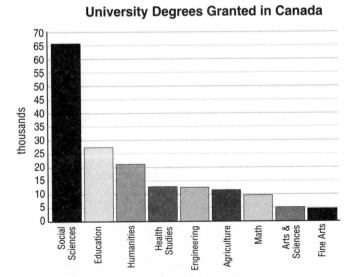

Source: Adapted from Statistics Canada Catalogue table -00580602

Challenge How many students are in your class? What per cent are male? female? Draw a pie chart like the ones in Exercise 4.

15

1. Look at **pages 26 and 27** in your dictionary. Write the time of each activity in numbers and words. Use your own paper.

    a. get dressed   **b.** eat breakfast   **c.** clean the house   **d.** go to bed

    Example: *get dressed:* _____6:30_____   _six-thirty_

2. Look at Nick's time management worksheet. The clocks show the time that he began each activity. Complete his worksheet.

a.    b.    c.   d.    e.   f.

TIME MANAGEMENT WORKSHEET			
ACTIVITY	TIME BEGAN	TIME ENDED	TOTAL TIME
a. get dressed	7:15 A.M.	8:00 A.M.	45 minutes
b. brush teeth	A.M.	8:01 A.M.	1
c. drive to work		9:00 A.M.	
d. lunch		1:15 P.M.	
e. class		9:15 P.M.	
f. talk to girlfriend		11:40 P.M.	

3. Complete the report. Use the information in Exercise 2.

Before our program, Nick was taking forty-five <u>seconds</u> / (<u>minutes</u>) to get dressed, from a quarter
                                                      a.

<u>to</u> / <u>after</u> seven until eight <u>P.M.</u> / <u>o'clock</u>. Now it takes him fifteen <u>hours</u> / <u>minutes</u> (he puts
  b.   **c.**   **d.**

his clothes out the night before). Because he finishes getting dressed by seven <u>-thirty</u> / <u>-fifteen</u>,
                                                                e.

Nick can eat breakfast, brush for three minutes, and catch an eight <u>hour</u> / <u>o'clock</u> bus instead
                                                                  f.

of driving. Nick studies on the bus. He also studies for the first forty minutes of his lunch hour,

from <u>half past</u> / <u>a quarter after</u> twelve until five <u>to</u> / <u>after</u> one. Nick used to talk to his girlfriend
                    g.   **h.**

until twenty to <u>eleven</u> / <u>twelve</u>. Now he calls her forty minutes earlier, at <u>twenty to</u> / <u>half past</u>
                   i.   **j.**

ten, and he gets more sleep.

4. What about you? How long does it take you to do everyday activities? Write five sentences.

5. Look at the time-zone map in your dictionary. Complete these notes.

a.
Flight 20 ✈
flying time: 6 hours
leave Montréal 10:30 a.m. (Eastern time)
arrive Vancouver 1:30 p.m. (Pacific time)

c.
Flight 34 ✈
flying time: 3 1/2 hours
leave Winnipeg 12:00 p.m. (Central time)
arrive Halifax _____ (Atlantic time)

b.
Flight 453 ✈
flying time: 7 hours
leave Edmonton 11:30 p.m. (Mountain time)
arrive St. John's _____ (Newfoundland time)

d.
Flight 733 ✈
flying time: 4 hours
leave Windsor 8:00 a.m. (Eastern time)
arrive Regina _____ (Central time)

6. Complete the article. Use the words in the box. (You will use two words more than once.)
Use your dictionary for help.

Atlantic	daylight saving	earlier	later	Pacific	standard	time zones

It's a Question of Time

In 1884, people in different countries agreed to have ____standard____ time. They
                                                         a.
divided the world into 24 _____. Some large countries have more than one.
                              b.
Canada, for example, has six. These include Eastern, Central, Mountain, _____,
                                                                              c.
Newfoundland and _____ time.
                        d.
     The time difference between one zone and the next is one hour. For example, when it's noon

Eastern time, it's 1:00 P.M. _____ time. (That's one hour _____.)
                                    e.   **f.**
At the same time, it's 11:00 A.M. Central time. (That's one hour _____.) An
                                                                        g.
exception is Newfoundland time. Newfoundland time is only thirty minutes later than

Atlantic time.

     Many countries change the clock in order to use more hours of light in the summer. This

is called _____ time. It begins the first Sunday in April and ends the last Sunday
               h.
in October. People then return to _____ time.
                                          i.

Challenge Look at **page 182** in this book. Follow the instructions.

1. Look at **page 19** in your dictionary. Compare June to December 2001. Which month…?

   a. has more days _____

   b. begins on a weekday _____

2. Read Eva's e-mail. Then complete her calendar for April.

> Subj: your visit
> Date: 4-10-99 12:07:11 EST
> From: EvaL@uol.com
>
> Hi Dania! It's Saturday night. I just returned to Vancouver yesterday. There were no classes for a week so I flew to Edmonton last Saturday to visit my parents. Classes begin again on Monday. It's a busy semester. I have English three times a week (Mondays, Wednesdays, and Fridays). I usually have language lab every Thursday, too. Next week, however, there's no language lab—I go to computer lab instead. In addition to English, I'm studying science. Science meets twice a week on the days that I don't have English. And there's science lab on Tuesdays.
>
> Last Sunday, daylight saving time began. Do you have that in Ontario? I like it a lot. The days seem much longer.
>
> I'm glad it's the weekend. Tomorrow I'm seeing Tom. (I told you about him in my last letter.) I've got to go now. On Saturdays I go to the gym to work out. We can go together when you come! I'm really looking forward to your visit. Just two weeks from today!
>
> Eva
> P.S. Bring your appetite! On Sunday there's a cake sale at the school cafeteria.

1999				April			1999
S	**M**	**T**	**W**	**T**	**F**	**S**	
				1	2	3	
4	5	6	7	8	9 *Return to Vancouver*	10	
11	12	13	14	15	16	17	
18	19	20	21	22	23	24	
25	26	27	28	29	30		

3. What about you? Write a letter to a friend. Describe your weekly schedule. Use your own paper.

4. Look in your dictionary. Write the season.

    a. Tim's birthday _____spring_____   **c.** the man and woman's anniversary _____

    b. Easter _____   **d.** the man's vacation _____

5. Read the information. Write the season next to each holiday.

	Canadian Statutory Holidays	
a. _____winter_____	Christmas	12/25
b. _____	Boxing Day	12/26
c. _____	Canada Day	07/01
d. _____	Labour Day	First Monday in September
e. _____	New Year's Day	01/01
f. _____	Thanksgiving Day	Second Monday in October
g. _____	Victoria Day	05/24
h. _____	Easter	March or April (Date Changes)
i. _____	Good Friday	Friday before Easter

6. Look at the chart in Exercise 5. Put the holidays in the correct time order in the columns below. Write the seasons and the months in words.

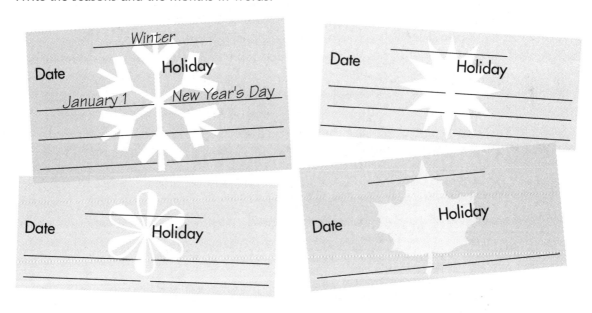

7. Look at the chart in Exercise 5. Which months do not have any statutory holidays?

    _____February_____, _____, _____, _____

Challenge Look at the chart on **page 182** in this book. Follow the instructions.

Money

1. Look in your dictionary. On your own paper, write the fewest coins and bills you can use to make....

   a. $7.05   **b.** $.64   **c.** $1.37   **d.** $380

   Example: *$7.05: a five-dollar bill, one toonie, and...*

2. Fill in the chart below. The first two are done for you.

NAME OF MONEY	VALUE	COLOUR OF THE MONEY	PERSON ON THE MONEY	ANIMAL OR BIRD ON THE MONEY
hundred dollar bill	$100	dark brown	Robert Borden (former Prime Minister)	Canada Goose
fifty dollar bill	$50	pink	W.L. Mackenzie King (former Prime Minister)	Snowy Owl
twenty dollar bill				
ten dollar bill				
five dollar bill				
two dollar coin (toonie)				
one dollar coin (loonie)				
quarter				
dime				
nickel				
penny (cent)				

Challenge There is usually more than one way to tell somebody about an amount of money. You can say it in two ways.

Example: $14.95 can be said either as:
"fourteen dollars and ninety-five cents" or "fourteen ninety-five"

Write two ways of saying each of the amounts of money listed below. Use your own paper.

a. $67.25   **b.** $134.89   **c.** $1.50

1. Look in your dictionary. Another customer bought sweaters at the same sale. Read the conversation and complete the receipt.

   Customer: I'll take the blue and the green.
   Clerk: Cash or credit card?
   Customer: Cash. Do you have change for $100?
   Clerk: Certainly.

Clothesmart
4 . 15 . 01
2
___ sweater
@ _____
_____ @ ____ %   1 . 40
Amount due   _____
Amount tendered   _____
_____   78 . 62

2. Circle the correct words to complete the shopper's advice column.

   Q Recently, I bought a microwave at the (regular) / sale price. A week later, I saw it at the
                                              a.

   same store for 20% less. Is there anything I can do?

   A Some stores will give you the cheaper price if you show your sales tax / receipt. That's
                                                                    b.

   why you should always keep / sell it.
                         c.

   Q I gave my nephew a sweater for his birthday. He wants to exchange / return it and use
                                                                    d.

   the money for a music CD. When I paid for / sold it, it was $19.99. Now the store is
                                          e.

   having a big sale, and it's only $9.99. How much will they give him?

   A Give him the receipt / change and total / price tag to show the store. He might
                         f.   **g.**

   get $19.99.

   Q I bought three pairs of jeans. The sales tax / price tag showed $14.99 each, but the
                                                  h.

   cash register showed only $26.97. The clerk said the jeans just went on sale. How did

   the cash register know?

   A The new price / tax was in the store computer. When the computer "read" the
                i.

   receipt / bar code (those black lines), the cash register showed the correct change / total.
        j.   **k.**

   What a nice surprise!

Challenge Write a question for the shopper's advice column.

   ▶ Go to page 170 for Another Look (Unit 1).

Age and Physical Description

1. Look in your dictionary. Use words from page 22 to write a sentence describing the person in each of these pictures.

    a. 21 _____He is average weight._____

    b. 17 _____

    c. 25 _____

    d. 12 _____

    e. 16 _____

    f. 22 _____

2. a. This is a page from a Canadian passport. Fill in the blanks with information about yourself.

CANADIAN PASSPORT   # 1234567

PHOTO

Name _____
            (Family Name)   (Given Name)   (Middle Name)

Sex ___   ___   Date of Birth _____
    (Male) (Female)

Height _____   Weight _____   Marital Status _____

Colour of Eyes _____   Colour of Hair _____

    b. Write one or two paragraphs describing yourself physically. Use your own paper if you need more space.

    _____
    _____
    _____
    _____
    _____

Challenge Use words from page 22 of your dictionary to write a paragraph describing what the most handsome man/most beautiful woman in the world would look like. Use your own paper.

Describing Hair

1. Look at the women at the bottom of your dictionary page. Who said...?

   a. "I use bigger rollers at home."   *the woman in picture C*

   b. "Wow! Great colour!"

   c. "Please cut it very short."

   d. "Will this perm take a long time?"

2. Complete the advice column with the words in the box.

perm	colour	cut	long	moustache	~~grey~~	wavy	beard	blow dryer

HAIRY PROBLEMS

Q I'm only twenty, but I've got a lot of _____*grey*_____ hair.
        a.

A Why not _____ it? Ask your hairdresser about the shade.
     b.

Q My boyfriend loves _____ hair, but I want short hair this summer.
        c.

A _____ it a little at a time. Stop when you both like the length.
  d.

Q I want _____ hair, but I hate rollers.
       e.

A _____ it. You'll have the style you want with no work.
  f.

Q I always use a _____ after I shampoo. Is hot air bad for my hair?
      g.

A Yes. Use a towel some of the time.

Q My husband says he spends too much time shaving.

A Tell him to grow a _____ and a _____. He'll have to shave less!
       h.   **i.**

3. Find and correct four more mistakes in this advertisement.

Mom has beautiful, shoulder-length, ~~curly~~ *straight* hair. Dad has long, curly blond hair. Erica has shoulder-length, wavy hair. They all have great haircuts from Kindest Cuts. **Still only $15.**

Challenge Look in a magazine, newspaper, or your picture dictionary. Find a hairstyle you like. Describe what a stylist did to create the style.

Family

1. Look at page 24 in your dictionary. Who said…?
   a. "I play softball with my two brothers."   _____Lily_____
   b. "My baby brother just started to walk."   _____
   c. "I don't have any brothers or sisters."   _____
   d. "Aunt Ana made a pretty dress for me."   _____

2. Complete the family tree. Show the people's relationship to Diana.

   May and Charles

   a. __mother-in-law__   b. _____

   Diana and Kevin   **Alvin and Mia**

   c. _____   d. _____   e. _____

   Tim   **Amy**   **Robert**   **Suzanne**

   f. _____   g. _____   h. _____   i. _____

3. Look at Diana's niece Suzanne in Exercise 2. Use information from the family tree to complete this paragraph from Suzanne's letter.

   This week my _____cousin_____ Amy turned sixteen, so my _____
   a.   b.
   Kevin and my _____ Diana gave her a big party. My _____
   c.   d.
   Robert and I played with the younger children, and my _____ were very
   e.
   busy too – Mom helped serve the food, and Dad took lots of pictures of Amy,
   their only _____. In the middle of the party someone shouted, "May
   f.
   is on the telephone." It was our _____ calling from San Francisco!
   g.

4. What about you? Draw your family tree. Use your own paper.

5. Look at page 25 in your dictionary. **True** or **False**?

a. David's father is Lisa's stepfather. _____True_____

b. Kim's mother is married to Lisa's father. _____

c. Mary and Kim are stepsisters. _____

d. Carol is divorced from Bill's stepfather. _____

6. Complete the entries from Lisa's diary. Use the words in the box. (You will use two words more than once.)

divorced	half sister	married	remarried
single father	stepfather	stepmother	

3/15/96-Dad moved away this week. He and Mom got ___divorced___.
a.
That means they're not _____ anymore. I feel bad, but
b.
Mom says I didn't do anything wrong.

4/1/96-Dad's new apartment is cool. He says he'll always be my
father, but now he's a _____, not a married one.
c.

10/4/98-Mom says she wants to get _____ someday. That
d.
man Rick seems nice.

12/10/98-Mom and Rick got _____! Rick's my _____
e. f.
now. I wonder—can I still visit Dad?

12/12/98-I had a great time at Dad's this weekend. We went to the
circus with Bill and Kim. When Dad and Sue get married, he'll be
Bill and Kim's _____, and Sue will be my _____.
g. h.

11/14/99-We have a new baby! Her name is Mary. I'm her
_____. Mom says I can help take care of her.
i.

Challenge Look at **page 183** in this book. Follow the instructions.

Daily Routines

1. Look in your dictionary. Complete the schedule.

TIME	Mai	David
6:00 A.M.	get up	wake up
6:30 A.M.	take a shower	get dressed
7:00 A.M.	make lunch	
8:00 A.M.		drive to work
10:00 A.M.	school	
6:00 P.M.	cook dinner	
6:30 P.M.		have dinner
10:30 P.M.		go to bed

2. Read this article about the family in your dictionary. Find and <u>underline</u> five more mistakes. Use your dictionary for help.

The Fast Track Family

David and Mai Lim want a lot from life, and their daily routine shows it. In the morning, David gets up <u>before</u> Mai. Mai takes a shower while David gets dressed. Then David eats breakfast with the kids and Mai makes lunch. At 7:30, Mai takes the kids to school. Mai, a full-time student, is in school all day. David stays home. Between 4:30 and 6:00, Mai goes to the market, cleans the house, and cooks dinner. During that time, David leaves work and picks up the kids at daycare. The family eats dinner together. Then Mai does homework, and David reads the paper. They go to sleep at 10:30. It's a busy schedule, but the Lims enjoy it. ■

3. Explain the mistakes in Exercise 2.

a. <u>David doesn't get up before Mai. He gets up after her.</u>

b. _____

c. _____

d. _____

e. _____

f. _____

4. Make questions from the scrambled words.

a. time   What   you   up   do   get

    <u>What time do you get up?</u>

b. eat   breakfast   When   you   do

_____

c. you   leave   When   the   house   do

_____

d. home   come   you   do   time   What

_____

e. to   bed   go   do   When   you

_____

5. What about you? Complete the chart with information about your daily routine. Then interview another person. Use questions like the ones in Exercise 4.

Your name: _____		Your partner's name: _____	
ACTIVITY	**TIME**	**ACTIVITY**	**TIME**

Challenge Compare the routines in Exercise 5. Write six sentences. Use *after, before,* or *while* in some of your sentences. **Example:** *I get up before Kyung, but we both leave for class at 8:00.*

Life Events

1. Look in your dictionary. How old was Martin Perez when he...?

   a. started school   5

   b. joined the army   _____

   c. became a citizen   _____

   d. got married   _____

   e. had his first child   _____

   f. bought his first house   _____

   g. had his first grandchild   _____

   h. died   _____

2. Complete this biography about inventor Alexander Graham Bell. Use the past tense form of the words in the boxes.

| move   live   die   ~~be born~~   immigrate |

Alexander Graham Bell was a fine teacher and a wonderful inventor. He _____was born_____ in Edinburgh, Scotland in 1847.
a.

At the age of fifteen, Alexander _____ to England where
b.

he _____ with his grandfather for one year. Bell's two brothers
c.

_____ from tuberculosis. Alexander _____ with his parents to Canada
d.   **e.**

in 1870. They hoped that the Canadian climate would keep Alexander well.

| go   get   is |

Alexander Graham Bell _____ to the United States in 1871. There he
f.

_____ a job as a teacher at the Boston School for the Deaf. He _____ a very
g.   **h.**

successful teacher and he became an American citizen.

| form   rent   marry |

Bell _____ a small apartment. One room served as a bedroom and the other
i.

room was his workshop. In this workshop, he invented the telephone in 1876. On July 9, 1877,

Bell and his partner, Thomas Watson, _____ the Bell Telephone Company. Two days later,
j.

Alexander _____ Mabel Hubbard. Mabel was one of Bell's former students.
k.

---

invent	include	die	continue

Although Alexander Graham Bell is best known for inventing the telephone, he also

_____ many other things. His inventions _____ a metal detector, an audiometer
    l.   m.

for measuring speech, and a hydrofoil (a fast boat). Bell returned to Canada in 1885. He

_____ to work until he _____ on August 2, 1922 in Baddeck, Nova Scotia.
    n.   o.

3. Read the statements about Alexander Graham Bell. **True** or **False**? Write a question mark (**?**) if the information isn't in the reading in Exercise 2.

    a. Alexander Graham Bell was born in Boston, USA.   _____False_____

    b. He moved to Canada in 1870.   _____

    c. Bell got married before he invented the telephone.   _____

    d. He was President of the National Geographic Society.   _____

    e. He died in Nova Scotia, Canada.   _____

4. Check (✓) the documents that Alexander Graham Bell probably had. Use the information in Exercise 2.

    _____ driver's licence   _____ marriage licence

    _____ passport   _____ American citizenship papers

5. Complete the timeline for Alexander Graham Bell. Use the information in Exercise 2.

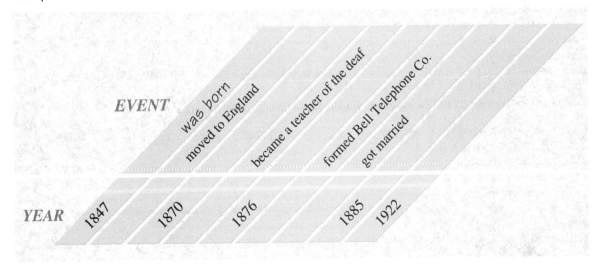

6. What about you? Draw a timeline with your own information. Then, write a short autobiography. Use your own paper.

Challenge Think of a famous person and look up biographical information about him or her. Draw a timeline and write a paragraph about the person's life.

29

Feelings

1. Look in your dictionary. Find and write the opposite of these words.

   a. comfortable   <u>uncomfortable</u>   **d.** sick   _____

   b. hot   _____   **e.** happy   _____

   c. nervous   _____   **f.** full   _____

2. Read the conversations. Complete each sentence with a word from the box.

   Ana: What's the matter?

   Hisae: I really miss my family.

   Hisae feels _____<u>homesick</u>_____ .
          a.

hurt	~~homesick~~	sick

   Alfons: Ow!

   Carla: What's wrong?

   Alfons: It's my heart!

   Alfons is _____ .
          b.

homesick	in love	in pain

   Tom: I can't eat _that!_

   Julia: Why not?

   Tom: It looks and smells just terrible!

   Tom is _____ .
          c.

disgusted	sick	nervous

   Laurel: There you are! It's almost 10:30!

   Andy: Sorry. The train was late.

   Laurel: I'm glad you're OK. I was worried.

   Laurel is _____ .
          d.

angry	confused	relieved

   Jennifer: Would you like some more?

   Bill: Oh, no thanks. I can't have another bite!

   Bill feels _____ .
          e.

full	hungry	thirsty

3. Circle the correct words to complete the story.

Min Hau had so many feelings his first day of school. When he left home, he felt

(scared) / excited . His mother looked nervous / calm , but his little brother just looked
    a.   **b.**

sad / sleepy . When he got to school, he walked into the wrong class. The teacher looked
    c.

bored / surprised , and Min Hau was very embarrassed / worried . He felt much better in math
    d.   **e.**

class. He was proud / shocked when he did a problem correctly. His teacher looked
                f.

happy / surprised . At lunchtime, he looked at his food and felt confused / disgusted .
    g.   **h.**

"What is this?" As he sat in the cafeteria, Min Hau was feeling awfully tired / lonely . Then
                                            i.

someone said, "Can I sit here?" Suddenly his feelings changed. Was he in love / in pain ?
                                                j.

4. What about you? How did you feel on your first day of school? Write sentences on your own paper.

Challenge Look at **page 183** in this book. Follow the instructions.

A Graduation

1. Look in your dictionary. Who said…?

a. "I'm happy to be here today. I remember my own graduation." _____guest speaker_____

b. "Please, everyone, look over here. Now, smile!" _____

c. "My four years here have been wonderful." _____

2. Complete the article. Use the words in the box.

applauded	audience	class	cried	diplomas
gowns	guest speaker	graduated	graduates	~~podium~~
speech	stage	took	valedictorian	

Mayor Attends Graduation

Mayor Rodriguez behind the
_____podium_____.
a.

GREENVILLE, JUNE 11—Yesterday was Bryant University's fiftieth graduation ceremony. The event took place in the school's large auditorium. This year's graduating _____ had 78 _____ .
        b.   **c.**
In their purple caps and _____ , they
        d.
walked proudly across the large _____
        e.
to receive their _____ .
        f.
The _____ , graduating senior, Cathy
        g.
Chan, gave a beautiful _____ .
        h.
   The _____ of proud friends and
        i.
family _____ loudly at the end.
        j.
Mrs. Chan _____ tears of happiness.
        k.
   This year's _____ was Greenville's
        l.
own mayor, Lillian Rodriguez. Mayor Rodriguez herself
_____ from Bryant in 1970. Rodriguez
        m.
spoke about jobs, schools, and family as the photographer
_____ pictures.
        n.

3. Look in your dictionary. Who said…?

a. "Can I give you some more chicken? Something to drink?"   _caterer_

b. "And next, we're going to hear a song called 'School's Out.'"   _____

c. "This is a great party. Thanks for inviting us!"   _____

4. Look at the pictures. Find and describe six more differences. Use your own paper.

Example: *There are ten guests on Brian's dance floor. There are eight guests on Ana's dance floor.*

Brian's Party

Ana's Party

Challenge Write a newspaper report of a graduation you have attended or the one in your dictionary.

▶ **Go to page 171 for Another Look (Unit 2).**

33

Places to Live

1. Look in your dictionary. Where can you hear…?

   a. "My roommate is studying chemistry."   university residence

   b. "I became homeless after I lost my job."   _____

   c. "We raise horses."   _____

   d. "All four houses look the same."   _____

2. Complete the letter. Use the words in the box.

| city   ~~farm~~   house   nursing home   suburbs   apartment   country |

Dear Fran,

   You asked me to tell you about the places I have lived. I hope I can remember them all. I grew up on a potato _____ **farm** _____ in Ireland. Not long after your grandfather and I got
   a.
married, we immigrated to Canada. For five years, we rented a little _____ in
                                                                    b.
an old building. I didn't like living in a big _____ like Toronto. I really prefer
                                             c.
living in the _____, where I grew up. I was happy when we bought our own
              d.
_____ in the _____, only 15 kilometres from the city. It had a
    e.   **f.**
yard and your father had his own bedroom. We lived there for 20 years. When your grandfather
stopped working, we wanted to travel. We bought a mobile home, and for a while, we
moved our little home every few years! After your grandfather died, I couldn't get around
very well or live alone anymore, so I moved here. When you were little, you used to think that
all the elderly people here in the _____ were your grandparents, too. We're
                                  g.
all looking forward to your next visit.

                                                    Love,
                                                    Grandma

3. Many Canadians move several times in their lives. What about you? Where have you lived?
   Make a chart like the one below. Use your own paper.

PLACE NAME	CITY, SUBURBS, OR COUNTRY	TYPE OF HOME	YEAR YOU MOVED THERE	HOW LONG YOU LIVED THERE
Edmonton	city	apartment	1998	3 years

_____ **Challenge** Write a paragraph about the places you've lived. Use information from Exercise 3.

34

1. Look in your dictionary. What are they doing?

   a. "How about $125 000?"   *making an offer*

   b. "Let's put the table there, in front of the love seat." _____

   c. "The keys to our new house! Thank you." _____

   d. "Thank you. Now we have the money for the house!" _____

2. Circle the correct words to complete the article.

Home Improvement

The rent is too high and the rooms are too small, but this time you're not going to just **(look for)**/get a loan for a bigger **a.** apartment. And you're not going to sign a lease /arrange the **b.** furniture and continue to pay rent every month. You're going to make the big move and rent an apartment /buy a house! **c.** You're excited but nervous. Here are some suggestions that will make things easier.

First, make a checklist. Are schools important? Shopping? Write it all down. Next, talk to a Realtor /manager. Explain **d.** how much you can pay and go over your checklist. With that information, he or she can take ownership of /look for houses **e.**

that match your needs. Be patient. Most buyers look at seven to twelve homes before they decide.

When you find your dream house, make an offer /move in **f.** quickly, or you might lose it to another buyer. If you and the sellers agree on the price, it's time to unpack /get a loan. **g.** This can take a long time. Again, be patient.

Finally the happy day comes. The seller hands you the keys and you sign a rental agreement /take ownership! Now **h.** all you have to do is move in, unpack /sign a lease, and **i.** arrange the furniture. Oh, and pay the rent /mortgage, **j.** of course.

3. What about you? Check (✓) all the items that are important to you.

• R E A L T Y •

TYPE	☐ APARTMENT	☐ HOUSE	☐ OTHER:_____
LOCATION	☐ CITY	☐ SUBURBS	☐ COUNTRY
NEAR	☐ SCHOOLS	☐ SHOPPING	☐ WORK
SPACE	☐ NUMBER OF ROOMS	☐ SIZE OF ROOMS	
COST	☐ RENT	☐ MORTGAGE	

Challenge Write a paragraph about a time you looked for and found a new home.

Apartments

1. Look in your dictionary. Where can you hear…?

   a. "We're going up now."   _in the elevator_

   b. "Come in. The water's great!"   _____

   c. "All I ever get are bills and ads."   _____

   d. "It's beautiful up here. What a great view!"   _____

   e. "Someone's car is in my space."   _____

   f. "Your things will be dry in five minutes."   _____

2. Circle the correct words to complete this ad.

The Glenwood Manor

1- and 2-Bedroom apartments now available!

We just hung out a fire escape /(vacancy sign!)
                                      a.

> Enjoy suburban living in the
> middle of the city!
> The Glenwood has it all…

Security
- 24-hour security / landlord
          b.
- Intercom / garbage chute on every floor
          c.

Comfort
- All apartments come with garbage bins / air conditioners
                                        d.
- Some apartments available with balconies / entrances
                                        e.
- Beautiful roof garden / security gate
               f.

Convenience
- 20-car courtyard / garage (Every apartment has its own free fire exit / parking space.)
         g.   **h.**
- Laundry room / Swimming pool on every floor (All new washers and dryers.)
              i.
- Elevator / Playground for children
              j.
- Lane / Rec room with exercise equipment
        k.

For more information, contact our manager / tenant: John Miller 555-4334
                                        l.

3. Complete this pamphlet. Use the words in the box.

deadbolt	door chain	doorknob	elevator	fire escape
intercom	~~neighbours~~	peephole	smoke detector	stairs

BETTER SAFE THAN SORRY!

■ Know your ___neighbours___ .
              a.
  Don't allow strangers into the

  building.

■ Always use your _____
                  b.
  to ask "Who's there?"

■ Look out your _____
              c.
  before you open your apartment

  door.

■ When you're at home, keep

  your _____ on.
            d.

■ Install a _____ .
           e.
  It's the strongest lock.

■ Keep a _____
            f.
  on the wall or ceiling between your

  bedroom and your apartment door.

  Check it every month!

■ In case of fire, do not use the

  _____ . (The heat
          g.
  can cause it to stop between

  floors.) Use the _____
              h.
  instead.

■ Feel the _____ of your
            i.
  apartment. If it's hot, the fire may be

  out in the hall. Use the _____
              j.
  _____ to leave your apartment.

For serious emergencies dial 911.
All other times call your local
police or fire department.

4. What about you? How safe is your home? Check (✔) the things your home has.

☐ smoke detector   ☐ fire escape   ☐ fire exit   ☐ intercom

☐ security system   ☐ security gate   ☐ deadbolt lock   ☐ peephole

☐ door chain   ☐ Other: _____

Challenge Describe the ideal apartment building.

A House

1. Look at the house in your dictionary. Choose the correct ad for it.

a.
> New 2BR, 2 bth house with 2-car gar, deck, large front & backyard. All new roof.

c.
> Small, pretty, 2BR, 1 bth house with 1-car gar, deck, front & backyard.

b.
> 🏠 Small, pretty, 3BR, 1 bth house with 2-car gar, deck, front & backyard.

d.
> Nice 2BR, 1 bth house with deck, large front porch, gar, backyard with pool.

Note: BR = bedroom   bth = bathroom   gar = garage

2. Look at the houses. Find and describe 11 more differences. Use your own paper.

Example: *10 Pine Street's chimney is on the right, but 12's is on the left.*

10 Pine Street   **12 Pine Street**

Challenge Find an apartment ad in the newspaper. Describe the apartment.

1. Look in your dictionary. What can you use to...?

   a. cook outdoors   _____barbecue_____

   b. clean leaves from the lawn   _____ or _____

   c. lie down and read   _____

   d. carry compost   _____

   e. water the lawn   _____

   f. cut branches from bushes   _____

   g. water the flowers near the patio   _____

   h. plant a tree   _____

2. Circle the correct words to complete the article. Look at **pages 132–134** in your dictionary for help.

We're planning to change our yard into a wildlife habitat—a home for birds and animals.

Next to our patio, we're going to plant (bushes) / flowerpots where rabbits and squirrels can hide.
                                                    a.

We want two big trowels / trees that will be homes for squirrels and bats, and a thick hedge / hose
                                b.   **c.**

in the back where rabbits and other small animals can live. To attract butterflies, we'll plant colourful

compost / flowers at the edge of the patio. The patio furniture / lawn will be very small because
               d.   **e.**

animals don't like open spaces—that means we'll have less to mow!

3. What about you? Plan your ideal yard. Check (✔) the items you would like.

   ☐ trees   ☐ a hammock   ☐ flowers   ☐ a compost pile

   ☐ a lawn   ☐ bushes   ☐ hedges   ☐ a patio

   ☐ a barbecue   ☐ Other: _____

Challenge Draw your ideal yard and write a paragraph describing it.

A Kitchen

1. Look in your dictionary. What is <u>it</u>?

    a. <u>It</u>'s on the right back burner of the stove.   _____kettle_____

    b. <u>It</u>'s on the counter, to the left of the sink.   _____

    c. <u>They</u>'re on the wall, under the cabinets.   _____

    d. <u>It</u>'s below the oven.   _____

2. Look at the chart. **True** or **False**?

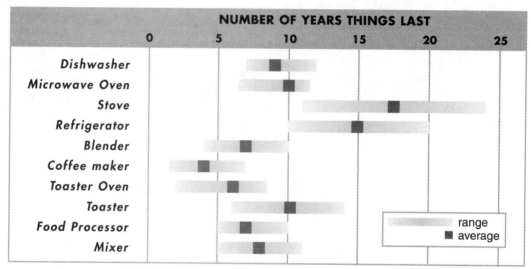

Based on information from *Consumer Reports 1997 Buying Guide*

    a. A lasts an average of ten years.   ____False____

    b. A lasts an average of about nine years.   _____

    c. A lasts longer than a .   _____

    d. The average life of a is shorter than the life of a .   _____

    e. A lasts from about ten to twenty years.   _____

    f. A doesn't last as long as a .   _____

3. What about you? List the kitchen appliances from Exercise 2 that you have. Use your own paper. How long have you had them? **Example:** *mixer—2 years*

Challenge   Which five kitchen appliances are the most important? Why?

1. Look in your dictionary. List the items on the table. Use your own paper.

Example: *5 placemats*

2. Complete the conversations. Use the words in the box.

| candles | ceiling fan | creamer | serving dish | ~~tablecloth~~ | tray | vase |

a. Alek: I'm setting the table. Are we going to use placemats?

   Ella: No. Put on the white _____tablecloth_____ instead.

b. Alek: Is it hot in here?

   Ella: Yes. Why don't you turn on the _____?

c. Alek: What beautiful flowers!

   Ella: I'll get a _____ for them.

d. Alek: Are we going to serve each guest a piece of fish?

   Ella: No. I'm going to put the fish on a _____ in the middle of the table. That way people can take as much as they want.

e. Alek: Where should I put the coffee cups?

   Ella: I'll carry them out on a _____ after we finish eating.

f. Alek: Could you pour some milk in the _____ and bring it out with the sugar bowl?

   Ella: Sure.

g. Alek: It was a lovely dinner party.

   Ella: Yes, it was. Can I blow out the _____ now?

3. What about you? Draw a picture of the table at a dinner you had. Label the items. Use your own paper.

Challenge Find a picture of a dining area in a newspaper or magazine. Describe it.

A Living Room

1. Look in your dictionary. **True** or **False**? Correct the underlined words in the false sentences.

      stereo system

a. There's a ~~TV~~ in the wall unit.   *False*

b. There's a <u>fire</u> in the fireplace.   _____

c. There's a painting over the <u>mantle</u>.   _____

d. The magazine holder is next to the <u>fire screen</u>.   _____

e. There are throw pillows on the <u>armchair</u>.   _____

2. Look at the pictures. Circle the correct words to complete the sentences.

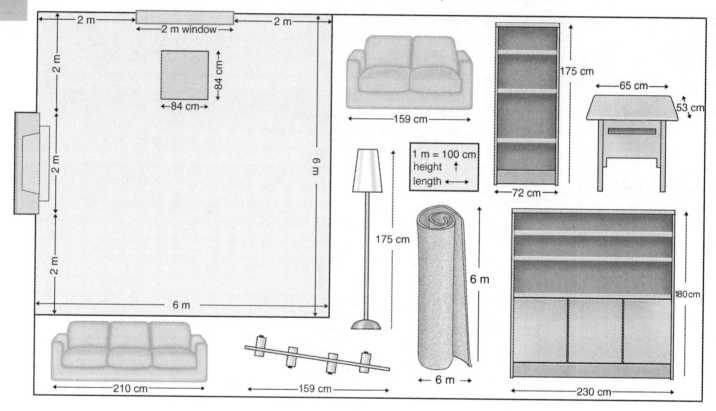

a. The (coffee table)/ end table is already in the living room.

b. The <u>bookcase / wall unit</u> can go to the left of the window.

c. The <u>sofa / love seat</u> fits to the right of the window.

d. The track lighting is the same length as the <u>love seat / fireplace</u>.

e. The carpet is <u>bigger than / the same size as</u> the living room.

f. The floor lamp is the same height as the <u>bookcase / wall unit</u>.

3. What about you? Draw a floor plan of your living room. Label the items. Use your own paper.

Challenge How would you decorate the living room in Exercise 2? Write sentences. **Example:** *I'd put the sofa in the middle of the living room, across from the window…*

1. Look in your dictionary. Which item is each person talking about?

   a. "Can I put my dirty jeans in <u>here</u>?"   <u>   hamper   </u>

   b. "Look at <u>that</u>! You weigh 25 kilos!"   <u>   </u>

   c. "I just used the <u>last roll</u>. Do we have any more?"   <u>   </u>

   d. "I'm going to hang your towel and washcloth <u>here</u>."   <u>   </u>

   e. "There's hair in <u>it</u>. The water's not going down."   <u>   </u>

   f. "Let's open <u>these</u> so we have more light."   <u>   </u>

2. Complete the article. Use the words in the box.

sink	hot water	medicine cabinet	soap dish	shower head
rubber mat	toilet	bath mat	wastebasket	~~bathtub~~	faucets

   ## Keep bath time safe and happy by following these safety rules:

   1. Never leave a young child alone in the <u>bathtub</u> . Even small amounts of water can
   a.
   be dangerous.

   2. Avoid burns from _____ . Turn the temperature on your water heater down
   b.
   to 40°C. Fix any dripping _____ , and don't forget the _____ —hot
   c. **d.**
   drops from above can hurt too.

   3. Prevent falls. Keep a _____ in the bathtub or shower stall
   e.
   and a nonslip _____ on the floor. Don't forget to put that
   f.
   slippery soap back in the _____ after you wash.
   g.
   Provide a stool so that children can reach the _____ safely to wash their hands
   h.
   and brush their teeth.

   4. Keep medicines locked in the _____ . Never throw old medicines away in a
   i.
   _____ where children can get them. Flush them down the _____ .
   j. **k.**

   Based on information from: Larson, D.: *Mayo Clinic Family Health Book.* (NY: William Morrow and Company, 1990)

3. What about you? What do you do to prevent injuries and accidents in the bathroom? Write sentences on your own paper.

   Example: *We put a rubber mat in the bathtub.*

   Challenge List items in a bathroom that usually cost $15.00 or less.

A Bedroom

1. Look in your dictionary. **True** or **False**? Correct the underlined words in the false sentences.

        pillow
a. The ~~flat sheet~~ is striped.   _____False_____

b. The clock radio is on the <u>bureau</u>.   _____

c. The <u>light switch</u> and the outlet are on the same wall.   _____

d. There is a <u>mirror</u> over the bed.   _____

e. The woman is lifting the <u>bedspread</u> and the dust ruffle.   _____

2. Read the letter and look at the picture. Complete Tran's list on your own paper.

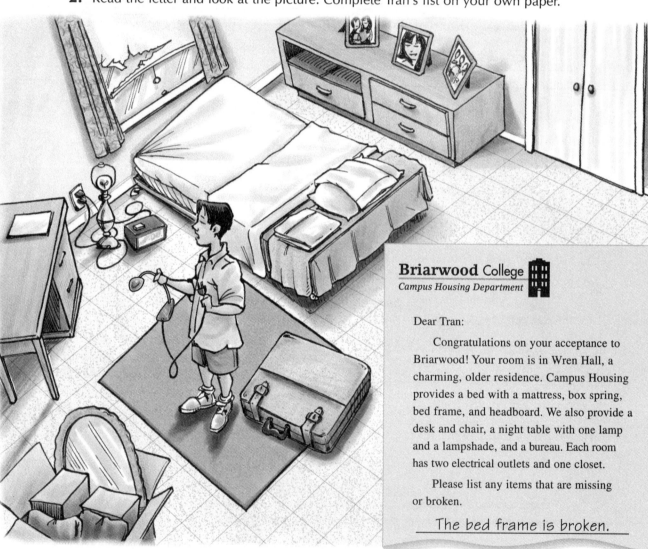

Briarwood College
Campus Housing Department

Dear Tran:

    Congratulations on your acceptance to Briarwood! Your room is in Wren Hall, a charming, older residence. Campus Housing provides a bed with a mattress, box spring, bed frame, and headboard. We also provide a desk and chair, a night table with one lamp and a lampshade, and a bureau. Each room has two electrical outlets and one closet.

    Please list any items that are missing or broken.

    The bed frame is broken.

3. Look at Exercise 2. What did Tran bring? Make a list on your own paper.

Example: *sheets*

_____ **Challenge** Write a paragraph describing your ideal bedroom.

1. Look in your dictionary. Cross out the word that doesn't belong. Write the category. Use the words in the box. (You will use one word more than once.)

safety	storage	playing	~~sleeping~~

a. _sleeping_	crib	~~puzzle~~	bunk bed	cradle
b. _____	baby monitor	smoke detector	bumper pad	blocks
c. _____	change table	chest of drawers	toy chest	picture book
d. _____	ball	diaper pail	doll	teddy bear
e. _____	colouring book	dollhouse	crayons	comforter

2. Complete the article. Use the words in the box.

mobile	change table	wallpaper	stuffed animals	~~crib~~
comforter	chest of drawers	diaper pail	night light	

Expecting a new family member? Here's what you'll need to make your baby's room a safe and happy place. The biggest item is the ___crib___ **a.** . The mattress must fit tightly, with no spaces that a baby's head can fit through. A pretty _____ **b.** will keep baby warm, but it should fit loosely on top of the mattress. You can change your baby on a bed, but a _____ **c.** is better for your back. You can keep diapers on the shelves below. Have a _____ **d.** nearby for the dirty ones. Finally, you will need a _____ **e.** for baby's clothing and extra blankets.

For decoration, hang a _____ **f.** where baby can watch it (some play music, too). Paint the room or put up colourful _____ **g.** , add some lovable _____ **h.** to hug, and plug a cheerful _____ **i.** into an electrical outlet for nighttime feedings.

3. What about you? Describe your favourite toy or game as a child.

Example: *When I was three, I loved my little teddy bear.*

_____

Challenge Look at **page 183** in this book. Follow the instructions.

Housework

1. Look in your dictionary. Correct the <u>underlined</u> words in these false sentences.

> *cleaning*
a. The woman in C is <s>emptying</s> the oven.

c. The girl in N is <u>washing</u> the dishes.

b. The man in L is <u>polishing</u> the floor.

d. The man in J is <u>sweeping</u> the floor.

2. Look at the room. Circle the correct words to complete the note.

Hi! As you can see, I wasn't quite able to do everything. I polished the (desk) dresser,
a.
but I didn't have a chance to dust the

desk / dresser. I **swept / vacuumed** the floor,
b.   c.
and I finally washed the **dishes / windows**.
d.
I also washed the **sheets / glasses**, but
e.
didn't make **lunch / the bed**. Sorry! By the
f.
way, could you **take out / empty** the garbage
g.
and put away the **dishes / books**?
h.

Thanks. See you after class,
Viktor

3. What about you? Which would you rather do? Write sentences on your own paper.

a. wash the dishes / dry the dishes

c. sweep the floor / vacuum the carpet

b. dust the furniture / polish the furniture

d. clean the oven / wash the windows

Example: *I'd rather dry the dishes than wash the dishes.*

Challenge Take a survey. Ask five people about their favourite and least favourite kinds of housework. Write their answers.

46

1. Look in your dictionary. Add a word to complete the list of cleaning supplies.

    a. dust _____mop_____   e. recycling _____

    b. rubber _____   f. scrub _____

    c. garbage _____   g. vacuum _____

    d. dish _____   h. furniture _____

2. Complete the conversations. Use the words from Exercise 1.

    a. **Ben:**   Water isn't good for the dining room floor, is it?

       Ann: No. Use the _____dust mop_____.

    b. **Paulo:**   Do you have any _____? I want to empty the wastebasket.

       Sara: Oh. I used the last one.

    c. **Ada:**   The _____ doesn't seem to be working well.

       Mario: Maybe the bag is full. Have you checked it?

    d. **Fei-mei:**   If you give me a _____, I'll dry the dishes.

       Da-ming: Great.

    e. **Luis:**   You know, that cleanser isn't good for your hands.

       Vera: You're right. Do we have any _____?

    f. **Taro:**   What should we do with the empty bottles?

       Rika: Don't throw them away. Put them in the _____ in the alley.

    g. **Amber:**   I dusted the desk, but it still doesn't look clean.

       Chet: Try some _____ on it.

    h. **Layla:**   The kitchen floor is really dirty.

       Zaki: I know. You have to get down and use the _____ on it.

3. Cross out the word that doesn't belong. Give a reason.

    a. dustpan   broom   ~~glass cleaner~~   wet mop
       _You don't use it to clean the floor._____

    b. steel-wool soap pads   dishwashing liquid   dish towel   bucket

       _____

    c. scrub brush   sponge   feather duster   wet mop

       _____

_____ **Challenge**   Imagine you have just moved into a new home. What do you need to: dust the furniture, clean the oven, wash the windows, mop the kitchen floor? Make a shopping list. You can use your dictionary for help.

Household Problems and Repairs

1. Look in your dictionary. Who should they call?

a.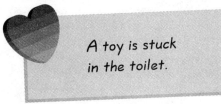

> A toy is stuck
> in the toilet.

_____the plumber_____

c.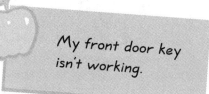

> My front door key
> isn't working.

_____

b.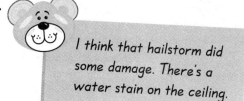

> I think that hailstorm did
> some damage. There's a
> water stain on the ceiling.

_____

d.

> Sorry, Mom. I kicked my
> soccer ball through the
> front window.

_____

2. Look at Tracy and Kyung's cabin. Complete the telephone conversations by describing the problem or problems for each repair service.

a. **Repairperson:** Bob Derby Carpentry. Can I help you?
   Tracy: _The door on our kitchen cabinet is broken_____.

b. **Repairperson:** Plumbing Specialists, Ron here.
   Kyung: _____,
   _____, and
   _____.

c. **Repairperson:** Quick Fixes Small Repairs. What can we do for you?
   Tracy: _____.

d. **Repairperson:** Chestertown Electricians. This is Pat.
   Kyung: _____.

e. **Repairperson:** Nature's Way Exterminators. What's the problem?
   Tracy: _____!

3. Look at the chart. **True** or **False**? Write a question mark (**?**) if the information isn't in the chart.

Pests	Where They Live	How to Prevent Them	How to Get Rid of Them
	on pets, carpets, furniture	Keep pets either inside or outside all the time.	Vacuum often. Comb pets daily. Wash them with water and lemon juice.
	behind walls, under roofs and floors	Repair cracks and holes in roofs and walls. Keep garbage in tightly closed garbage cans.	Poison is dangerous to humans. Put traps along walls instead. Put a piece of bacon in the trap.
	in wood; especially wet or damaged places	Repair cracks and holes. Repair leaks in pipes. Check every 1–2 years.	Call the exterminator. You need a professional to get rid of these pests, which destroy your house by eating the wood.
	gardens and lawns	Repair wall cracks. Clean floors and shelves often; wipe spilled honey or jam immediately.	Find where they enter the house and repair that hole. Put mint leaves in food cupboards.
	behind walls, in electric appliances	Clean carefully; keep food in closed containers. Repair all cracks and holes.	Make a trap by putting a banana in a wide-mouthed jar. Put petroleum jelly around the inside of jar to keep trapped bugs inside. Place in corners or under sinks.

a. To prevent most pests, you must repair household problems. _____True_____

b. You have to use poison to get rid of mice and rats. _____

c. Sometimes cockroaches get into the toaster oven. _____

d. Fleas like sweet food. _____

e. You have to buy cockroach traps. _____

f. Ants carry diseases. _____

g. Mint leaves help get rid of termites. _____

h. Termites are very common in warm, wet climates. _____

i. Mice eat people's food. _____

j. You should put a piece of fruit in a mousetrap. _____

Challenge Write some other ways of dealing with household pests.

▶ **Go to page 172 for Another Look (Unit 3).**

1. Look in your dictionary. Complete each statement.

   a. The _____lemons_____ are 3 for a dollar.

   b. The man is hanging a basket of _____.

   c. The green banana is _____.

   d. The _____ banana has brown spots.

2. Look at the pictures. Complete the chart with the names of the fruit.

Buying fresh fruit is an art. Here are some tips:

Fruit	Best During	Buy Ones That Are
a. ___watermelon___	June, July, August	cut open, dark red inside
b. _____	June and July	dark red and big
c. _____	July and August	bright orange, with soft skins
d. _____	December–June	heavy
e. _____	the whole year	not soft (Let them get ripe at home.)
f. _____	April 15–July 15	dry and dark red (Size is not important.)
g. _____	July and August	dark green

Based on information from: Murdich, J.: *Buying Produce: The Greengrocer's Guide to Selecting and Storing Fresh Fruits and Vegetables.* (NY: Hearst Marine Books, 1986)

3. Look at Exercise 2. **True** or **False**? Write a question mark (**?**) if the information isn't in the chart.

   a. The best mangoes are very heavy. _____?_____

   b. Don't buy a watermelon unless it has been cut open. _____

   c. Raspberries become rotten very quickly. _____

   d. Small strawberries taste better. _____

   e. Fresh apples are best in the summer. _____

   f. The best juice oranges come from Florida. _____

   g. When you buy cherries, size is important. _____

   h. You should buy avocados that are completely ripe. _____

   i. Summer is a good time to buy lemons. _____

   j. Apricots should be bright orange when you buy them. _____

   k. A ripe cantaloupe is soft at both ends. _____

4. What about you? List your favourite fruits. When do you buy them? Use your own paper.

Challenge Make a chart like the one in Exercise 2 for your favourite fruits.

1. Look in your dictionary. Put these vegetables in the correct category.

lettuce	spinach	carrots	zucchini	~~radishes~~	corn	parsley
~~chili peppers~~	squash	turnips	eggplants	cucumbers		string beans
beets	tomatoes	green peppers	cabbage	peas	yams	~~artichokes~~

ROOT VEGETABLES   **LEAF VEGETABLES**   **VEGETABLES WITH SEEDS**

radishes   artichokes   chili peppers

_____ _____ _____ _____

_____ _____ _____ _____

_____ _____ _____ _____

_____ _____ _____ _____

2. Complete the recipe with the amounts and names of the vegetables in the picture. (Look at **page 58** in your dictionary for ways to prepare foods.)

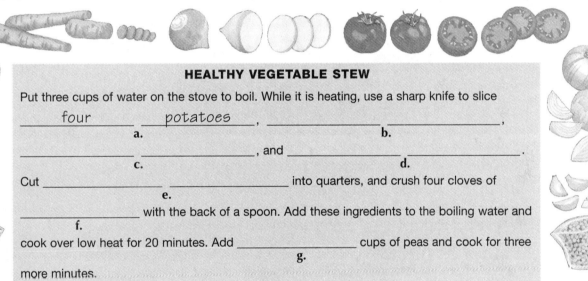

HEALTHY VEGETABLE STEW

Put three cups of water on the stove to boil. While it is heating, use a sharp knife to slice

_____four_____ _____potatoes_____, _____ _____,
     a.   **b.**

_____ _____, and _____ _____.
         c.   **d.**

Cut _____ _____ into quarters, and crush four cloves of
              e.

_____ with the back of a spoon. Add these ingredients to the boiling water and
  f.

cook over low heat for 20 minutes. Add _____ cups of peas and cook for three
                                             g.

more minutes.

3. What about you? Check (✓) the ways you like to eat vegetables.

VEGETABLE	STIR-FRIED	SAUTÉED	STEAMED	BAKED	BOILED	RAW
broccoli						
cauliflower						
scallions						
mushrooms						
Other: _____						

Challenge Write the recipe for a vegetable dish.

Meat and Poultry

1. Look in your dictionary. Cross out the word that doesn't belong. Write the category.

a. ____poultry____ ~~bacon~~ breast thigh wing

b. _____ sausage bacon chop tripe

c. _____ leg chop wing shank

d. _____ liver gizzard tripe steak

2. Complete the article with information from the charts.

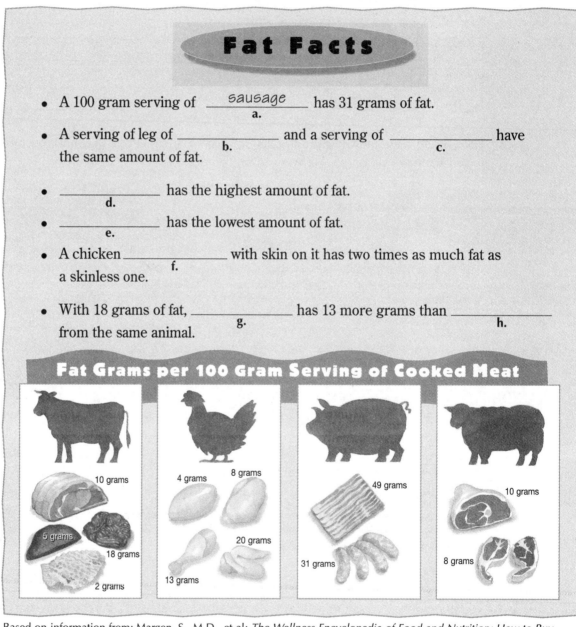

Fat Facts

- A 100 gram serving of ____sausage____ has 31 grams of fat.
    a.

- A serving of leg of _____ and a serving of _____ have
    b.   c.
the same amount of fat.

- _____ has the highest amount of fat.
    d.

- _____ has the lowest amount of fat.
    e.

- A chicken _____ with skin on it has two times as much fat as
    f.
a skinless one.

- With 18 grams of fat, _____ has 13 more grams than _____
    g.   h.
from the same animal.

Fat Grams per 100 Gram Serving of Cooked Meat

10 grams

5 grams

18 grams

2 grams

4 grams

8 grams

20 grams

13 grams

49 grams

31 grams

10 grams

8 grams

Based on information from: Margen, S., M.D., et al: *The Wellness Encyclopedia of Food and Nutrition: How to Buy, Store, and Prepare Every Variety of Fresh Food.* (NY: Random House, 1992.)

Challenge Keep a record of the meat you eat in one day. Figure out the fat content. Use the
information in Exercise 2.

1. Look in your dictionary. **True** or **False**? Correct the <u>underlined</u> words in the false sentences.

   potato salad
   a. There's a spoon in the ~~pasta salad~~.   <u>False</u>

   b. Salami is <u>meat</u>.   _____

   c. The potato salad is next to the <u>cheddar cheese</u>.   _____

   d. The Swiss cheese is between the cheddar cheese
      and the <u>processed cheese</u>.   _____

   e. The <u>rye bread</u> has seeds in it.   _____

   f. There are some <u>whole halibut</u> for sale.   _____

   g. The trout is <u>frozen</u>.   _____

   h. The <u>sole</u> has no bones.   _____

2. Look at the seafood prices and the recipe cards. How much will the seafood for each recipe cost? (See dictionary **page 57** for information about weights and measures.)

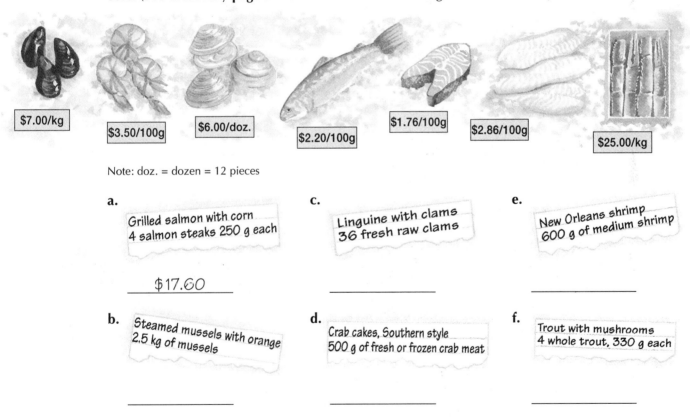

$7.00/kg

$3.50/100g

$6.00/doz.

$2.20/100g

$1.76/100g

$2.86/100g

$25.00/kg

Note: doz. = dozen = 12 pieces

a.
   Grilled salmon with corn
   4 salmon steaks 250 g each

   <u>$17.60</u>

b.
   Steamed mussels with orange
   2.5 kg of mussels

   _____

c.
   Linguine with clams
   36 fresh raw clams

   _____

d.
   Crab cakes, Southern style
   500 g of fresh or frozen crab meat

   _____

e.
   New Orleans shrimp
   600 g of medium shrimp

   _____

f.
   Trout with mushrooms
   4 whole trout, 330 g each

   _____

3. What about you? Order lunch from the deli for yourself and a friend. Use your own paper.

   Example: *One ham and cheddar cheese sandwich on whole wheat bread with a side order of coleslaw. One turkey breast on white bread.*

Challenge Plan a party menu for your class. Use a deli menu and the information from Exercise 2. How much will you buy? How much will it cost?

The Supermarket

1. Look in your dictionary. Cross out the word that doesn't belong. Write the section of the store.

a. <u>canned goods</u> soup ~~sugar~~ beans tuna

b. _____ bananas tomatoes oranges rolls

c. _____ yogurt eggs milk ice cream

d. _____ pop bottled water sour cream apple juice

e. _____ rice bread cake cookies

f. _____ butter gum potato chips candy bars

g. _____ chicken cheese turkey steak

h. _____ oil flour spaghetti cake mix

i. _____ aluminum foil plastic wrap paper towels pet food

2. Complete the article. Use the words in the box.

bagger	basket	beans	bottle return	cart	cash register
cashier	checkouts	coffee	~~cookies~~	line	manager
margarine	paper	plastic	produce	vegetables	

SAVE TIME AND MONEY: Some Shopping Tips

- Never shop when you're hungry. Those chocolate ___<u>cookies</u>___ will be hard
  a.

  to resist on an empty stomach.

- Do you really need a large shopping _____, or is a smaller shopping
  b.

  _____ enough? Having too much room may encourage you to buy
  c.

  more than you need.

- Shop with a list. That makes it easier to buy only what you need.

- Keep a price book of items that you buy frequently. *Example:* If you drink a lot of

  _____, compare prices at different stores.
  d.

- Always check the unit price. *Example:* It may be cheaper to buy a large can of

  _____ than a small can. The important question: How much does it
  e.

  cost *per 100 millilitres?*

- Watch for sales. Buy a lot of the items you need.

54

- Buy the store brand. *Example:* A container of Supermarket Brand _____
  f.

  will probably cost less than the famous brands.

- If the _____ doesn't look fresh, buy frozen _____.
  g.   h.
  They'll look and taste better.

- Avoid standing in _____. Try to shop when the store is less crowded.
  i.

  If all the _____ aren't open, speak to the store _____.
  j.   k.

- Always watch the _____ when the _____ is ringing
  l.   m.

  up your order. Is the price the same as the one on the item? Mistakes can happen!

- Don't throw away those empty cola bottles without looking! In some provinces, you

  can get a refund. Take them to the _____.
  n.

- If the _____ gives you a choice between a _____ or
  o.   p.

  _____ bag, consider paper—it can be recycled. If the store only has
  q.

  plastic bags, use them again!

---

3. What about you? Which of the shopping tips in Exercise 2 do you follow? Which ones will you try? What other ways do you save money when you go food shopping? Write about them. Use your own paper.

Challenge   Make a list of ten food items that you often buy. Go to two stores and compare prices.

Example:

Item

1. <u>can of beans</u>

Store A: <u>Shop & Save</u> / Item Size: <u>398 mL</u> / Price: <u>69¢</u> / Unit Price: <u>17¢ per 100 mL</u>

Store B: <u>B&D</u> / Item Size: <u>398 mL</u> / Price: <u>59¢</u> / Unit Price: <u>14¢ per 100 mL</u>

2. _____

Store A: <u>Shop & Save</u> / Item Size: _____ / Price: ___ / Unit Price: _____

Store B: <u>B&D</u> / Item Size: _____ / Price: ___ / Unit Price: _____

Containers and Packaged Foods

1. Look in your dictionary. Complete the flyer.

RECYCLE—It's Your Duty!

The packaging for many items on your grocery list belongs in your recycling bin, not your garbage can.
Follow the recycling guidelines as you use these items.

YES	NO
a. ☑ plastic or glass _____bottles_____ (pop, juice)	**f.** ☒ plastic _____bags_____ (bread)
b. ☑ plastic or glass _____ (jam)	**g.** ☒ plastic _____ (yogurt)
c. ☑ cardboard _____ (cereal)	**h.** ☒ cardboard _____ (paper towels)
d. ☑ cardboard _____ (eggs, milk)	**i.** ☒ plastic _____ (cookies)
e. ☑ metal _____ (tuna, soup)	**j.** ☒ plastic _____ (toothpaste)

Note: Recycling guidelines are different in different places.

2. Look at the groceries that Mee-Yon bought this week. Which items have packaging that she can recycle? Which items don't? Complete the lists below. Use information from Exercise 1.

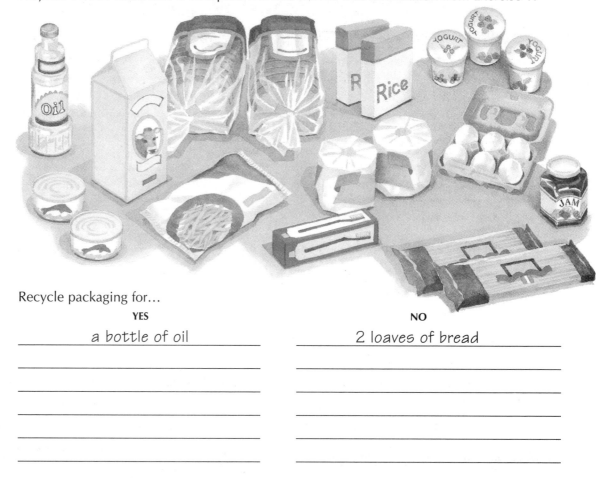

Recycle packaging for...

YES	NO
_____a bottle of oil_____	_____2 loaves of bread_____
_____	_____
_____	_____
_____	_____
_____	_____
_____	_____

3. What about you? Look in your refrigerator and kitchen cupboards. List items that you can and can't recycle. Use information from Exercise 1.

Challenge Where are the recycling centres in your community? What kinds of containers does each one accept?

56

1. Look in your dictionary. Circle the larger amount.

a. 3 teaspoons / (3 tablespoons)

d. 5 millilitres / 1 tablespoon

b. 100 millilitres / 1 litre

e. 500 grams / 1 kilogram

c. 1 cup / 500 millilitres

f. 250 millilitres / ½ cup

2. Look at the nutrition facts. Answer the questions. Use your dictionary for help.

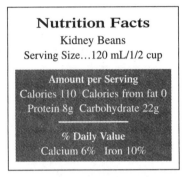

Nutrition Facts
Kidney Beans
Serving Size...120 mL/1/2 cup

Amount per Serving
Calories 110 Calories from fat 0
Protein 8g Carbohydrate 22g

% Daily Value
Calcium 6% Iron 10%

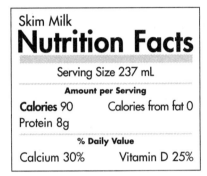

Skim Milk
Nutrition Facts

Serving Size 237 mL

Amount per Serving
Calories 90   Calories from fat 0
Protein 8g

% Daily Value
Calcium 30%   Vitamin D 25%

Nutrition Facts

Rice
Serving Size 1/4 cup raw (about 1 cup cooked)

Amount per Serving
Calories 170   Calories from fat 0
Protein 4 grams   Carbohydrate 38 grams

% Daily Value
Calcium.......... 2%   Iron............... 8%

CHOCOLATE CANDY
Nutrition Facts
Serving Size 1 piece (15 g)
AMOUNT PER SERVING
Calories 90   Calories from fat 30
Total fat 4g • Protein 1g

Note: g = grams   % Daily Value = % of the total amount you should have in one day   1 cup = 237 mL

a. Which has more protein, a cup of beans or a cup of milk?   _a cup of beans_

b. How many pieces of chocolate candy are there in 400 grams?   _____

c. How many millilitres of milk give 100% of the daily value of Vitamin D?   _____

d. How much fat is there in 90 grams of chocolate candy?   _____

e. A serving of rice and beans contains a quarter cup of beans and a half cup of cooked rice. How much carbohydrate is there in a serving?   _____

f. What per cent of the daily value of iron is there in a serving of rice and beans?   _____

g. How many litres of milk do you need for 50 servings?   _____

h. What per cent of the daily value of calcium do you get from 475 mL of milk and two servings of rice?   _____

Challenge Look at **page 184** in this book. Follow the instructions.

Food Preparation

1. Look in your dictionary. Complete the cookbook definitions. (*Hint:* The words are in alphabetical order.)

   a. _____bake_____ : Cook by dry heat in an oven. (cake, potatoes)

   b. _____ : Cook over an open fire with a sauce brushed on, often outside.

   c. _____ : Make mixture smooth by quick motion with a spoon, fork, or whisk. (eggs)

   d. _____ : Cook in very hot liquid (100°C for water).

   e. _____ : Cook in contact with direct heat under the broiler.

   f. _____ : Cut into pieces with a knife or other sharp tool.

   g. _____ : Cook in hot oil in a large pot or pan.

   h. _____ : Cut into very small pieces using small holes of a grater. (cheese)

   i. _____ : See *barbecue*.

   j. _____ : Combine ingredients, usually with a spoon.

   k. _____ : Take off outer covering. (onion, carrot)

   l. _____ : Cook in a small amount of hot butter or oil. (onion, garlic)

   m. _____ : Cook slowly in liquid just below the boiling point.

   n. _____ : Cook over boiling water, not in it. (vegetables)

2. Look at Andy's recipe. It got wet, and now he can't read parts of it. Complete the recipe. Use the words in the box.

add	bake	~~grease~~	mix	pour	slice

   Baked sole in sour cream

   filet of sole   1/4 c. mayonnaise
   butter   1/2 c. sour cream
   salt, pepper, paprika mushrooms

   Grease a baking dish. Place the fish in the dish, top with butter.
       a.
   _____ salt, pepper, and paprika. _____ the mayonnaise and
       b.   **c.**
   sour cream. _____ over the fish. _____ the mushrooms, and
               d.   **e.**
   add to the dish. _____ in 350° oven for 45 minutes.
                    f.

_____ **Challenge** Write one of your favourite recipes.

58

1. Look in your dictionary. **True** or **False**? Correct the <u>underlined</u> words in the false sentences.

counter
a. There's a casserole dish on the ~~stove~~.   _____False_____

b. One of the cooks is using a <u>can opener</u>.   _____

c. Another cook is putting <u>pasta</u> into a colander.   _____

d. The cook with the rolling pin is making a <u>pie</u>.   _____

e. One of the cooks used the <u>vegetable peeler</u>.   _____

f. There's a <u>turkey</u> in the roasting pan.   _____

g. There are five <u>rolls</u> on the cookie sheet.   _____

h. There's <u>butter</u> in the frying pan.   _____

2. Circle the correct words to complete the cookbook information.

Some utensils you need in your kitchen:

a. <u>Grater /</u>(**Whisk:**) for beating eggs, cream, etc.

b. <u>Steamer / Colander:</u> for removing water from cooked pasta, vegetables, etc.

c. <u>Ladle / Spatula:</u> for spooning soup, sauces, etc., out of a pot

d. <u>Paring / Carving knife:</u> for cutting up small fruits and vegetables

e. <u>Tongs / Lids:</u> for covering pots and pans

f. <u>Plastic storage containers / Strainers:</u> for keeping food fresh

g. <u>Pots / Pot holders:</u> for handling hot utensils

h. <u>Egg beaters / Wooden spoons:</u> for stirring soup, sauces, etc.

i. <u>Double boiler / Roasting rack:</u> for slow cooking on top of the stove

j. <u>Cake and pie pans / pins:</u> for baking desserts

Challenge Look in your dictionary. Make a list of the five most important kitchen utensils. Explain your choices.

Fast Food

1. Look in your dictionary. Where can you hear…?

   a. "How's your taco?"   _____booth_____

   b. "I'll have a hamburger with fries, and a large pop." _____

   c. "After this hot dog, I'm going to the salad bar."   _____

2. Look at the chart. **True** or **False**? Write a question mark (**?**) if the information isn't there.

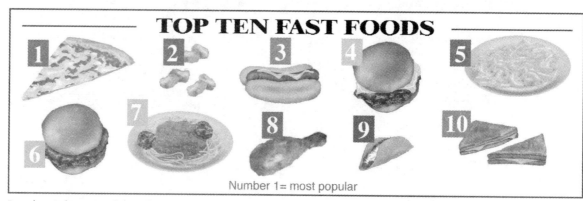

TOP TEN FAST FOODS

Number 1 = most popular

Based on information from: Choron, S. and H.: *The Book of Lists for Kids.* (NY: Houghton Mifflin Co., 1995)

   a. Hot dogs are the most popular food.   _____False_____

   b. Cheeseburgers are more popular than hamburgers.   _____

   c. French fries are among the ten most popular foods.   _____

   d. Muffins are more popular than doughnuts.   _____

   e. Pizza is more popular than spaghetti.   _____

   f. Nachos are one of the top ten fast food items.   _____

   g. Frozen yogurt is very popular.   _____

3. Match the ingredients labels with the condiments.

   __3__ a. **INGREDIENTS:** VINEGAR, MUSTARD SEED, SALT, TURMERIC   **1.** ketchup

   _____ b. **INGREDIENTS:** SOYBEAN OIL, WHOLE EGGS, VINEGAR, WATER, EGG YOLKS, SALT, SUGAR, LEMON JUICE, NATURAL FLAVOURINGS   **2.** mayonnaise

   _____ c. **INGREDIENTS:** CUCUMBERS, CORN SYRUP, VINEGAR, ONIONS, WATER, SALT, SUGAR, SPICES, PEPPERS   **3.** mustard

   _____ d. ■ **INGREDIENTS:** TOMATO CONCENTRATE (WATER, TOMATO PASTE), CORN SYRUP, VINEGAR, SALT, SPICES   **4.** relish

4. What about you? List your "top ten" fast foods. Use your own paper.

   Challenge Take a survey of your classmates' top ten fast foods.

1. Look in your dictionary. Cross out the word that doesn't belong. Write the category.

a. _desserts_	pudding	~~mashed potatoes~~	pie	cake
b. _____	garlic bread	waffles	scrambled eggs	pancakes
c. _____	coffee	decaf coffee	syrup	tea
d. _____	chef's salad	sandwich	sausage	soup
e. _____	bacon	pasta	baked potato	fried fish

2. Look at the pictures. Circle the correct words to complete one of the orders.

"I'll have pasta / (soup), steak / a chef's salad, and a cup of coffee / tea."
  a.   **b.**   **c.**

"I'd like fried fish / roast chicken with mashed potatoes / rice pilaf, and a cup of tea / coffee.
           d.   **e.**   **f.**

Pudding / Pie for dessert, please."
  g.

"I'll have pancakes / waffles and ice cream / syrup with bacon / sausage and a cup of
           h.   **i.**   **j.**

tea / decaf coffee."
  k.

3. Look again at the pictures in Exercise 2. Write the *other* orders in the correct category.

a. **Breakfast:** "I'll have _scrambled eggs, toast, and a cup of coffee_____."

b. **Lunch:** "I'd like _____."

c. **Dinner:** "I'll have _____."

4. What about you? Order a meal from Exercise 2.

_____.

Challenge Imagine you own a coffee shop. Write your own menu.

A Restaurant

1. Look at the top picture on pages 62 and 63 in your dictionary. Who said...?

   a. "Your table will be ready in a minute, Mr. and Mrs. Pyle."   *hostess*

   b. "Would you like spinach or broccoli with that?"   _____

   c. "This salad is delicious."   _____

   d. "We also have chocolate, coconut, and mango ice cream."   _____

   e. "Here are some more dirty dishes!"   _____

   f. "The glasses are all clean, and I'm almost done with these plates."   _____

2. Circle the correct words to complete this restaurant review.

☆ ☆ ☆

A.J. Clarke's 290 Park Place 555-3454

As soon as I walked into Clarke's, I was impressed by the handsome pink and green <u>(dining room)</u> / kitchen **a.** that can serve about 50 <u>chefs / diners</u> **b.**. The hostess <u>seated / served</u> **c.** my guest and me at a quiet table in the corner where we immediately got a <u>bread basket / soup bowl</u> **d.** filled with warm, freshly baked rolls. The service was great. The <u>patron / busperson</u> **e.** continued to <u>pour / clear</u> **f.** water throughout the meal.

And what a meal it was! The <u>bill / menu</u> **g.** had something for everyone. Our <u>dishwasher / server</u> **h.**, Todd, recommended the fish of the day, tuna. My friend <u>ordered / served</u> **i.** the chicken l'orange. After Todd <u>carried / took</u> **j.** our orders, he brought us two salad <u>forks / plates</u> **k.** with the freshest lettuce I've ever eaten.

This was followed by two large—and delicious— <u>bowls / plates</u> **l.** of onion soup. Our main dishes did not disappoint us. The tuna was so tender that you could cut it without the <u>steak knife / teaspoon</u> **m.** that came with it. The chicken, too, was wonderful.

When we were finished, the busperson <u>cleared / set</u> **n.** the table. Time for dessert! Todd <u>carried / left</u> **o.** out the dessert <u>fork / tray</u> **p.**, which was filled with several cakes and pies—all baked in the restaurant's own <u>kitchen / dishroom</u> **q.**. Raspberry pie with whipped cream and a <u>cup / saucer</u> **r.** of delicious hot coffee ended our perfect meal.

We happily <u>paid / poured</u> **s.** our bill and <u>left / took</u> **t.** Todd a nice tip. My tip to you: Eat at A.J. Clarke's. Reservations recommended.

---

3. Look at the picture and complete the description.

A formal ___place setting___
                        a.

A _____ **b.** is in the centre, usually with the _____ **c.** on top of it. The flatware is on both sides. To the left of the plate are (from closest to farthest) a _____ **d.** and a _____ **e.**

To the right of the plate are a _____ **f.**, a _____ **g.**, and sometimes a shellfish _____ **h.**. Above and to the right of the plate are a _____ **i.** and two _____ **j.**

There is also a small _____ **k.** above and to the left of the dinner plate. The butter _____ **l.** is set on top of it.

4. What about you? Most people's table settings do not look like the formal one in Exercise 3! Draw your table setting. How is it the same? How is it different? Write sentences on your own paper.

Example: *We put the napkin under the fork.*

Challenge Write a description of a meal you had at a restaurant or at someone's home.

▶ **Go to page 173 for Another Look (Unit 4).**

63

Clothing I

1. Look in your dictionary. Who said...? Identify the people by their clothes.

   a. "Only one more kilometre."

     <u>The man in the sweatshirt and sweatpants.</u>

   b. "You look so good in your new turtleneck."

     _____

   c. "It's 6:05. Where's the bus?"

     _____

   d. "Mommy, can Ricky and I sit in the first row?"

     _____

   e. "Your tickets, please."

     _____

   f. "You look nice in that dress."

     _____

   g. "Where's the women's washroom, please?"

     _____

   h. "Daddy, look there!"

     _____

   i. "Here's the last letter."

     _____

2. Circle the correct words to complete the article.

Back to Basics

Building a basic wardrobe? Here are a few items of clothing that you can wear almost anywhere—from a job interview to a walk in the park.

FOR MEN:

A navy blue (suit)/ tuxedo. Wear it with a white   shirt / knit shirt
          a.   **b.**

for formal occasions.

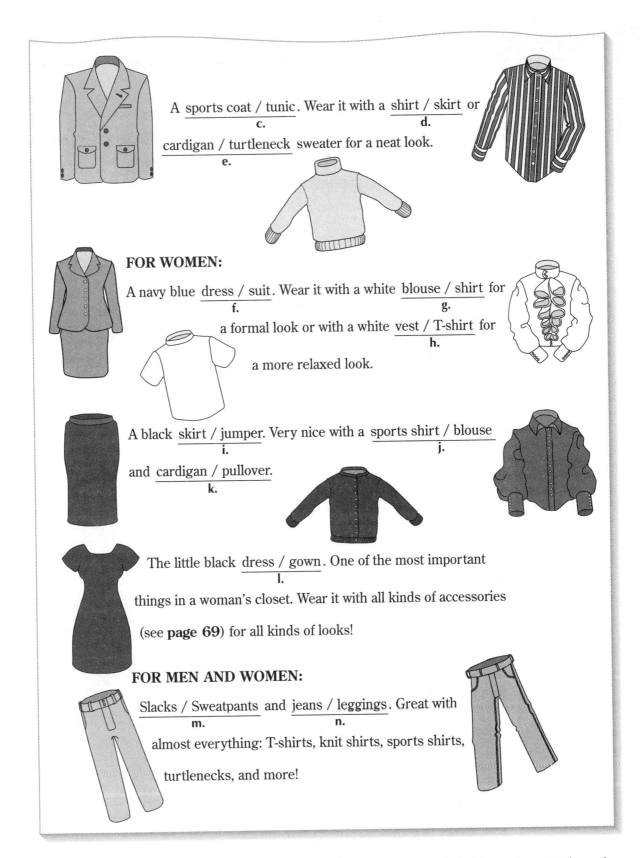

A <u>sports coat / tunic</u>. Wear it with a <u>shirt / skirt</u> or
     c.   **d.**

<u>cardigan / turtleneck</u> sweater for a neat look.
     e.

FOR WOMEN:

A navy blue <u>dress / suit</u>. Wear it with a white <u>blouse / shirt</u> for
           f.   **g.**

a formal look or with a white <u>vest / T-shirt</u> for
                   h.

a more relaxed look.

A black <u>skirt / jumper</u>. Very nice with a <u>sports shirt / blouse</u>
      i.   **j.**

and <u>cardigan / pullover</u>.
   k.

The little black <u>dress / gown</u>. One of the most important
         l.

things in a woman's closet. Wear it with all kinds of accessories

(see **page 69**) for all kinds of looks!

FOR MEN AND WOMEN:

<u>Slacks / Sweatpants</u> and <u>jeans / leggings</u>. Great with
      m.   **n.**

almost everything: T-shirts, knit shirts, sports shirts,

turtlenecks, and more!

3. What about you? What do you think are the most important items of clothing to have? Where do you wear these clothes?

Example: *slacks and a sports shirt—I wear them to work, to school, and at home.*

Challenge Choose five people from your dictionary. Describe their clothes. **Example:** *The administrative assistant on page 136 is wearing a blue skirt and a pink blouse.*

Clothing II

1. Look in your dictionary. Cross out the word that doesn't belong. Write the weather condition.

a. _____raining_____   poncho   rain boots   umbrella   ~~toque~~

b. _____   overcoat   cover-up   scarf   jacket

c. _____   straw hat   bathing suit   parka   sunglasses

d. _____   down jacket   tights   ski mask   baseball cap

2. Correct the ad.

It's windy out there, but Jillian is dressed for the weather in a
jacket
warm brown leather ~~parka~~, earmuffs, and a striped scarf. That

straw hat protects her from the autumn wind.

Jillian

3. Write ads for Abdulla, Polly, and Julio's clothing. Use Exercise 2 as a model.

Abdulla

a. _____
_____
_____

Polly

b. _____
_____
_____

Julio

c. _____
_____
_____

Challenge   What do you like to wear in different weather conditions? Write short paragraphs like the ones in Exercise 3.

66

1. Look in your dictionary. Find the words that complete *a pair of....*

<u>bike shorts</u> _____ _____ _____

_____ _____ _____ _____

_____ _____ _____ _____

2. Read the note. Then complete each list with the correct name and items to pack. Continue on your own paper.

> *Dear Ann,*
> *Thanks for agreeing to take care of Bobby this weekend. I have to go out of town, and Julio is going skiing. Inga can't babysit because she's going on a bike trip. We appreciate your help!*
> *Love,*
> *Amanda*

a. for Bobby
    two sleepers

b. for _____

c. for _____

d. for _____

<u>**Challenge**</u>   You're going on a trip next weekend. List the underwear and sleepwear you'll take.

Shoes and Accessories

1. Look at items 25–43 on **page 69** in your dictionary. Read the sentences. Write the names of the items the people are talking about.

   a. "I always keep my coins in one—separate from my bills."   _change purse_

   b. "According to this one, it's 8:20."   _____

   c. "What does the *NJ* on it stand for?"   _____

   d. "Ow! This is sharp! I just stabbed myself with it."   _____

   e. "Wow! This has even more room than the backpack!"   _____

   f. "John gave one to me. I put his photo in it."   _____

   g. "Oh, no. I forgot to put my credit card back in it."   _____

2. Complete the ad.

Newport Mall—*Your one stop for fall fashions!*

Men's striped _____tie_____
     a.

▶ The Neck Stop

Black _____ and silver _____
          b.   c.

▶ Accessories East

Brand name _____
                  d.

▶ Foot Smart

Gold _____ and
            e.

pierced _____
              f.

▶ E.R. Jewellers

Leather _____
              g.

▶ The Bag House

68

3. Look at the shopping list. Where can you buy these items? Use the stores from Exercise 2.

To buy –   bow tie   The Neck Stop
             brown purse   _____
             gold bracelet   _____
             backpack   _____
             pearls   _____
             black boots   _____

4. Circle the correct words to complete this card.

If the Shoe Fits

Always try on (shoes) / scarves at the end of the day—your feet are bigger then!
a.

Ask yourself: Is there enough room at the sole / toe? There should be at least
b.

1½ cm between the end of your foot and the beginning of the shoe. And remember,

you need different kinds of shoes for different kinds of activities. Women may want

to wear high heels / oxfords to an evening party, but tennis shoes / pumps are a
c.   **d.**

better choice for the office. The lower the heel / pin, the more comfortable the
e.

shoe. Both women and men can relax at home in a pair of hiking boots / loafers,
f.

but you'll want shoes with belts / shoelaces for walking. And if running is part of
g.

your daily routine, track shoes / sandals are the best bet.
h.

Foot Smart at the Newport Mall

5. What about you? How do you feel about…? Circle the number that's true for you.

	LIKE ←――――――――→ DON'T LIKE				
a. high heel shoes	1	2	3	4	5
b. hats	1	2	3	4	5
c. suspenders	1	2	3	4	5
d. bow ties	1	2	3	4	5
e. pierced earrings	1	2	3	4	5

Challenge Which accessories make good gifts? Explain who you would buy them for and why.
    Example: *I'd buy a backpack for my girlfriend because she loves to hike.*

Describing Clothes

1. Look in your dictionary. Cross out the word that doesn't belong. Write the category.

a. <u>sweater styles</u>	V-neck	crewneck	~~casual~~	turtleneck
b. _____	nylon	plaid	paisley	polka-dotted
c. _____	large	extra large	small	too small
d. _____	leather	wool	plain	linen
e. _____	rip	sleeveless	stain	too big

2. Look in your dictionary. Write the type of material next to each description.

Material Matters

a. ___linen___ This was the first woven material. Ancient people learned how to make thread from the blue-flowered flax plant and weave it into cloth. Today it is often used to make jackets and suits.

b. _____ Very early, people learned how to make animal skins into this material. They rubbed the skins with fat to make them soft. Later they learned to use plants to soften the skins.

c. _____ For thousands of years, only the Chinese knew how to make clothing from this beautiful material. Around 500 A.D., two men stole several eggs of the insects that make the thread. They took the eggs to the West, and the secret was out!

d. _____ This is the most important material in the world. It is used everywhere for all kinds of clothing and many other products. It comes from a plant that grows in hot climates.

e. _____ This material is also used all over the world. It is made from the hair of an animal. It is soft, warm, and naturally waterproof!

f. _____ This synthetic material comes from the laboratory, not from a plant or animal. It's used to make pantyhose and many other items of clothing.

3. Look at the pictures. Circle the correct words to complete the article.

SUITABLE DRESSING

Men's formal business suits never seem to change very much these days.

However, it took a long time for men to get to this basic piece of clothing.

Here's how it happened.

During the 1500s in Europe, fashionable men wanted to look fat. Their

pants, called pumpkin breeches, were (short)/ long and baggy / tight. They
                       a.   **b.**

wore short / long, light / heavy, sleeveless / long-sleeved jackets, and
      c.   **d.**   **e.**

they even stuffed their clothes with cereal and horsehair to look bigger!

In the 1700s, men preferred to look thinner and taller. The rich and stylish

wore their pants shorter / longer and very tight / baggy, and they wore
                  f.   **g.**

shoes with low / high heels and big buckles. Jackets became longer / shorter
         h.   **i.**

and looser / tighter, and men wore fancy / plain shirts under them.
     j.   **k.**

After the French Revolution in 1789, it became dangerous to dress like the

rich. Instead, many men dressed like workers in long / short pants and loose
                                    l.

jackets. This outfit was a lot like the modern suit, but the parts did not match.

The man in the picture, for example, is wearing striped / checked brown
                                   m.

pants with a polka-dotted / paisley vest and a solid / plaid jacket.
          n.   **o.**

Finally, at the end of the 1800s, it became stylish to match the pants,

jacket, and vest. As you can see, the traditional formal / casual three-piece
                                      p.

business suit has not changed much since then.

4. What about you? How have styles changed in your country in the past 100 years? Write at least
three sentences. Use your own paper.

Challenge Describe traditional clothing for men or women from a culture you know well. What
materials, colours, and patterns do people wear? **Example:** *In Oman, women wear short
tunics and long, baggy pants. The weather is very hot, so clothing is usually cotton or silk…*

Doing the Laundry

1. Look in your dictionary. **True** or **False**?

   a. A man is doing the laundry.   _True_

   b. He's at the dry cleaners.   _____

   c. The clothes in the laundry basket are ironed.   _____

   d. There's a clean shirt on the ironing board.   _____

   e. Someone hung a pair of jeans on the clothesline. _____

2. Circle the correct words to complete the laundry room instructions.

◯ CLEANMACH INDUSTRIES, INC.

Washing Instructions

1. Pour **detergent** / spray starch into bottom of <u>washer / dryer</u>.
          a.   b.
2. <u>Sort / Fold</u> clothes and place loosely and evenly in the machine. DO NOT OVERLOAD.
   c.
3. Choose the correct temperature.
4. Close door. <u>Hanger / Washer</u> will not operate with door open.
                 d.
5. Insert coin(s) into slot.
6. To add <u>bleach / dryer sheets</u>: Wait until <u>laundry basket / washer</u> has filled.
               e.   f.
DO NOT POUR directly onto clothes.
7. If you use <u>fabric softener / detergent</u>, add it when the rinse light goes on.
          g.

Drying Instructions

1. Clean the <u>iron / lint trap</u> before using the dryer.
          h.
2. <u>Load / Unload</u> the machine. DO NOT OVERLOAD. Overloading causes <u>dirty / wrinkled</u> clothes.
   i.   j.
3. Add <u>dryer sheets / clothespins</u> if you wish.
          k.
4. Close door. <u>Dryer / Washer</u> will not operate with door open.
          l.
5. Choose the correct temperature.
6. Insert coin(s) into slot. Push start button.
7. Remove <u>dry / wet</u> clothes immediately.
   m.

FOR SERVICE CALL (800) 555-3452

Challenge Look at some of your clothing labels. Write the laundry instructions.

1. Look in your dictionary. What can you use to…?

    a. repair a rip when you don't have needle and thread   _safety pin_

    b. cut material   _____

    c. hold pins and needles   _____

    d. remove threads from a hem or a seam   _____

    e. measure your waist   _____

    f. close the front of a windbreaker   _____

    g. close the top of a dress (above the zipper)   _____

    h. protect your finger when you sew   _____

2. Look at the picture. Circle the correct words to complete the instructions.

Tailor Made

Please make these alterations:

Move the top button / <u>buttonhole.</u> It should be
                   a.
below the <u>collar</u> / pocket.
         b.

Let out the <u>collar</u> / waistband.
         c.

<u>Shorten</u> / Lengthen the sleeves.
     d.

The right <u>cuff</u> / pocket is missing—please sew it on.
         e.

<u>Let out</u> / Take in the seams on the skirt and
    f.
hem / <u>lengthen</u> it so it's right at the knee.
    g.

3. What about you? Would you prefer to sew by hand or by machine? Why?

_____

_____

Challenge   Design a piece of clothing. Draw it and write a description.

▶ **Go to page 174 for Another Look (Unit 5).**

The Body

1. Look in your dictionary. Match each pair with the connecting part.

_4_	**a.** hand / arm	**1.**	elbow
_____	**b.** foot / calf	**2.**	ankle
_____	**c.** calf / thigh	**3.**	waist
_____	**d.** head / shoulders	**4.**	wrist
_____	**e.** upper arm / lower arm	**5.**	knee
_____	**f.** chest / abdomen	**6.**	neck

2. Yoga is a very old form of exercise and meditation. Circle the correct words to complete the instructions.

PALMING Rub your (palms) / gums together until your hands feel warm.
a.

Then hold them over your nose / eyes .
b.

BEE BREATH Place your hands / legs gently on your feet / face as follows:
c.   d.

thumbs / teeth on your ears / eyebrows , first finger / toe on your
e.   f.   g.

eyelashes / toenails of your closed eyes, second on your chin / nose , third and
h.   i.

fourth on your top and bottom lips / eyelids . When you breathe out, gently
j.

close your ears with your thumbs and put your tongue / bone against the
k.

top of your throat / mouth to make a "zzzz" sound.
l.

THE BOW Lie on your abdomen / artery . Reach back and hold your
m.

heels / ankles . Pull your thighs / hips and chest / buttocks off the floor.
n.   o.   p.

Your skeleton / pelvis rests on the floor.
q.

THE MOON Kneel with your buttocks / rib cage on your arms / heels .
r.   s.

Put your hands / hair against your breast / back and hold your right
t.   u.

wrist / vein . Bend forward until your chin / forehead touches the floor.
v.   w.

3. Read the article. Label the foot with the matching parts of the body.

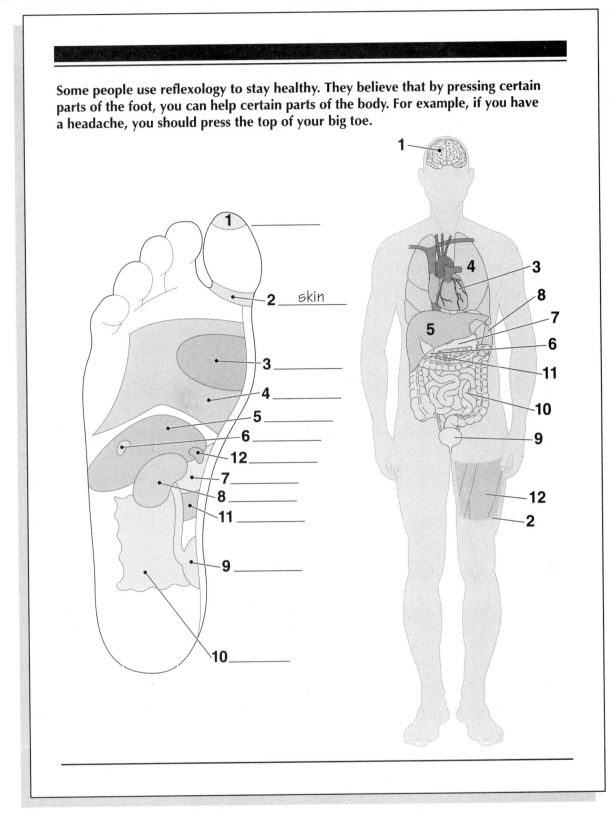

Some people use reflexology to stay healthy. They believe that by pressing certain parts of the foot, you can help certain parts of the body. For example, if you have a headache, you should press the top of your big toe.

1 _____

2 __skin_____

3 _____

4 _____

5 _____

6 _____

12 _____

7 _____

8 _____

11 _____

9 _____

10 _____

4. What about you? What do you do to relax and stay healthy? What parts of the body are these activities good for? Write at least five sentences. Use your own paper.

Challenge Write instructions for your favourite exercise.

Personal Hygiene

1. Look at the people in your dictionary. What is each person doing?

   a. "This air is really hot."   ____drying her hair____

   b. "This cap really keeps my hair dry!"   _____

   c. "This mouthwash tastes great."   _____

   d. "I don't want to get a sunburn."   _____

   e. "I think all the shampoo is out of my hair now."   _____

   f. "Ouch! I cut my cheek."   _____

   g. "I don't use a brush when it's still wet."   _____

2. Number the steps in a manicure. Then write the item to use for each step. Look in your dictionary for help.

   ### FOUR STEPS TO BEAUTIFUL HANDS

_____	a. When they are the right length, smooth and shape them.	_____
___1___	b. First, take off the old polish.	_nail polish remover_
_____	c. Finally, put the new colour on your fingernails.	_____
_____	d. After you remove it, cut your nails.	_____

3. Circle the correct words to complete the article.

Putting on makeup takes time, but it's worth it for a special evening. Here's how:

Use (hair clips)/ shampoo to hold your hair off your face. Then wash your
    a.
face with a gentle soap / deodorant . While your skin is still a little wet, put
                        b.
shaving cream / moisturizer on your face and neck. When it's dry, put on
            c.
foundation / conditioner —don't forget your eyelids and neck. Next apply
        d.
rouge / eye shadow , starting at the inside corner of the eyelid. With
        e.
a comb / an eyeliner , make a smooth line right above the eyelashes.
            f.
Next, apply hair gel / mascara to make your eyelashes look long and
                    g.
thick, and eyebrow pencil / hair spray to fill in the line of your eyebrows.
                h.
Brush on blush / cologne to give your cheeks a healthy colour. Outline your
            i.
lips first and then fill in the lines with lipstick / toothpaste . Finish off with
                                                    j.
a dusting of talcum / face powder.
                k.

4. Complete the crossword puzzle. Each clue is two words.

Clues

12 Across + 1 Down	You don't need water when you shave with it.
2 Down + 18 Down	It holds your hair in place.
3 Across + 10 Down	Use it after every meal.
5 Down + 6 Across	Be careful when you shave with them—they're sharp.
8 Across + 17 Across	Colour your fingernails and toenails with it.
9 Across + 4 Down	It will make your eyes look bigger.
11 Across + 7 Down	Put it on your skin when you're finished shaving.
10 Across + 13 Down	It makes your skin feel smooth and soft.
14 Down + 19 Across	Style your hair with it.
16 Across + 15 Down	Remove food from between your teeth with it.

Now use the circled letters to answer this question:

What can you take to relax?   A ___ ___ ___ ___   ___ ___ ___ ___

5. What about you? What is your personal hygiene routine in the morning? List the steps. Use your own paper. Use Exercise 2 as a model.

Example: *First, I…*

Challenge Write detailed instructions for one of the following tasks:

washing and styling your hair   flossing and brushing your teeth   shaving

Symptoms and Injuries

1. Look in your dictionary. Which symptom or injury are they talking about?

    a. "This one in the back hurts."   _____toothache_____

    b. "The thermometer says 39°C."   _____

    c. "I ate too much ice cream."   _____

    d. "Next time I'll wear gloves when I rake the leaves."   _____

    e. "I need another blanket."   _____

    f. "Thanks for your handkerchief."   _____

2. Circle the correct words to complete the article.

Home Health Hints

Sick or injured? Try some of these tips:

- After a day in the sun, put oatmeal in your bathwater for a <u>swollen finger</u> / (<u>sunburn.</u>)
  a.
- A <u>sprained / cut</u> ankle or wrist is a common sports injury. Use RICE—Rest, Ice,
  b.
  Compression (wrapping in a tight elastic bandage), and Elevation (raising the injured part).
- Rub deodorant on <u>blisters / insect bites</u> caused by bees or spiders.
  c.
- Eating bad food can make you feel nauseous. You might even <u>vomit / faint.</u>
  d.
  Drinking warm cola can help you feel better.
- It's hard to swallow with a <u>backache / sore throat</u>. Soft ice cream helps the pain.
  e.
- Put an ice pack on a <u>rash / bruise</u> the first day. After 24 hours, use a heating pad.
  f.
  As it gets better, the area changes from blue, to red, to yellow.
- For <u>headaches / nasal congestion</u>, take hot baths and drink fluids to breathe more regularly.
  g.
- It's not bad to <u>cough / sneeze</u>—it gets bacteria out of your lungs. But an
  h.
  over-the-counter syrup helps you stop when you want to sleep.

Remember, these problems can be serious. If you feel very bad or if the problem continues or gets worse, see your doctor or other health professional.

3. What about you? What do you do when you have a(n)…?

SYMPTOM OR INJURY	REMEDY
stomachache	_____
earache	_____
rash	_____
Other: _____	_____

Challenge Find out about blisters. Write about how to prevent and treat them.

1. Look in your dictionary. Complete the chart.

Illness or Condition	What is it?	Contagious?	What are some symptoms?
a. _____asthma_____	a medical condition	No	tight feeling in chest, difficulty breathing; wheezing, coughing
b. _____	a common childhood illness	Yes	fever, blisters on face and body, and inside mouth, nose, or throat
c. _____	a very common infection of the nose, throat, etc.	Yes	nasal congestion or runny nose, sore throat, cough, low fever, tiredness, watering eyes
d. _____	a condition caused by the pancreas not making enough insulin	No	tiredness, thirst, increased hunger, and weight loss
e. _____	an infection most common in infants and children	No	nervousness, earache, "full" feeling in the ear, fever, difficulty hearing
f. _____	a common illness	Yes	chills, fever, muscle aches, cough, sore throat, runny nose, headache
g. _____	a condition often caused by hard and narrow arteries	No	(Often no symptoms in the beginning.) Later: chest pains, heart attack
h. _____	the virus that causes AIDS	Yes	swollen glands, sore throat, fever, skin rash
i. _____	a common childhood illness	Yes	fever, cough, red eyes, red rash on forehead and around ears, and, later, whole body
j. _____	a common childhood illness	Yes	swollen glands (between ear and jaw), fever, headache, sore throat
k. _____	a throat infection	Yes	fever, throat pain, headache, general sick feeling, ear pain, swollen glands in neck, bright red throat
l. _____	a lung disease	Yes	(Often no symptoms in the beginning.) Later: flu-like symptoms, low fever, loss of weight, tiredness, cough (with blood), chest pain, difficult breathing

Based on information from: Griffith, H. W.: *Complete Guide to Symptoms, Illness, and Surgery*, 3rd ed. (NY: The Body Press/Perigee Books, 1995)

2. What about you? Check (✓) the illnesses or conditions you had as a child.

☐ measles ☐ mumps ☐ chicken pox ☐ asthma

☐ allergy ☐ Other: _____

_____ **Challenge** Find out about high blood pressure. What is it? Is it contagious? What are some symptoms?

1. Look in your dictionary. **True** or **False**? Correct the <u>underlined</u> words in the false sentences.

    exercising

a. The couple in D is ~~taking medicine~~.   *False*

b. The man with a cane is in a <u>pharmacy</u>.   _____

c. The girl in E is getting <u>acupuncture</u>.   _____

d. The man in A is <u>getting bed rest</u>.   _____

e. The <u>audiologist</u> is putting eyeglasses on a girl.   _____

f. The <u>orthopedist</u> is putting on a cast.   _____

2. Which medicine are they talking about? Read the labels. Write the type of medicine after each statement. Use the words in the box.

capsules	**cough syrup**	**ointment**

CORTICARE

INDICATIONS:
Use on insect bites and rashes caused by poison ivy or poison oak.

DIRECTIONS:
Apply a small amount of Corticare 1 to 3 times a day.

WARNING: FOR EXTERNAL USE ONLY

ABC/pharmacy

RX:2596   Date filled:6/9/01

BLACK, RONALD
Take 1 three times a day with food. Finish entire prescription.

BEMOX 250 MG.

DR. SUSAN BROWN   Qty: 30

DRUGWORLD

RX:789   Date filled:1/1/97

CHARNOV, RUDY
Take 2 tsp. by mouth every 4 hours

POLYRISTINE CS

DR. PAUL RIME
Amount:120 ml. Exp.12/31/98

👁 DO NOT **DRIVE** WHILE TAKING THIS MEDICATION

a. It's a liquid.   *cough syrup*

b. You can use this three times a day.   _____

c. The dosage is one, three times a day.   _____

d. This is an over-the-counter medication.   _____

e. Take this for ten days.   _____

f. The expiry date has already passed.   _____

g. Don't put this in your mouth!   _____

h. There's no warning label.   _____

i. Have some yogurt with this.   _____

j. This will make you feel sleepy.   _____

3. Circle the correct words to complete the diary entries.

Feb. 11—Woke up in the hospital with crutches / (casts) on both my legs! I can't
a.
remember anything about the accident. Jim's OK, thank goodness. He has
a sling / walker on his arm, but that's all. Here comes the nurse...
b.

Feb. 14—Jim visited me today and pushed me around the hospital in a
wheelchair / humidifier. He didn't come before because he had to
c.
use nasal spray / get bed rest for a few days, but he's fine now.
d.

March 24—They took off the casts / glasses and put on hearing aids / braces. Now
e.   f.
I can hold my air purifier / walker in front of me, and move around on my own.
g.
After a couple of weeks, I'll be ready for a pair of crutches / contact lenses.
h.

April 8—I can stand! I work with Carlos, my physio therapist / chiropractor,
i.
every day. I have to learn to use my legs again. The exercises hurt a lot. I put
an antacid / a heating pad on my painful muscles after therapy. At first I used
j.
pain relievers / throat lozenges, but I don't like to change my diet / take medicine.
k.   l.

April 25—Acupuncture / Immunization is helping! It's amazing! A needle in my
m.
shoulder makes my knees feel better. Now I use eye drops / prescription medication
n.
only when I really need it.

April 28—Tomorrow I go home! It's been more than two months! I still need to use
a cane / tablet, but Carlos says it won't be long now until I can walk without any help.
o.

4. What about you? What over-the-counter medicine do you have at home? Look at the labels and make a chart like the one below. Use your own paper.

Form	Dosage	Indications	Warning
tablets	1–2 tablets every 4–6 hours	to prevent nausea	Do not take if you have a breathing problem.

Challenge Write about an accident or illness that you (or someone you know) have recovered from. What were the treatments and medications? What were the steps to recovery?

81

Medical Emergencies

1. Look in your dictionary. What happened? Write the medical condition.

   a. The little girl in the laundry room _____swallowed poison_____.

   b. The woman in the snow _____.

   c. The man with the toaster _____.

   d. The boy in the doctor's office _____.

   e. The man pouring coffee _____.

   f. The girl under the blue blanket _____.

   g. The woman at the dinner table _____.

2. Circle the correct words to complete the article.

How Safe Are You at Home?

Not very. As you probably know, most accidents occur at home. The chart below shows the number of people who were (injured) / unconscious in just one year using
a.
everyday products.

Estimated number of injuries in the home

Product	Estimated injuries
Stairs, steps	1 055 355
Bicycles	604 066
Knives	460 625
Bathtubs/showers	151 852
Drugs/medications	115 814
Razors/shavers	43 691
Hot water	43 457
TVs	36 457
Irons	16 447
Pesticides	16 281

Based on information from: Consumer Product Safety Commission (1993)

Falls are the number one cause of all household injuries. More than a million and a half people fell / had an allergic reaction while
b.
using stairs, steps, or bicycles. Some of the 151 852 injuries occurring in the bathtub or shower were also caused by falls.

How else are people getting hurt? In addition to falls, some people drowned / swallowed poison
c.
or burned themselves / got frostbite while
d.
bathing or showering. More than 500 000 people cut themselves and bled / couldn't breathe while
e.
using knives or razors, and over 100 000 people burned themselves / overdosed on drugs
f.
or got an electric shock / had an allergic reaction
g.
while taking medicine. ◆

3. What about you? How can you prevent some of the injuries in Exercise 2? Use your own paper.

   Example: *To prevent frostbite, I wear gloves when it's very cold.*

   Challenge Look at the chart in Exercise 2. How do you think people hurt themselves using TVs? irons? pesticides?

1. Look in your dictionary. Complete the information from a first-aid manual.

Always keep your medicine chest or first aid kit well supplied. Include:

a. _____gauze_____ for holding pads in place, or (if sterile) for covering cuts

b. _____ for removing pieces of glass or wood from the skin

c. _____ for preventing movement of a broken or sprained arm, finger, etc.

d. _____ for covering large cuts and burns

e. _____ for holding pads and gauze in place

f. _____ for preventing infection of cuts

g. _____ for covering small cuts

h. _____ for pouring on a new cut to help prevent infection

i. _____ for putting around a sprained ankle

j. _____ for treating rashes and allergic skin reactions

k. _____ for reducing pain and swelling

Note: A deep cut that continues to bleed may need _____ . Contact your doctor
l.
or go to a clinic or hospital emergency room. People with special medical conditions such as diabetes,

heart disease, or serious allergies, should wear a _____ to identify the problem.
m.

2. Write the name of the lifesaving techniques. Use the words in the box.

| CPR | ~~Heimlich manoeuvre~~ | artificial respiration |

a. __Heimlich manoeuvre__   Named after the doctor who invented it, this technique is
used on people who are choking on food or another object.

b. _____   Performed mouth-to-mouth, this technique is used on
people who have stopped breathing.

c. _____   This technique is used on people who have stopped
breathing as a result of a heart attack, choking, or drowning.
It involves mouth-to-mouth breathing and heart compression
(massage) and should only be done by people with training.

3. What about you? Are there first-aid items that you use that are not in your dictionary?
Write about them.

_____ for _____

Challenge Write the first-aid steps for a cut finger. (The finger is bleeding, but the cut is not deep.)

Clinics

1. Look at the medical clinic in your dictionary. What are the people talking about?

   a. "It was hard to read after the third line."   _____eye chart_____

   b. "According to <u>this</u>, your weight is 80 kg."   _____

   c. "Can you please fill <u>this</u> out for me?"   _____

   d. "According to <u>this</u>, your pressure is fine."   _____

   e. "Relax. <u>This</u> will only hurt a little."   _____

   f. "According to <u>this</u>, you have a low fever."   _____

   g. "When I listen through <u>this</u>, your lungs sound clear."   _____

2. Complete the pamphlet. Use the words in the box.

cavities	braces	dentist	fillings	hygienist
	orthodontist	patients	~~tartar~~	

COMMON DENTAL QUESTIONS

Q: What is _____tartar_____ ?
   a.

A: A hard substance that forms on your teeth.

Only a _____ or
   b.

dental _____
   c.

can remove it.

Q: I never get

_____.
   d.

Do I still need to

make appointments

every year?

A: Yes. Dentists also check for

other problems including gum disease and

cancer.

Q: My daughter just got _____ to
   e.

straighten her teeth. Am I too old for them?

A: No. Today more than one out of

four _____ visiting
   f.

the _____ is
   g.

an adult.

Q: I have a lot of old

silver and gold

_____. Is
   h.

there anything I can do about

their appearance?

A: They can be replaced by newer types that look

more like your own teeth.

_____ **Challenge**   Write two more questions about dental care like the ones in Exercise 2. Try to find
the answers.

1. Look in your dictionary. What are the people doing?

    a. "Open wide and say *ahh*."   *looking in his throat*

    b. "Can the doctor see me in the morning?"   _____

    c. "Look straight at me."   _____

    d. "You don't have a fever."   _____

    e. "I'm getting all the tartar off."   _____

    f. "I'm almost finished. Then I'll fill it."   _____

    g. "You won't feel any pain after this."   _____

2. Complete the pamphlet. Use the words in the box.

~~check your blood pressure~~	draw blood	examine your eyes
listen to your heart	look in your throat	take an X-ray

• **Dr. Gregory Sarett** •

The Medical Exam—What to Expect

    Dr. Sarett will check your height and weight. He will also _*check your blood pressure*_

                                       a.

to see if it is too high or too low. Then, using a stethoscope, he will _____

                                       b.

while you are lying down and while you are sitting up. He will use

the stethoscope to listen to your lungs and abdomen, too. Then,

using an ophthalmoscope (an instrument with a light), he will

_____. If there is a problem, he may suggest you see an ophthalmologist.
           c.

    He will also _____, nose, and ears. The doctor may do other
                        d.

tests. He may, for example, _____ and send it to a lab for testing.
                              e.

He may _____ of your chest. At the end of the exam, he will discuss
                 f.

the results and make recommendations. You should feel free to ask him any questions before, during, or

after the exam.

3. What about you? How often do you go for a…?

    a. medical checkup _____   **b.** dental checkup _____

Challenge   Write a paragraph about what to expect during a dental exam.

A Hospital

1. Look in your dictionary. **True** or **False**? Correct the underlined words in the false sentences.

a. The obstetrician's patient is wearing a ~~hospital gown~~. *dress*   ___False___

b. There's a medical waste disposal inside the patient's room.   _____

c. The bedpan is next to the hospital bed.   _____

d. The X-ray technician is drawing blood from the patient.   _____

e. There's a glass on the bed table.   _____

f. A volunteer is carrying books to a patient.   _____

g. An RN is carrying food.   _____

h. A registered nursing assistant is talking to the dietitian.   _____

i. Two orderlies are taking a patient on a stretcher into the emergency room.   _____

j. The anaesthetist in the operating room is wearing a surgical cap.   _____

2. Circle the correct words to complete the information from a hospital pamphlet.

The Operation — What to Expect

In most cases, orderlies will take you to the emergency /(operating)
a.
room on a gurney / tray. They will then carefully move you to the
b.
nurse's station / operating table, where the surgery will take place.
c.
Your surgical team (the anaesthetist, surgical nurses, and, of

course, the dietitian / surgeon) will be there. In order to avoid
d.
infection, they will wear surgical caps / gloves on their heads, and
e.
sterile latex gloves / gowns on their hands. All the instruments will be
f.
sterilized, too. During the operation, the anaesthetist / volunteer
g.
will monitor all your medical charts / vital signs (blood pressure,
h.
breathing, and heart rate). An IV / RN, attached to a vein in your
i.
arm, will provide you with fluids, and, if necessary, medication.

3. Write the full forms for these abbreviations.

    a. RN   <u>registered nurse</u>   **c.** IV   _____

    b. RNA   _____

4. Read each statement. Decide which doctor is talking. Fill in the blank.

anaesthetist	**pediatrician**	**cardiologist**
internist	~~**radiologist**~~	**obstetrician/gynecologist**
opthalmologist	**psychiatrist**	**general practitioner**

    a. "The X-ray indicates that his collar bone is fractured."   <u>radiologist</u>

    b. "His heart is beating a bit too fast."   _____

    c. "Keep a patch on his eye and it should be fine."   _____

    d. "Young children often run a fever. She should be fine!"   _____

    e. "These pills will help you get over your depression."   _____

    f. "Congratulations! You're going to have twins!"   _____

    g. "I think you have the flu. Rest and drink fluids."   _____

    h. "The gas will keep you asleep during surgery."   _____

    i. "I think that her liver has been damaged."   _____

5. What about you? Which of these doctors have you visited? Why? Use your own paper to write your answers.

6. What about you? Who would you prefer? Check (✔) the columns.

	MALE	FEMALE	NO PREFERENCE
a. internist			
b. cardiologists			
c. psychiatrists			
d. ophthalmologists			
e. orderlies			
f. obstetricians			
g. pediatricians			
h. nurses			

Challenge   Find out the names of other kinds of medical specialists. What do they do?
                 Example: *An orthopedist is a bone doctor.*

      ▶ Go to page 175 for Another Look (Unit 6).

City Streets

1. Look in your dictionary. Where can you get...?

	PLACE	LOCATION
a. a sandwich	coffee shop	Main and Elm
b. a cake		
c. a haircut		
d. the best view of the city		
e. traveller's cheques		
f. a carton of milk		
g. oil for your car		
h. a new couch		
i. a used car		
j. a hammer		
k. a room for the night		

2. Complete the tourist information. Use the words in the box.

> city hall   hospital   hotel   library   office buildings
> park   post office   school   ~~skyscraper~~

PLACES OF INTEREST IN TORONTO

Courtesy CN Tower/Trizec Hahn

CN Tower Although not officially a _____skyscraper_____,
a.

the CN Tower is the tallest free-standing structure in the world.

Standing at 553 m in height, this building towers over the

_____ around it.
b.

"Sick Kids" is an affectionate nickname for the 383 bed _____ For Sick
c.

Children. "Sick Kids" provides a variety of medical and surgical treatments for children up to eighteen

years of age.

Canada's First _____ **and Museum** See how letters were written with a quill
d.

and sealed with wax before the use of envelopes and postage stamps. Learn how they were sent.

Toronto _____ With over 28 million reference items in annual circulation, this is the
        e.
largest reference system in Canada. Each year, over 19 million people visit at least one of the 98

branches of this system.

Toronto _____ opened in September of 1965.
        f.
It is one of the most unique buildings in the city. In winter, skaters

enjoy the ice rink in front of the building.

The Royal York This famous _____ has 1365 guest rooms. It offers accommodations
                g.
to people from all over the world. Three generations of the British Royal Family have stayed at the Royal

York. It is their home when they are in Canada.

Ontario Place This beautiful _____ extends
                        h.
over three islands on the shore of Lake Ontario. It adds a

touch of "green" to the city. It contains walking paths,

waterslides, play areas, and the Cinesphere where you can

watch IMAX movies.

Black Creek Pioneer Village See the hundred-year-old buildings which include a doctor's office,

hotel, blacksmith, and craft shops. There is even a _____ where pioneer children learned
                                    i.
to read, write, and do arithmetic (math).

3. What about you? Would you want to live near a...? Check (✔) the boxes.

	YES	NO	WHY?
police station	☐	☐	_____
park	☐	☐	_____
fire station	☐	☐	_____
health club	☐	☐	_____
parking garage	☐	☐	_____
theatre	☐	☐	_____
Other: _____	☐	☐	_____

Challenge Make a list of places for tourists to visit in your city or town. Include some information
about each place.

An Intersection

1. Look in your dictionary. Where can a shopper use these coupons?

a.

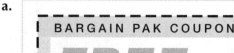

BARGAIN PAK COUPON

FREE
Burger, Fries, and
Medium Drink
When you buy a lunch
combo at the regular price.

fast food restaurant

b.

Offer expires: 11/30

Brite Aid Coupon

½ PRICE
This Month Only

All *Brite Aid*
Children's Cold Medicines

_____

c.

Bargain Pak Coupon

FALL SPECIAL

20% OFF

Winter Coats, Sweaters, Jackets
not valid after 11/30

_____

d.

Manufacturer's Coupon

SAVE $1.50

When you buy two boxes of Nuts 'n Bran
or Apple Oatmeal Cereal

_____

e.

STORE COUPON

GLOSSIES

Free Roll of Film

with every processing order of
two rolls or more

_____

f.

STORE COUPON

Buy 12
Get 1 FREE

(With a FREE cup of coffee)

Baked Fresh Daily!

_____

2. Where can you hear…? Use your dictionary if you need help.

Dad: I can't read the menu.
Tim: Drive forward a little.

a. _____ drive-thru window _____

Anne: How much change do I need?
Clerk: Two quarters for ten pages.

b. _____

Bob: Where's the bleach?
Kim: On top of the dryer.

c. _____

Pete: Do you get Spanish papers?
Owner: *El Diario* comes on Tuesdays.

d. _____

3. Look at the picture. <u>Underline</u> eight more mistakes in the newspaper article.

Local News

Last week, Fran Bates rode her <u>motorcycle</u> into Mel Smith's car. There were no injuries. A customer entered the nail salon with a dog and was asked to leave. Two children opened the mailbox on Elm Street. Chief Dane closed it and called their parents. A shopper parked a car in the crosswalk on Main Street and received a parking ticket.

The town council met yesterday and voted to fix the streetlight at Main and Elm. Pedestrians say they cannot cross the street safely. Officer Dobbs reported that the parking meter on that corner should also be fixed. May Miller mentioned a problem outside her convenience store. She said the buses don't come often enough. Finally, the council voted for another drive-thru window. Shoppers have complained about long lines for the one in service.

4. Rewrite the article correctly. Use your own paper.

Example: *Last week Fran Bates rode her bicycle…*

Challenge Look at the picture in Exercise 3. Write about other problems.

A Mall

1. Look in your dictionary. Check (✔) the activities you can do at this mall. Write the kind of store you can do them in. (Do not use *department store*.)

☐ Buy cough syrup _____

☑ Buy a birthday card _____card shop_____

☐ Look at CD players _____

☐ Get clothes dry-cleaned _____

☐ Rent movies _____

☐ Plan a vacation _____

☐ Get new eyeglasses _____

☐ Buy flowers _____

☐ Buy a dictionary _____

☐ Buy a dog _____

☐ Mail letters _____

☐ Buy chocolates _____

2. Two teenagers are shopping at another mall. Look at the mall directory on page 93 of this book. Read the conversations and write the kind of place for each one.

a. **Server:** What flavour?

   Bee: Strawberry, please. _____ice cream stand_____

b. **Amy:** What do you think? Too curly?

   Bee: No. It's a terrific perm. _____

c. **Amy:** I love that new song by Kicking Pumpkins.

   Bee: Let's go buy the CD. _____

d. **Bee:** Hey! That's Jim coming down.

   Amy: Let's meet him at the bottom. _____

e. **Bee:** Let's go here for your high heels.

   Amy: Good idea. I usually don't like what they have at Crane's. _____

f. **Amy:** Do you like these earrings?

   Bee: Yeah. You look good in gold. _____

g. **Bee:** What do you want to eat? We have three choices.

   Amy: I think I'd like Mexican food. _____

h. **Amy:** Excuse me. Where's the main entrance?

   Clerk: Right behind you. _____

3. Look at Exercise 2. Circle the numbers and symbols on the map and draw Amy and Bee's route.

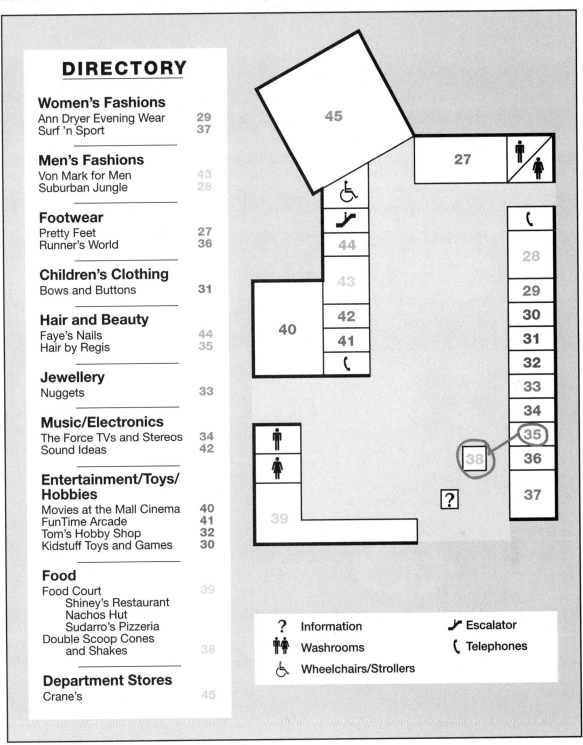

DIRECTORY

Women's Fashions
Ann Dryer Evening Wear   29
Surf 'n Sport   37

Men's Fashions
Von Mark for Men   43
Suburban Jungle   28

Footwear
Pretty Feet   27
Runner's World   36

Children's Clothing
Bows and Buttons   31

Hair and Beauty
Faye's Nails   44
Hair by Regis   35

Jewellery
Nuggets   33

Music/Electronics
The Force TVs and Stereos   34
Sound Ideas   42

Entertainment/Toys/Hobbies
Movies at the Mall Cinema   40
FunTime Arcade   41
Tom's Hobby Shop   32
Kidstuff Toys and Games   30

Food
Food Court   39
    Shiney's Restaurant
    Nachos Hut
    Sudarro's Pizzeria
Double Scoop Cones
    and Shakes   38

Department Stores
Crane's   45

? Information
♟ Washrooms
♿ Wheelchairs/Strollers
〲 Escalator
℡ Telephones

4. What about you? Is there a mall near your home? Imagine that you're going there this weekend. What stores will you go to? What will you do there? (If there isn't a mall nearby, you can use the one in your dictionary.)

Example: *I'll go to the toy store and buy some puzzles for my niece.*

Challenge Where would you prefer to shop, downtown (the business centre of a town or city) or at a shopping mall? Think about weather conditions, the transportation you can use to get there, the kinds of shops, prices, and entertainment. Write at least five sentences.

A Childcare Centre

1. Look at the childcare centre in your dictionary. Correct the underlined words in these false sentences.

   a. A little boy is sitting in a ~~carriage~~. (*stroller*)

   b. A childcare worker is dropping off her daughter.

   c. The children's clothes are on the floor.

   d. A childcare worker is sitting in a high chair and looking at a picture book.

   e. Another worker is changing a baby's diaper in a playpen.

2. Circle the correct words to complete the instructions to childcare workers.

KidCo   October 4

Don't (feed) / dress Stefan or give him a diaper pin / bottle after 2:20 p.m.
   a.   **b.**
His mother wants to nurse / play with him when she comes at 5:30.
                           c.

Peter's first day at KidCo! His father will drop him off / pick him up at
                                        d.
7:30 a.m. If he cries when his father leaves, rock him / tie his shoes and
                                        e.
read him a story / play with him. His favourite book is "The Cat in the Hat."
              f.

Rachel has an ear infection. Please change her diapers / pick her up and
                                        g.
hold her whenever she cries. Call her mother if she has a fever.

Steven tells a story / takes a nap from 11:00 to noon. When he wakes up,
                    h.
drop off / feed him his lunch and then let him play in the playpen / baby food.
    i.   **j.**

Tracy gets a rash from wipes / walkers and carriages / disposable diapers. When
                            k.   **l.**
you tell her a story / change her diapers, please use a washcloth and cloth diapers.
               m.

César just started to dress / rock himself and tie / hold his shoes!
                           n.   **o.**
He needs extra time to get ready before he goes outside to play.

3. Cross out the word that doesn't belong. Give a reason.

a.   high chair   ~~baby backpack~~   potty seat

<u>Babies don't sit on a backpack.</u>

b.   pacifier   bib   diaper

_____

c.   formula   baby food   disinfectant

_____

d.   diaper pail   rattles   toys

_____

e.   carriage   stroller   teething ring

_____

4. Complete these thank you notes. Use the words in the box.

baby carrier	bib	car safety seat	~~high chair~~	playpen

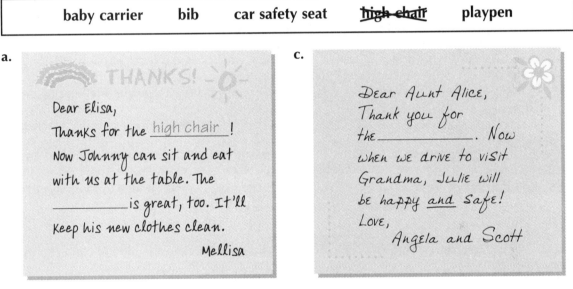

a.
THANKS!

Dear Elisa,
Thanks for the <u>high chair</u> !
Now Johnny can sit and eat
with us at the table. The
_____ is great, too. It'll
keep his new clothes clean.
                  Mellisa

c.
Dear Aunt Alice,
Thank you for
the _____. Now
when we drive to visit
Grandma, Julie will
be happy <u>and</u> safe!
Love,
      Angela and Scott

b.
A B C D E F G

Dear Lili and Quon,
We all love the
_____! Louisa sits
in it for hours playing with
her blocks.
What a great gift!
Jason
                  H I

d.
Thank You

Dear Bill,
The _____ is great!
I put Tommy in it yesterday
when I went to the market.
He slept happily and my hands
were free to do the shopping.
Thanks so much!
Love,
Amanda

Challenge Look in your dictionary. Choose a baby gift for someone you know. Explain your choice.

95

Canada Post

1. Look in your dictionary. What are the people talking about?

a. "That's not enough. You need to put another <u>one</u> on."   <u>   stamp   </u>

b. "<u>She</u> usually comes around 11:30."   _____

c. "<u>It</u> says May 7th."   _____

d. "Open <u>it</u>! It could be the vase we ordered."   _____

2. Circle the correct words to complete the information about Canada Post services.

<u>**Letter / Package:**</u> **a.**	First-class mail weighing 30 grams or less.
<u>**Postmark / Postage rate:**</u> **b.**	In Canada $.46 USA $.55 International $.95 (20 grams or less)
<u>**Postcard / Postmark:**</u> **c.**	Same rate as for first-class letter mail.
Priority Courier:	The fastest way to send a letter or package. The post office usually <u>delivers / receives</u> priority courier mail in one or two days. **d.** Rate: letter $9.65+ package $12.00+
Express Post:	This is a way to <u>send / stamp</u> mail faster. The post office usually **e.** delivers Express Post mail in one to four days to places in Canada. Rate $3.77+.
Registered Letter:	When you send important mail, you can get a mailing receipt. The <u>sender's / letter carrier's</u> post office keeps a record. Someone must **f.** sign for this mail at the <u>address / envelope</u> where it has been sent. **g.** Fee: $4.00+ postage for a regular letter.
Parcel Post:	For <u>letters / packages</u>, it takes up to ten days to receive items that **h.** are mailed to places in Canada. Rate varies.

Note: Rates can change. Check your local post office.

3. What about you? What kinds of mail service do you use? How much do they cost?

_____

Challenge You're in Manitoba. Use the information in Exercise 2 to figure out the postage for….

    a. a letter to Japan   _____   **c.** a registered letter to Nova Scotia _____

    b. a 30 gram letter to New York City _____   **d.** a postcard to Poland   _____

1. Look in your dictionary. Complete the sentences.

a. The _____teller_____ is helping a customer.

b. The _____ is wearing a uniform.

c. Rita Rose keeps her jewellery in a _____ in the bank's _____.

d. The customer at the bank machine is using a _____ number.

2. Look at the monthly statement. Complete the sentences. Use the words in the box.

deposit	~~chequing account~~	balance	savings account
bank card	withdrew	transferred	deposit slip

Monthly Statement

March 31–April 30, 2002

Jamal Al-Marafi   Account Number: 0125-00

Opening Balance
$1,117.20

Date	Transaction	Amount	Balance
3/31/02	Quikcash ATM #123	50.00	1,067.20
4/01/02	Deposit	1,283.47	2,350.67
4/20/02	Transfer to Chequing	850.00	1,500.67
4/29/02	Withdrawal	100.00	1,400.67

Account Number: 0135-08

Opening Balance
$849.00

Date	Transaction	Amount	Balance
4/05/02	Cheque #431	732.00	117.00
4/11/02	Quikcash ATM #123	75.00	42.00
4/20/02	Transfer from Savings	850.00	892.00

a. Jamal's _chequing account_ number is 0135-08.

b. His _____ number is 0125-00.

c. On April 11, Jamal used his _____ to get cash.

d. When Jamal got his $1,283.47 pay cheque, he made a _____.

e. He used a _____ for his April 1 transaction.

f. On March 31, the _____ in Jamal's chequing account was $849.00.

g. On April 29, Jamal _____ $100.00.

h. He _____ $850.00 from savings to chequing on April 20.

Challenge Find out about a local bank. Which services are free? Which ones have fees? How much are they?

A Library

1. Look in your dictionary. What do the underlined words refer to?

   a. You can look up the Nile River in <u>this book</u>. _____atlas_____ or _____

   b. <u>It</u> has a lot of small drawers. _____

   c. You'll need <u>it</u> to check out your book. _____

   d. The library clerk is <u>there</u>. _____

2. Complete the reference librarian's answers. Use your dictionary for help.

   Patron: Do you have the movie *Romancing the Stone*?

   Librarian: Yes. The ___videocassettes___ are right there.

a.

   Patron: I'm looking for a job. Do you have this weekend's job ads?

   Librarian: The Sunday _____ is in the _____ section.

b.   c.

   Patron: Where can I find information about fashion and makeup?

   Librarian: We get several fashion _____ every month. Try those.

d.

   Patron: In 1990 the *Gazette* had an article about our city. I'd like to read it.

   Librarian: We have the *Gazette* on _____ from 1890 to 1997. You can

e.

   read it on the _____.

f.

   Patron: Do you have audiocassettes by The What? I love their music.

   Librarian: No, but we have their new _____. It's next to the records.

g.

   Patron: I'm doing a report on Gandhi, but I don't know anything about him.

   Librarian: You should read an article in an _____ first.

h.

   Patron: I'm looking for Grisham's new book. I don't remember what it's called.

   Librarian: You don't need to know the _____. Just type the author's name

i.

   into the _____ and press *Enter*.

j.

Challenge What items does your library have? Make a chart like the one below.

ITEM	EXAMPLE	CAN CHECK IT OUT?	HOW LONG?
book	*The Runaway Jury, by John Grisham*	yes	two weeks

1. Look in your dictionary. Who is…?

    a. wearing handcuffs   _the suspect_

    b. pointing to the defendant   _____

    c. typing   _____

    d. sitting next to the defence counsel in court   _____

    e. sitting in jail   _____

    f. standing in a corner in the courtroom   _____

2. Circle the correct words to complete the interview with a former convict.

INTERVIEW

PS Magazine: Dan Long, you've received awards for your work with young people. But you yourself ~~went to prison~~ / *stood trial for several years.*
                                          a.

Dan Long: Yes—for burglary. I was <u>released / arrested</u> three years ago. It
                                      b.
was the happiest day of my life.

*PS: Tell us about your experience with the legal system. You didn't have
a job. How did you <u>hire a lawyer / stand trial</u>?*
                                  c.

DL: I didn't. I got one through Legal Aid. And she was good. In fact,
when we <u>gave the verdict / appeared in court</u>, she got the <u>guard / judge</u> to
                           d.   **e.**
lower the bail to $1000.

PS: So what happened when you <u>sentenced the defendant / stood trial</u>?
                                        f.

DL: She did her best, but the <u>Crown counsel / defence</u> counsel had a lot of
                                     g.
evidence against me.

PS: Were you surprised when the <u>police officer / jury</u> gave the verdict?
                                        h.

DL: No, but I was when the judge <u>sentenced / released</u> me. Seven years!
                                   i.
Now I tell young people what it's like to spend years in <u>jail / court</u>.
                                         j.

Challenge Write the story of the man in the dictionary who was arrested.

Crime

1. Look in your dictionary. Put each crime in the correct category.

CRIMES AGAINST PEOPLE	CRIMES AGAINST PROPERTY (BUILDINGS, CARS, ETC.)	SUBSTANCE ABUSE CRIMES (DRUGS AND ALCOHOL)
gang violence	_____	_____
_____	_____	_____
_____		
_____		

2. Look at the line graphs. Complete the sentences. Use the words in the box. (You will use two words more than once.)

assaults	burglaries	murders	vandalism

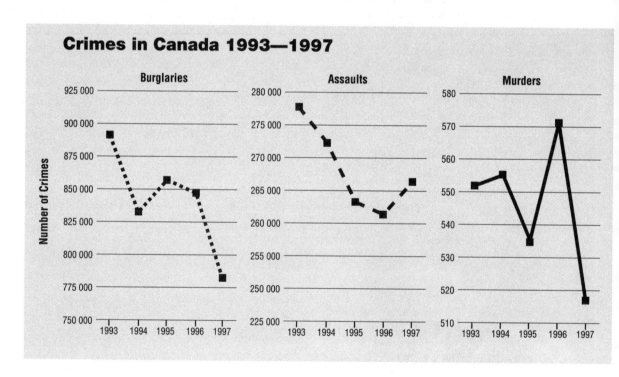

(Information from CANSIM, Statistics Canada)

a. In 1993, there were about 278 000 _____assaults_____ in Canada.

b. In 1995, there were about 862 000 _____ .

c. Between 1993 and 1994, the number of _____ went down.

d. In 1993/1994, the number of _____ changed less than other crimes.

e. The number of _____ went up between 1996 and 1997.

f. The chart does not have information about _____ .

Challenge Look at **page 184** in this book. Complete the chart.

1. Look in your dictionary. Complete the newsletter with the correct advice.

Safety Tips

a. _____Lock your doors._____

A deadbolt lock is your best protection. Door chains are also good.

b. _____

If you're at a party or a bar, choose a "designated driver."

c. _____

Always ask, "Who's there?" If you don't know them, don't let them in!

d. _____

It's easy for a criminal to grab something that is just hanging from your arm or shoulder.

e. _____

For men, the best place is an *inside* jacket pocket. For women, a *closed* purse.

f. _____

There's safety in numbers. Muggers usually look for *easy* victims.

g. _____

Remember: criminals don't want witnesses, so lights are your friends. Also, this way *you* can see who's on the street, and you won't be surprised!

h. _____

If you witness a crime or become a crime victim, dial 911 immediately!

The East Village Neighbourhood Watch—Looking Out for You!

2. Look at the picture. What safety mistakes is the man making? Use the information in Exercise 1.

  a. _He isn't staying on well-lit streets._

  b. _____

  c. _____

3. What about you? Which of the safety tips in Exercise 1 do you follow? Make a list. Use your own paper.

Challenge   Interview five people. Find out about the safety tips they follow.

1. Look in your dictionary. Which disaster is the news reporter talking about?

    a. "The same mountain erupted five years ago."   <u>volcanic eruption</u>

    b. "All homes near the beach were destroyed by the water."   _____

    c. "The two vehicles were badly damaged, but luckily, the drivers were not hurt in the crash at the intersection of Tenth and Elm."   _____

    d. "Store detectives found the little girl sitting on the floor."   _____

    e. "The twister destroyed several farms in its path."   _____

2. Complete the newspaper articles. Use the words in the box.

airplane crash	blizzard	drought	~~earthquake~~	explosion
fire	firefighters	hurricane	search and rescue team	

a.

Disaster Strikes Kobe, Japan

TOKYO, Jan. 17—An _____<u>earthquake</u>_____ measuring 7.1 on the Richter scale hit the city of Kobe, Japan, killing more than 5,000 people and injuring 26,500 others. More than 100,000 buildings were destroyed.

b.

_____ # KILLS 229

PEGGY'S COVE, Sept. 02—A Swiss Air jet en route to Geneva from New York went down in the Atlantic Ocean just off the coast of Peggy's Cove. All 229 passengers and crew were killed. The cause of the disaster is still not known.

c.

INFERNO IN LONDON UNDERGROUND

LONDON, Nov. 17—Thirty died and 21 were seriously injured in a _____ in one of the busiest subway stations in the world. "As soon as I got on the escalator, I could smell burning," said one witness. Seconds later she saw the red flames and dark smoke. _____ rushed to the scene.

d.

BOMB _____ IN OKLAHOMA CITY KILLS 170

OKLAHOMA CITY, Apr. 19—A car bomb went off outside a federal office building killing 169 people. A member of the _____ also died while trying to save the victims. The bomb destroyed most of the nine-storey building and damaged many other buildings in the area.

e.

High Winds in Jamaica

KINGSTON, Sept. 18— _____ Gilbert the most powerful Atlantic storm ever recorded, struck the island of Jamaica and Mexico's Yucatan Peninsula leaving more than 200 dead. Winds reached 350 kilometres an hour. Whole trees flew through the air.

f.

THE _____ OF '77

Niagara, Jan. 20—This giant snowstorm tied up traffic on the 401 highway. The Burlington Skyway was closed for several hours due to exceptionally strong winds. Drifting snow created dangerous driving conditions throughout the Niagara Region for three days.

g.

A Long Dry Winter

SANTA BARBARA, March 23—As a result of 73% less rain than usual over the last year, California is experiencing its worst _____ since the 1930s. The state is going to stop water deliveries to farms in an effort to save water.

Challenge Write a paragraph about an emergency or a natural disaster.

▶ Go to page 176 for **Another Look (Unit 7)**.

Public Transportation

1. Look in your dictionary. What are they talking about? Where are they?

   a. "It goes in this way."   transit pass   subway

   b. "This says there's one at 3:02."   _____   _____

   c. "Use this to change at Avenue A."   _____   _____

   d. "It says $3.50 so I'll tip 50¢."   _____   _____

2. Circle the correct words to complete the letter.

Dear Gray,

   I'm glad you decided to visit us in Plum Island. You can get here by public transportation, but take a book with you—it's a long trip!

   First, take a (bus) / taxi to Wyckoff Street. It's fast, and the meter / fare is only 75¢.
   a.   **b.**
I think one leaves every half hour. Check the schedule / route when you get to the
                                                c.
track / bus stop. When you get off at Wyckoff, go down the stairs to the ferry / subway and
d.   **e.**
buy a token / transfer. Take the WW or the Y train to Central Station. The Y only stops
       f.
there at certain hours. Check with the conductor / meter before you get on. At the
                                          g.
taxi stand / train station, buy a round-trip fare card / ticket to Harbour Point. It costs $45.00
       h.   **i.**
and it takes about three hours. Sit in the front of the train / ferry or you'll get off in
                                                          j.
somebody's garden. The track / platform at Harbour Point is only a few yards long. There's a
                          k.
taxi stand / subway station across the route / tracks from the station. Tell the driver / passenger
       l.   **m.**   **n.**
you're taking the ferry / subway to Plum Island. They don't use meters / schedules,
                   o.   **p.**
but it costs $5.00. See you soon!

                                                      Enrico

3. What about you? What kinds of public transportation do you use? Make a chart. Use your own paper.

   Example:

TYPE	FARE	HOW DO YOU PAY?	WHERE DO YOU GO?
ferry	$ .80 round trip	fare card	from home to work

Challenge Describe some advantages and disadvantages of public transportation.

1. Look in your dictionary. Where are they going?

    a. "Turn right here."   <u>around the corner</u>

    b. "This is our exit."   _____

    c. "Park Avenue and Third Street, please."   _____

    d. "Why don't they have an escalator?"   _____

2. Look at the map of Toronto. Circle the correct words to complete the directions.

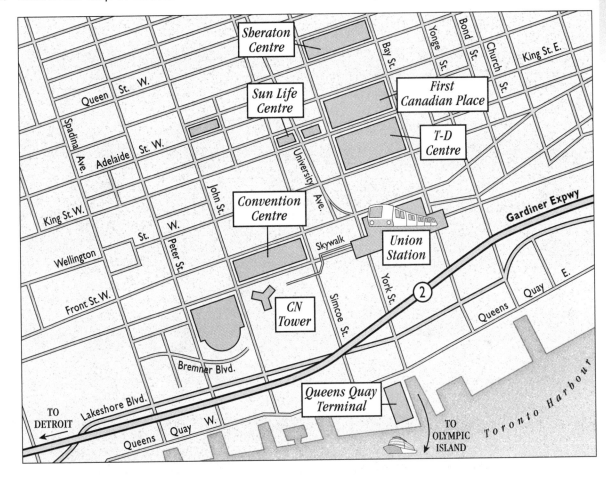

    a. To go from Union Station to Toronto Harbour, get off /(go under) the expressway on
         York Street.

    b. To go from the Convention Centre to the Sun Life Centre, get <u>into / out of</u> the taxi on
         King Street.

    c. To go from Queen's Quay Terminal to Olympic Island, go <u>across / around</u> Toronto Harbour.

    d. To go from Union Station to Detroit, get <u>onto / off</u> the expressway at York Street.

    e. To go from CN Tower to Union Station on foot, go <u>over / under</u> the Skywalk.

Challenge Write directions from your home to: school   the bus station   Other: _____

Cars and Trucks

1. Look in your dictionary. Read these ads. Write the kind of car or truck for sale.

a.
| used to remove cars from the highway |

<u>tow truck</u>

c.
| 16 wheels, orange cab |

_____

e.
| yellow with black interior, small rip in top |

_____

b.
| great small-family car, blue exterior |

_____

d.
| bike rack, sleeps 4 |

_____

f.
| beautiful green town car |

_____

2. Look at the cars and answer the questions. (Do not write the make and model.)

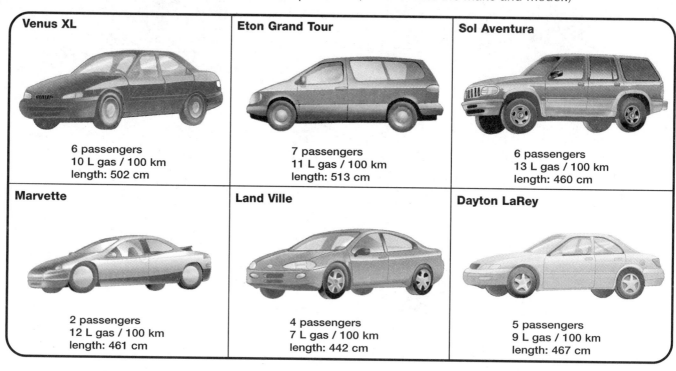

Venus XL
6 passengers
10 L gas / 100 km
length: 502 cm

Eton Grand Tour
7 passengers
11 L gas / 100 km
length: 513 cm

Sol Aventura
6 passengers
13 L gas / 100 km
length: 460 cm

Marvette
2 passengers
12 L gas / 100 km
length: 461 cm

Land Ville
4 passengers
7 L gas / 100 km
length: 442 cm

Dayton LaRey
5 passengers
9 L gas / 100 km
length: 467 cm

Which…

a. uses the most gas?   <u>sport utility vechicle</u>

b. carries the fewest passengers?   _____

c. is best for a big family?   _____

d. is the shortest in length?   _____

e. is cheapest to drive?   _____

f. carry the same number of passengers?   _____ and _____

3. What about you? Look in your dictionary. Which car would you choose? Why? Use your own paper.

Example: _I would choose a pickup. I carry a lot of things, but not many passengers._

Challenge Look at newspaper ads. Find the price range of the car you chose in Exercise 3.

1. Look at **pages 88 and 89** in your dictionary. Begin at the southeast corner of Main and Elm streets. Follow the directions below. Where are you?

   a. Go one block north. _____Elm and First_____

   b. Then go one block east. Turn left. Go straight for one block. _____

   c. Then go one block east. Turn right. Go two blocks south. _____

   d. Then go west for two blocks. _____

2. Complete the written part of a test for a driver's licence. Circle the letters of the correct answers.

   1. When you see a STOP sign, you must _____.
      a. go more slowly
      b. come to a complete stop
      c. turn right

   2. When you see this sign, you _____.
      a. must drive exactly 50 km/h
      b. can drive 45 km/h
      c. can drive 60 km/h

      SPEED LIMIT 50

   3. This sign means _____ crossing.
      a. pedestrian
      b. railroad
      c. school

   4. A NO EXIT sign means _____.
      a. you can't enter the street
      b. the street is very dangerous
      c. the street ends and there is no outlet

   5. This sign means you should look for _____.
      a. bridges
      b. rivers
      c. trains

   6. When you see this sign, you cannot make a _____.
      a. left turn
      b. right turn
      c. U-turn

   7. This sign indicates _____.
      a. handicapped parking
      b. a hospital
      c. no parking any time

Challenge Draw some other traffic signs. Explain their meanings.

Parts of a Car and Car Maintenance

1. Look in your dictionary. How many ... does the red car have?

a. hubcaps   _4_   e. gauges   _____

b. sideview mirrors   _____   f. rearview mirrors   _____

c. licence plates   _____   g. windshield wipers   _____

d. jacks   _____   h. spare tires   _____

2. Complete the conversations. Use the words in the box.

accelerator	air conditioning	front seat	~~gas gauge~~	glove compartment
licence plate	radio	rearview mirror	stick shift	temperature gauge

a. **Passenger:** Look, the _____ gas gauge _____ is almost on empty.

    Driver: There's a gas station. I'll stop there.

b. **Driver:** Where would you like to sit?

    Passenger: In the _____, next to you.

c. **Driver:** It would be nice to hear a traffic report.

    Passenger: I'll turn on the _____.

d. **Passenger:** It's getting hot in here.

    Driver: We can turn on the _____.

e. **Passenger:** Do we have a map?

    Driver: There should be one in the _____.

f. **Passenger:** That truck is getting very close!

    Driver: That's OK. I'm watching it in the _____.

g. **Passenger:** Step on the _____. You're going much too slow.

    Driver: OK.

h. **Passenger:** Look at the _____.

    Driver: Oh. The radiator needs coolant.

i. **Passenger:** That car is leaving the accident scene!

    Driver: Quick! Write down the _____ number!

j. **Passenger:** Do you like using a _____ ?

    Driver: Yes. I've always driven a car with a standard transmission.

3. Circle the correct words to complete information from a driver's manual.

Basic Driving

- The bumper / (steering wheel) gives you control over your car.
  a.
- Always have the correct amount of air in your hubcaps / tires. Check the pressure.
  b.
- When you step on your brake pedal / clutch, your car should stop quickly and smoothly.
  c.
- Jumper cables / Turn signals tell other drivers which direction you are going to go.
  d.
- Brake lights / Tail lights tell other drivers that you are slowing or stopping.
  e.
- Your hood / horn lets other drivers and pedestrians hear that you are there.
  f.
- Lug wrenches / Headlights are important in night driving, rainy weather, and in fog.
  g.
- The heater / windshield should be free of cracks and breaks. Use your
  h.
  gear shift / windshield wipers to clean it.
  i.

Preventing Injuries

- Check your odometer / speedometer to see how fast you are going.
  j.
- New cars come with air bags / spare tires that open in case of an accident.
  k.
  They keep you from hitting your head against the dashboard / trunk or steering wheel.
  l.
- Back seats / Seat belts and shoulder straps help prevent injury or death in case of
  m.
  an accident. Always use them.
- Use your door jacks / locks to keep your doors from opening in an accident.
  n.

Air and Noise Pollution Control

- When your car needs fuel, get lead-free gas / coolant.
  o.
- Keep your engine / cigarette lighter in good condition with regular maintenance.
  p.
- Make sure there is enough coolant in the battery / radiator.
  q.
- Change the air / oil and filter regularly.
  r.
- If your car is making a lot of noise, you may need to replace your ignition / muffler.
  s.

Challenge Look at **page 184** in this book. Follow the instructions.

1. Look in your dictionary. Who's speaking? About what?

    a. "My other bag isn't on <u>it</u>!"   _passenger_   _carousel_

    b. "<u>Number 24</u> is to your right."   _____   _____

    c. "You didn't sign <u>it</u>."   _____   _____

    d. "Put <u>it</u> over your face."   _____   _____

2. Circle the correct words to complete the travel tips.

✈ ESL International Travel Tips

Before Your Flight

★ Arrive at <u>customs</u>/<u>(the airline terminal)</u> at least two hours before your flight.
      a.

★ Check the <u>departure monitor</u>/<u>control tower</u> for information about your flight.
      b.

★ After going through security, go to the <u>check-in counter</u>/<u>baggage claim area</u>.
                                    c.

  Show your ticket to the <u>pilot</u>/<u>airline representative</u>.
                             d.

★ Go to your <u>gate</u>/<u>carousel</u>.
         e.

★ Wait in the <u>cockpit</u>/<u>boarding area</u>.
          f.

On the Plane

★ Put your carry-on bags in the <u>luggage carrier</u>/<u>overhead compartment</u>.
                                    g.

★ Pay attention as your <u>airline representative</u>/<u>flight attendant</u> shows you how to
                               h.

  put on your <u>oxygen mask</u>/<u>helicopter</u> and gives you other safety information.
                    i.

★ Keep your <u>seat belt</u>/<u>tray table</u> fastened around your waist in case of turbulence.
                 j.

★ Fill out <u>a declaration form</u>/<u>an arrival monitor</u> before you land.
                         k.

After You Land

★ Go to the <u>check-in counter</u>/<u>baggage claim area</u> to get your luggage from the
                           l.

  <u>luggage carrier</u>/<u>carousel</u>.
           m.

★ Take your bags through <u>customs</u>/<u>the boarding area</u>.
                     n.

Have an enjoyable trip, and thanks for flying ESL Airlines!

Challenge Find out about a job in an airport. Would you like this job? Why or why not?
Write a paragraph.

1. Look in your dictionary. **Before** or **After**? Circle the correct word.

    a. The passenger went through security before / (after) he checked his bags.

    b. He fastened his seat belt before / after he looked for the emergency exit.

    c. He requested a blanket before / after they experienced turbulence.

2. Look at the flight information. **True** or **False**? Write a question mark (**?**) if the information isn't there.

✈   HAPPY TRAVELS   ✈

ORTIZ/VILMA   PAGE 1 OF 1 FILE #142-34-02-54-2

RECONFIRM RESERVATIONS 72 HRS PRIOR TO EACH FLIGHT. FAILURE TO DO SO MAY RESULT IN MISSING YOUR FLIGHT OR HAVING THE SPACE CANCELLED BY THE AIRLINE.

AIRWAY AIRLINES		FLIGHT 613	10MAR SUN	
DEPART	0755A	REGINA REG		CHECK-IN REQUIRED
ARRIVE	1048A	THUNDER BAY THU		MEALS: SNACK

AIRWAY AIRLINES		FLIGHT 695	10MAR SUN	
DEPART	1115A	THUNDER BAY THU		SEAT 23D NON-SMOKING
ARRIVE	0155P	MONTREAL MON		MEALS: SPECIAL LOW-SALT

---

    a. The passenger bought her ticket from Happy Travels.   _____True_____

    b. This is a boarding pass. _____

    c. Her destination is Regina. _____

    d. The arrival time in Thunder Bay is 11:15 A.M. _____

    e. The departure time from Regina is 7:55 A.M. _____

    f. Passengers will board flight 613 at 7:35 A.M. _____

    g. Passengers can have two carry-on bags. _____

    h. Flight 613 takes off Sunday morning. _____

    i. It lands on Sunday afternoon. _____

    j. There's a stopover of about 30 minutes. _____

    k. The passenger has to change planes in Montréal. _____

    l. She doesn't have to check in for flight 613. _____

    m. She is in seat 23D on flight 695. _____

    n. The seat is next to an emergency exit. _____

    o. The passenger requested a special meal. _____

    p. Passengers will claim their baggage at carousel 4. _____

Challenge   Write a paragraph about a plane trip you (or someone you know) took.

▶ **Go to page 177 for Another Look (Unit 8).**

Types of Schools

1. Look in your dictionary. Read the teachers' comments and write the type of school the student is attending.

   a. Carrying that heavy book paid off. Good luck in college. _____high school_____

   b. You'll be a great mechanic, Marcia. _____

   c. Your English has improved a lot this semester, Ms. Rivera. _____

   d. José enjoys playing with blocks. _____

2. Complete the school directory. You can use your dictionary for help.

Name and Type of School		Public/Private/Separate
a. Baychester _____High School_____ (Grades 9–12) 966 students • free		_____public_____
b. Berg County _____ (Continuing Education) ESL, Citizenship classes • 147 students • free		_____
c. Country Day _____ (Ages 3–5) 874 students • $6000/yr.		_____
d. EMI _____ (Computer Training) 235 students • $670 per semester		_____
e. Gale _____ (Undergraduate, Graduate) 8230 students • $6000 per semester		_____
f. Hartwood _____ (Grades 1–5) 830 students • free		_____
g. St. Mary's _____ (Grades 6–8) 267 students • $1125/yr.		_____

3. Write the letter of the school from Exercise 2 that each person attends.

   a. Our 13-year-old son needs small classes, but we can't pay much. _____a_____

   b. I work in a fast food restaurant during the day, and I get job training at night. _____

   c. I graduated from college in my country. I study English at night. _____

   d. My granddaughter is only four. She loves going to school. _____

   e. We have two children in elementary school. Our taxes pay for their education. _____

   f. I plan to go to law school after I graduate. _____

4. What about you? What types of schools did you attend for each level? What did you like or dislike about them? Write sentences. Use your own paper.

   Example: *I attended a public preschool. I liked it because we went on a lot of trips.*

Challenge Look at the pie chart on **page 184** in this book. Answer the questions.

1. Look in your dictionary. Write the dates.

    a. The student got feedback from another student.   <u>   Oct. 1   </u>

    b. The teacher gave a writing assignment.   <u>   </u>

    c. The student turned in his composition.   <u>   </u>

2. Read the composition. **True** or **False**? Write a question mark (**?**) if the information isn't in the composition.

> I arrived in this country in 1997. I c~~o~~me *a* with my parents, my brother, and my little sister. At first I wasn't very happy. I didn't know anyone beside ^*s* my family, and I missed my friends a lot. My mother told me, "Don't worry! Things will get better."
>
> When I began ~~the~~ school, things improved a little. I made some friends right away. We studied together and spent time together on the weekends. Since we were all from different countries we had to speak English. That really helped a lot! Now I can even write a composition in English. I guess my mother was ~~write.~~ *right*

    a. Someone edited the paper.   <u> True </u>

    b. This is a first draft.   <u>   </u>

    c. There are two paragraphs in this composition.   <u>   </u>

    d. There are only six sentences in the second paragraph.   <u>   </u>

    e. The student used question marks.   <u>   </u>

    f. The student used three apostrophes in the first paragraph.   <u>   </u>

    g. The student used a semicolon.   <u>   </u>

    h. There is a colon before the quotation marks.   <u>   </u>

    i. The period comes *before* the last quotation marks.   <u>   </u>

    j. The last sentence of the second paragraph ends with an exclamation mark.   <u>   </u>

    k. There are two commas in the second sentence of the first paragraph.   <u>   </u>

    l. The student turned in his paper late.   <u>   </u>

3. What about you? Check (✔) the things you usually do when you write a composition.

    ☐ write a first draft   ☐ edit it   ☐ get feedback   ☐ rewrite the paper before I turn it in

Challenge Write a composition of three paragraphs about how you felt when you came to this country or started this school. Write a first draft, edit it, get feedback, rewrite it, and turn it in to your teacher.

Government and Citizenship in Canada

1. Complete the information about the Canadian Government. Use the words in the box. Use your dictionary for help.

Councillor	Premier	~~Federal~~	Mayor	**Members of Parliament**
	Provincial	**Members of Provincial Parliament**		Territorial
	Municipal	representatives	election	Prime Minister

There are three levels of Government in Canada. They are the ***Federal, Provincial or Territorial*** and ***Municipal.***

The ___Federal___ ***Government*** takes care of things that affect the whole country. These may include
      a.

citizenship, currency, defence, national budget, and foreign policy. Elected representatives to this branch of

government are called _____ (MPs). The leader of the ***Federal Government*** is called the
          b.

_____ .
   c.

The ***Provincial or Territorial Government*** takes care of things that affect the province or territory. These

may include education, licencing drivers, and health care. Elected representatives may have different titles,

depending on where they are from. They may be called _____ (MPPs) or another title. The
               d.

leader of a _____ or _____ ***Government*** is usually called a _____ .
     e.   **f.**   **g.**

A _____ ***Government*** takes care of things that affect a city or a locality such as police and
   h.

fire forces, garbage and snow removal, and making city by-laws. An elected member of this government may

be called a _____ . The leader of a ***Municipal Government*** is usually called a _____
        i.   **j.**

or Reeve.

The Candian people choose their leaders of government. They do this by voting for _____ in
                                                    k.

an _____ . The person who gets the most votes is elected.
   l.

2. Circle the correct words to complete the sentences.

   a. You must be (18)/ 12 years old to apply for Canadian citizenship.

   b. You must be a permanent / temporary resident of Canada.

   c. You must know a lot of / basic information about Canada.

   d. You must speak English and French / English or French.

   e. You must have lived here for one / three of the last four years.

   f. As a citizen you have both rights and responsibilities / pleasures.

Challenge Compare a level of the Canadian Government with another country's government that you know. **Example:** *In Canada, the Prime Minister rules the country. In Jordan, a king does.*

Canadian History Timeline

1. Look in your dictionary. Complete the chart. There may be more than one right answer for each!

		EXAMPLE	YEAR(S)
a.	Exploration	Jacques Cartier makes three voyages to the New World	1534-1541
b.	War	_____	_____
c.	Celebration	_____	_____
d.	Settlement	_____	_____
e.	Trade Agreement	_____	_____
f.	Rebellion	_____	_____

2. Circle the letter of the correct answer. Use your dictionary for help.

History 101

Name _____

1. The Canadian Pacific Railway was completed in _____.

    a. 1867   (b.) 1885   c. 1917

2. The October Crisis (FLQ) in Québec happened _____ the people of Québec voted to remain in Canada.

    a. before   b. during   c. after

3. The Red River Rebellion happened _____ Canada bought Rupert's Land.

    a. before   b. at the same time   c. after

4. The Vikings came to the East Coast of Canada _____ the year 1000.

    a. before   b. during   c. after

5. Canada fought with the British against the Americans during _____.

    a. World War II   b. The Battle of the   c. the War of 1812
                              Plains of Abraham

6. Canada has been an official world peacekeeper for about _____.

    a. 50 years   b. 10 years   c. 100 years

7. Women won the right to vote in Canada during _____.

    a. the Great Depression   b. World War I
    c. the Red River Rebellion

8. Canada celebrated its Centennial year in _____.

    a. 1967   b. 1867   c. 1687

Malak

3. Complete the paragraphs with the name of the events in the box. Write the dates in the parentheses ( ). Use your dictionary for help.

Constitution	**The Great Depression**	**maple leaf flag**
internment of the Japanese	**right to vote**	~~**Confederation**~~

---

a. In 1857 Queen Victoria chose Ottawa to be the capital of Canada. Beautiful new Parliament Buildings were built on a hill overlooking the Ottawa River. Although opened in 1866, they were designed to be used by the Federal Government when <u>Confederation</u> created the new Dominion of Canada in <u>(1867)</u>.

b. Following the attack on Pearl Harbour (USA) during World War II, some Canadians feared that Japanese people living in Canada would help with an invasion of our country. The government announced the _____ from the west coast to inland camps in <u>(_____)</u>. Many Canadians opposed this mass evacuation.

c. The Suffragist movement won a victory! Canadian women won the _____ in May of <u>(_____)</u>. Every female British subject over the age of 21 could now vote in elections, providing she met property requirements where they existed.

d. As a result of the North American Stock Market crash of 1929, and combined with dust storms in the wheat-growing areas of the prairies, many people were out of work. _____ of <u>(____-____)</u> forced many people into poverty. Thousands lacked the basics of food, clothing, and shelter.

e. Over 10 000 people stood on Parliament Hill today, as the Union Jack flag of England was taken down from the flag pole. The new Canadian _____ was raised as people cheered on February 15, <u>(_____)</u>.

f. A happy crowd of 32 000 people watched as Queen Elizabeth signed the new Canadian _____ on April 17, <u>(_____)</u>. This document officially cut Canada's last colonial tie to Britain.

4. What about you? Draw a timeline, like the one in your dictionary, for some of the major events in your country's history. Use your own paper.

Challenge Look in your dictionary. Choose two events. Look them up in an almanac, encyclopedia, or history textbook. Write paragraphs like the ones in Exercise 3.

1. Look in your dictionary. **True** or **False**? Correct the <u>underlined</u> words in the false sentences.

   a. There's a waterfall in the ~~forest~~.   rain forest
   _____False_____

   b. An ocean is <u>larger</u> than a pond and a bay.
   _____

   c. A <u>peninsula</u> has water all around it.
   _____

   d. There's a <u>canyon</u> between the mountains.
   _____

   e. There are flowers in the <u>valley</u>.
   _____

   f. There is a <u>mountain range</u> in the desert.
   _____

   g. Hills are <u>lower</u> than mountains.
   _____

2. Complete the descriptions. Use the words in the box. Look at the world map on **pages 124 and 125** in your dictionary if you need help.

desert	island	lake	mountain peak	ocean	river	~~waterfall~~

   ## WORLD FACTS

   a. **Angel Falls** (807 metres) is the highest _____waterfall_____ in the world. It is located on the Churun River in southeast Venezuela.

   b. The **Pacific** is the largest and the deepest (10 924 metres) _____ in the world. It covers almost one third of the earth's surface.

   c. Located in Tibet and Nepal, **Everest** (8848 metres) is the highest _____ in the world. In 1953, Hillary and Norgay were the first to reach the top.

   d. At 6670 kilometres, the **Nile**, in Africa, is the longest _____ in the world. Water from the Nile supplies electricity and helps agriculture in Egypt and the Sudan.

   e. The **Sahara** in Africa is the biggest _____ in the world. At 9 000 000 square kilometres, it is almost as large as the United States. It gets only from 13 to 25 centimetres of rain a year and sometimes has dry periods that last for years.

   f. Surrounded by water, **Greenland** (2 175 600 square kilometres) is the largest _____ in the world. It lies in the Arctic Circle and is a part of Denmark, although it is 2090 kilometres away.

   g. The **Caspian Sea** (378 400 square kilometres) is the largest _____ in the world. It's called a sea because its water is salty.

_____ **Challenge** Write some facts about a rain forest, a canyon, and a peninsula.

Mathematics

1. Look in your dictionary. Complete the diagram.

shapes

circle

circumference   radius   angle

2. Circle the correct words to complete the sentences.

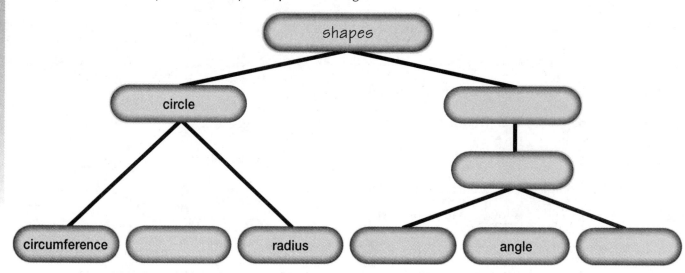

   a. A rectangle / (square) has four equal sides.

   b. An oval / A triangle has three sides.

   c. The diameter is always longer / shorter than the radius.

   d. A diagonal line is curved / straight.

   e. The distance between two parallel / straight lines is always equal.

   f. Parallel / Perpendicular lines sometimes look like the letter T.

   g. The type of mathematics that studies shapes is called geometry / trigonometry.

   h. A cube / square is a solid.

3. Complete the analogies.

   a. circle : sphere = square : _____ cube _____

   b. triangle : three = rectangle : _____

   c. addition : subtraction = multiplication : _____

   d. oval : shape = cone : _____

   e. triangle : shape = _____ : solid

   f. division : quotient = subtraction : _____

4. What about you? Which operations or types of math do you use? When do you use them?

   Example: *I use multiplication to change dollars to pesos.*

   _____

   _____

_____ **Challenge** Draw a circle. Include the diameter and the radius. Write the measurements. Calculate the circumference. (Circumference = diameter × π)

1. Look in your dictionary. Write the type of science class on these notes.

a.
<u>Physics</u> *101*
Formula for Einstein's theory of relativity: $\mathcal{E} = MC^2$

b.
_____ 101
$H_2 + Cl_2 \rightarrow 2HCl$ (2 atoms of hydrogen + 2 atoms of chlorine → 2 molecules of hydrochloric acid)
<u>Lab assignment</u>: Do experiment on p. 23. Record the results. <u>Must</u> wear goggles!

c.
_____ 101
<u>Lab</u>: Examine slide of frog's egg through microscope. Bring dissection kit for tomorrow.

2. Complete the list of laboratory equipment. Use the words in the box.

balance   Bunsen burner   ~~crucible tongs~~   forceps   funnel   graduated cylinder

a. ____crucible tongs____ : to pick up hot objects

b. _____ : to hold large amounts of material

c. _____ : to heat substances

d. _____ : to weigh chemicals

e. _____ : to pour liquids into a narrow container

f. _____ : to pick up very small things

3. Look at the lab experiment. Complete the list of laboratory equipment.

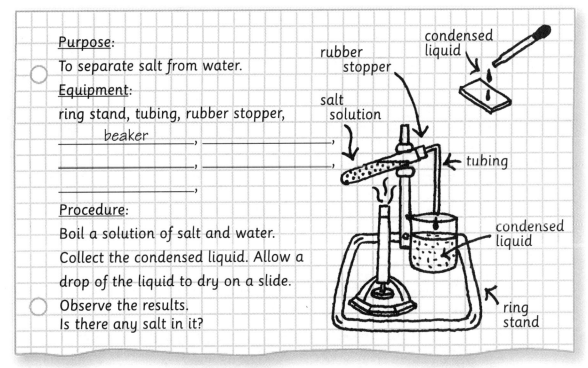

○ <u>Purpose</u>:
To separate salt from water.
<u>Equipment</u>:
ring stand, tubing, rubber stopper,
_____beaker_____ , _____ ,
_____ , _____ ,
_____ ,
<u>Procedure</u>:
Boil a solution of salt and water.
Collect the condensed liquid. Allow a
drop of the liquid to dry on a slide.
○ Observe the results.
Is there any salt in it?

rubber stopper
condensed liquid
salt solution
tubing
condensed liquid
ring stand

Challenge Look at **page 185** in this book. Follow the instructions.

Music

1. Look in your dictionary. Cross out the word that doesn't belong. Write the category.

   a. _____brass_____   French horn   ~~bass~~   trombone   tuba

   b. _____   clarinet   tambourine   piano   drums

   c. _____   cello   violin   guitar   organ

   d. _____   flute   oboe   xylophone   saxophone

2. Look at the bar graph. Circle the correct words to complete the sentences.

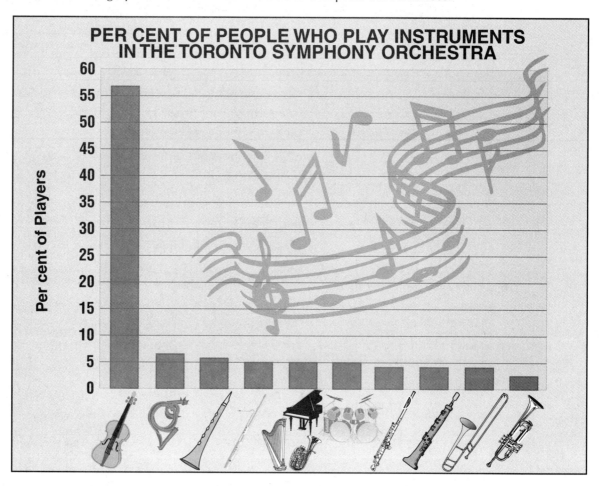

   a. Almost 60 per cent of players play the oboe / (violins)

   b. More people play the clarinet / trumpet than the flute.

   c. Fewer than six per cent of the people play the horns / other instruments.

   d. The strings / drums are the most popular instruments.

   e. The oboe is not as popular as the bassoon / trumpet.

   f. The flute is not as popular as the trombone / strings.

   g. The third most popular instrument is the trumpet / clarinet.

   Challenge   Ask your classmates about the instruments they play. Draw a bar graph like the one in Exercise 2.

1. Look in your dictionary. Write the school subject for each course description. Read quickly. You don't need to understand every word!

Courses

a. _____Computer Science_____ This basic class introduces students to hardware and software systems, and applications such as Microsoft® Word and Microsoft® Excel. There are two hours of lecture and two hours of lab each week.

b. _____ Three levels of ESL classes are offered in Conversation, Grammar, Reading, and Writing. In addition to three hours of class, there are two half-hour language lab sessions each week.

c. _____ Classes are offered in Spanish, French, and Japanese. Students learn grammar, conversation, reading, and writing. In addition to three hours of class, there are two half-hour language lab sessions each week.

d. _____ Students study plays and practice basic acting techniques, directing, and stage design. At the end of the school year they perform in a one-act play.

e. _____ Students choose among a variety of fitness and sports activities including basketball, volleyball, weightlifting, and aerobics. Activities take place in the gym and on the track. Two days a week. Proper sports clothing is required.

f. _____ In this class students study the history of the family, family issues, statistics on single-parent families, etc. and the future of the family.

g. _____ Students learn to operate common hand- and power-tools and to make basic home repairs, including car repairs.

h. _____ Basic drawing and painting. No experience necessary.

i. _____ Students learn basic concepts of money and credit, profit and loss, supply and demand, business cycles, banking, and the stock market.

j. _____ Students learn about the legal system in this country and how laws are made and enforced.

k. _____ Students learn office procedures and skills such as dictation, keyboarding, and use of the fax, the adding machine, and other office equipment.

l. _____ Students learn how to read music and sing a variety of songs from rock to opera. They perform at holidays and graduation.

2. What about you? Look at the classes in Exercise 1. Which classes do you think students should have to take (core courses)? Which classes do you think should be electives? Make two lists. Use your own paper.

Challenge Look at your lists in Exercise 2. Give reasons for your opinions.

1. Look in your dictionary. Cross out the word that doesn't belong. Complete the chart.

a. Provinces in _____	Alberta	~~Alaska~~	Nova Scotia	Québec
b. _States_ in the United States	Florida	Hawaii	Michigan	Baja California
c. States in Mexico	Louisiana	Durango	Sonora	Jalisco
d. _____ in Central America	Belize	Guatemala	Ontario	Panama
e. Regions of Mexico	Atlantic Provinces	Yucatan Peninsula	Chiapas Highlands	Gulf Coastal Plain
f. _____ of the United States	Midwest	Prairie Provinces	West Coast	Rocky Mountains
g. Bodies of Water	Gulf of Mexico	Southern Uplands	Atlantic Ocean	Caribbean Sea
h. _____	Costa Rica	Puerto Rico	Cuba	Bahamas

2. Look in your dictionary. Complete these sentences.

a. Texas is in the _____southwest_____ region of the United States.

b. Nicaragua lies between _____ and _____ in Central America.

c. _____ and the Dominican Republic share the same Caribbean island.

d. _____ is the smallest Canadian province.

e. _____, Mexico is northwest of Coahuila.

f. The west coast of British Columbia touches the _____ Ocean.

g. Newfoundland lies in the _____ _____.

h. The U.S. state of _____ is made of many islands.

i. Campeche lies in the _____ region of Mexico.

j. _____ is the largest island in the Caribbean Sea.

3. Look at the map. It shows where some products of Mexico come from. **True** or **False**? Correct the <u>underlined</u> words in the false sentences. Use your dictionary for help.

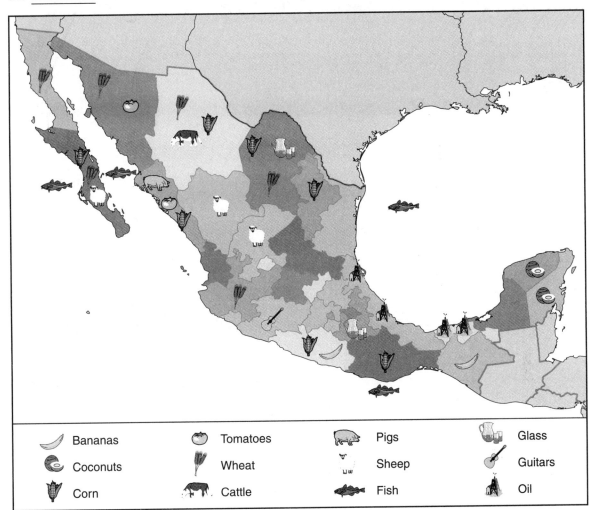

Bananas		Tomatoes		Pigs		Glass
Coconuts		Wheat		Sheep		Guitars
Corn		Cattle		Fish		Oil

a. Tomatoes are grown in the ~~south~~ *north* of Mexico.   False

b. <u>Coconuts</u> grow in the Yucatan Peninsula.   _____

c. Bananas grow in the <u>north</u> of Mexico.   _____

d. Fishing is done in both the <u>Gulf of Mexico</u> and the <u>Pacific Ocean</u>.   _____

e. Oil is found in the <u>west</u>.   _____

f. There is <u>more</u> wheat in the north than in the south.   _____

g. Guitars are made in <u>Michoacan</u>.   _____

h. <u>Pigs</u> are raised in Sinaloa.   _____

4. What about you? Draw a map showing some of the products of your country. Write eight sentences. Use your own paper.

Challenge Look at the map in Exercise 3. Write five more sentences about Mexican products.

The World

1. Look in your dictionary. Circle the correct words to complete the sentences.
   a. There are six /(seven) continents.
   b. Tanzania is in Africa / South America.
   c. Greenland, the biggest island in the world, is part of Europe / North America.
   d. Africa is bigger / smaller than South America.
   e. Syria is in Africa / Asia.
   f. Chad, in central Africa, has five / six neighbours.
   g. Located on two continents, China / Russia is the biggest country in the world.
   h. Afghanistan, in Asia, has five / six neighbours.
   i. Poland, in Europe, is bigger / smaller than the Czech Republic.
   j. Kazakhstan / Turkey is on the Black Sea.

2. Look in your dictionary. Write comparisons with *than*. Use the correct form of the words in parentheses ( ). Choose your own comparison for **g**.
   a. IN AFRICA: Uganda / Angola (big)
      Angola is bigger than Uganda.

   b. IN EUROPE: Italy / Finland (warm)
      _____

   c. IN ASIA: Thailand / Laos (small)
      _____

   d. IN SOUTH AMERICA: Chile / Argentina (wide)
      _____

   e. AUSTRALIA / ANTARCTICA (cold)
      _____

   f. NEAR SOUTH ASIA: The Red Sea / The Arabian Sea (narrow)
      _____

   g. IN NORTH AMERICA: _____ / _____ (_____)
      _____

3. Look in your dictionary. For each continent, find a country that is landlocked (it has no water around it).

   Africa: _____Chad_____   South America: _____

   Europe: _____   Asia: _____

124

4. Look in your dictionary. Complete these world facts. Write the names of the countries and the bodies of water.

a. _____ Mexico _____

Location: southern North America

Borders: U.S. to north, Gulf of Mexico to east, Belize and Guatemala to south, _____ Ocean to west

b. _____

Location: island off southeast Africa in western _____ Ocean

Borders: about 500 km east of Mozambique

c. _____

Location: central Europe

Borders: Germany and Czech Republic to north, Hungary and Slovakia to east, Slovenia and _____ to south, Switzerland and Liechtenstein to west

d. Laos

Location: southeast Asia

Borders: Myanmar to northwest, _____ to north, Vietnam to east, Cambodia to south, _____ to southwest

e. _____

Location: Western Africa

Borders: Guinea to north, Atlantic Ocean and _____ to west, Ivory Coast to east

f. _____

Location: northwestern South America

Borders: Colombia to north, Peru to east and south, _____ to west

g. Belarus

Location: northeastern Europe

Borders: Lithuania and _____ to north and northwest; Russia to north, northeast, and east; _____ to south, Poland to west

h. _____

Location: southwestern Asia

Borders: Turkmenistan to northwest, Tajikistan to north, China to northeast, Pakistan to east and south, _____ to west

5. What about you? Write a description of your country like the ones in Exercise 4. (If your country is in Exercise 4, choose a country you have visited.) Use your own paper.

Challenge Choose five other countries. Write descriptions like the ones in Exercise 4.

Energy and the Environment

1. Look in your dictionary. Circle the correct words to complete these sentences.

   a. Nuclear /(Solar) energy comes directly from the sun.

   b. Coal, oil, and natural gas / radiation are sources of energy.

   c. Another source of energy is acid rain / wind.

   d. Hydroelectric power / Geothermal energy comes from water.

   e. A danger of nuclear energy is radiation / smog.

   f. Old batteries / Paper bags are examples of hazardous waste.

   g. Acid rain / An oil spill kills trees.

   h. ♲ means radiation / recycle.

2. Look at suggestions for ways to save the earth. Check (✓) the correct column(s).

	HELP SAVE...			HELP PREVENT...			
	Energy	Water	Trees	Air Pollution	Water Pollution	Hazardous Waste	Pesticide Poisoning
a. Buy a "low-flow" showerhead.	✓	✓					
b. Use less detergent.					✓		
c. Use public transportation.							
d. Recycle newspapers.							
e. Keep refrigerator at 4°C or 5°C, not lower.							
f. Turn the tap off while you brush your teeth.							
g. Get your car checked regularly.							
h. Recycle batteries or use rechargeable ones.							
i. Turn off lights when you're not using them.							
j. Use "natural" methods to control cockroaches, ants, etc.							

3. What about you? List the things in Exercise 2 that you do. Use your own paper.

   Example: *I use public transportation to save energy and help prevent air pollution.*

Challenge List other things people can do to help save the earth.

1. Look in your dictionary. Complete the chart.

Planet Name	Symbol	Distance from the Sun (in kilometres)	Diameter (in kilometres)
a. _____Mars_____	♂	228 million	6 791
b. _____	♀	108 million	12 104
c. _____	⊕	150 million	12 755
d. _____	♄	1492 million	120 657
e. _____	♇	5.8 billion	2 200
f. _____	♃	779 million	142 796
g. _____	♅	2.9 billion	51 116
h. _____	♆	4.5 billion	49 494
i. _____	☿	58 million	4 877

2. Circle the correct words to complete these sentences. You can use your dictionary for help.

   a. There are nine moon /(planets)/ stars in the solar system.

   b. Uranus was the first planet discovered with a magnet / microscope / telescope.

   c. The astronaut / astronomer / space station William Herschel first observed Uranus in 1781.

   d. Thousands of asteroids / constellations / galaxies orbit the sun between Mars and Jupiter.

   e. Constellations / Galaxies / Comets look like pictures in the sky.

   f. The Earth's galaxy / orbit / space (a group of billions of stars) is called the Milky Way.

   g. It takes 27 days for the moon to go from a new moon to a full moon and back to

   a crescent moon / new moon / quarter moon again.

3. What about you? Describe what you can see when you look at the night sky. Use your own paper.

   Example: *I can see the constellation called the Big Dipper…*

Challenge Look in an encyclopedia, almanac, or science book. Find out more about three planets. How long does a day last? How long does it take to orbit the sun?

▶ **Go to page 178 for Another Look (Unit 9).**

Trees and Plants

1. Look in your dictionary. Which trees or plants have…? You will use some answers more than once.

COLOURFUL FLOWERS	BERRIES	NEEDLES	LEAVES THAT CAN GIVE YOU A RASH
dogwood	poison sumac	spruce	poison oak

2. Circle the correct words to complete the article. You can use your dictionary for help.

Trees

Trees are the biggest flowers /(plants) in the world. As long as they live, they
  a.
never stop growing. The pine/Sitka spruce, can reach a height of 60 metres.
  b.
Its cone/trunk can have a diameter of 4.5 **metres**.
  c.

The limbs/roots, which grow underground, are the fastest growing part of a
  d.
tree. They collect water and send it up the berries/trunk to the leaves/vines.
  e.   f.

There are two main categories of trees. *Broad-leaf trees*, such as the maple/pine,
  g.
have leaves that turn beautiful colours and then drop to the ground in the fall.
They often have many large branches that grow from the lower trunk.

Needle-leaf trees, such as the birch/pine, stay green all year and are called
  h.
evergreens. They carry seeds in cones/berries. The trunk/twig usually goes to
  i.   j.
the top of the tree.

A third category of tree is the *elm/palm*. It is almost all leaves/limbs and does
  k.   l.
not have branches/roots.
  m.

All trees have flowers. Some are very colourful and beautiful like those of the
magnolia/willow. Others, such as those of the dogwood/oak, are so small
  n.   o.
that many people do not notice them.

Challenge Make a list of at least five tree products.

128

1. Look in your dictionary. Complete the order form for this bouquet.

Westside 🌹 *Florist*

Order Form

1 mixed bouquet:

a. 2   irises

b. 4

c. 3

d. 1

e. 2

f. 2   orchids

2. Look in your dictionary. Complete the sentences with information from the chart.

FLOWER	GROWN FROM	SEASON	COMMENTS
		spring–fall	remove thorns for bouquets
		late spring–late summer	water often
		summer–early winter	plant seedlings in June
		early spring	very short stems
		October–June	3–4 buds on each stem
		winter–spring	good houseplant
		spring–summer	lovely perfume

a. _____Lilies_____ and _____ grow from bulbs.

b. _____, _____, and _____ grow from seeds.

c. _____ have thick white petals and smell very nice.

d. You can buy _____ in the spring, fall, and all winter.

e. Don't hurt your finger when you make a bouquet of _____!

Challenge Write about flower traditions in your country. **Example:** *In North America, men often give red roses to their wives or girlfriends on Valentine's Day.*

Marine Life, Amphibians, and Reptiles

1. Look in your dictionary. Match the animals that look similar. Write the numbers.

_____3_____ **a.** frog   **1.** garter snake

_____ **b.** salamander   **2.** porpoise

_____ **c.** dolphin   **3.** toad

_____ **d.** walrus   **4.** crocodile

_____ **e.** alligator   **5.** lizard

_____ **f.** eel   **6.** sea lion

2. Complete the conversations at an aquarium. Use the words in the box. Use your dictionary for help.

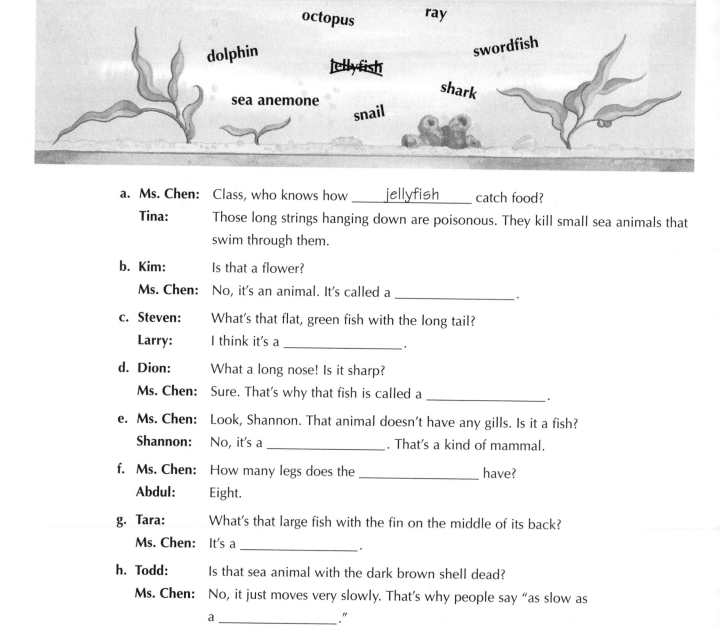

octopus   ray
dolphin   ~~jellyfish~~   swordfish
sea anemone   shark
snail

a. Ms. Chen: Class, who knows how _____jellyfish_____ catch food?

    Tina: Those long strings hanging down are poisonous. They kill small sea animals that swim through them.

b. Kim: Is that a flower?

    Ms. Chen: No, it's an animal. It's called a _____.

c. Steven: What's that flat, green fish with the long tail?

    Larry: I think it's a _____.

d. Dion: What a long nose! Is it sharp?

    Ms. Chen: Sure. That's why that fish is called a _____.

e. Ms. Chen: Look, Shannon. That animal doesn't have any gills. Is it a fish?

    Shannon: No, it's a _____. That's a kind of mammal.

f. Ms. Chen: How many legs does the _____ have?

    Abdul: Eight.

g. Tara: What's that large fish with the fin on the middle of its back?

    Ms. Chen: It's a _____.

h. Todd: Is that sea animal with the dark brown shell dead?

    Ms. Chen: No, it just moves very slowly. That's why people say "as slow as a _____."

3. Circle the correct words to complete the article.

Animal Defences

Animals have many ways of protecting themselves. Some have colours that make them hard to

see. One fish, the cobra / (flounder) can change its colour to match the environment. Two sea animals,
                 a.

the squid / sea lion and the otter / octopus, squirt ink into the water and hide in its dark cloud.
     b.   **c.**

Some poisonous amphibians / gills and reptiles warn enemies to keep away. For example,
            d.

the bright colours of some frogs / fins tell other animals that they are not safe
            e.

to eat, and the garter snake / rattlesnake makes a loud sound with the end of
           f.

its tail before it bites. The turtle's / trout's hard shell and the sharp needles of
           g.

the sea urchin / anemone are another kind of protection.
      h.

Sea mammals like dolphins / swordfish are intelligent and use language to warn each other of
          i.

danger. Scientists have even recorded the songs that whales / worms sing to each other as they
            j.

travel around the world. Other members of this group, such as walruses and sea lions / sea horses,
            k.

live in large communities to protect their babies.

4. Circle the correct letter for each statement. Write the letters in the circles below. You can use
your dictionary for help.

		TRUE	FALSE
a.	Salamanders have fur.	A	(O)
b.	Whales can swim.	L	Z
c.	All sea mammals have gills.	J	O
d.	Some mammals have fins.	R	L
e.	Rattlesnakes are poisonous.	E	B
f.	All reptiles have legs.	G	C
g.	Bass have scales.	D	P
h.	Scallops and shrimp are black.	E	I
i.	Jellyfish look like fish.	T	C

(O) ◯ ◯ ◯ ◯ ◯ ◯ ◯ ◯

Now unscramble the letters to find the name of an animal: _____

Challenge Look at **page 185** in this book. Follow the instructions.

Birds, Insects, and Arachnids

1. Look in your dictionary. Complete the diagram with the words in the box.

| ~~feathers~~ | claws | six or eight legs | a beak | two legs | wings |

Both

Birds   **Insects and Arachnids**

feathers

2. Look in your dictionary. Write the name of the bird, insect, or arachnid.

   a. It makes honey from flowers. Unlike the wasp, it dies after it stings. _____honeybee_____

   b. It looks like a big duck and is raised for food and feathers. _____

   c. It's very small. It eats blood and often lives in the fur or skin of mammals. It can make people sick. _____

   d. It's brown with an orange breast. _____

   e. It's very small and red, and it has black polka dots. _____

   f. It has sharp claws and big eyes in the front of its head. _____

   g. It begins its life as a caterpillar. _____

   h. It has a long bill for eating nectar from flowers. It moves its wings 1000 times a second. _____

   i. It catches insects by making holes in trees with its beak. _____

   j. It doesn't fly, but swims in icy water to catch fish. _____

   k. It lives near water. It flies and bites people. _____

   l. It looks like a small grasshopper, and eats cloth like a moth. It makes music by rubbing its wings together. _____

   m. It has beautiful blue feathers and eats insects and fruit. _____

   n. It likes human food and causes many diseases. A spider often catches it in its web. _____

   o. It's very big with long, colourful feathers. _____

3. What about you? What are some common birds, insects, and arachnids where you live? Make a list. Use your own paper.

Challenge Look up information about a bird, insect, or arachnid in your list from Exercise 3. Where does it live? What does it eat? How does it help or hurt people?

1. Look in your dictionary. Which animals...?

   a. are babies   ___kitten___   _____

   b. have wings   _____   _____   _____

   c. live in water   _____

   d. have stripes   _____

   e. live in holes   _____

   f. give us milk   _____   _____   _____

   g. lay eggs   _____

   h. carry people   _____   _____

2. Look at the chart and complete the sentences.

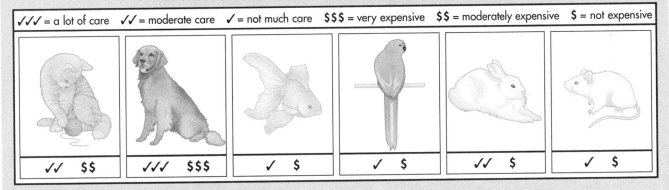

CARE AND COST OF COMMON PETS

✓✓✓ = a lot of care   ✓✓ = moderate care   ✓ = not much care $$$ = very expensive $$ = moderately expensive $ = not expensive

✓✓ $$	✓✓✓ $$$	✓ $	✓ $	✓✓ $	✓ $

   a. _____Dogs_____ need the most care. In addition to giving them food and water, you have to train them and play with them. They are also the most expensive.

   b. _____ need less care than dogs. With enough water and food, they can be left alone during the day. They are less expensive than dogs, but more expensive than other pets.

   c. If you like birds, think about getting one or more _____. They aren't expensive and don't need much care. They like to climb, so give them a tall cage with a ladder.

   d. Perhaps the easiest and cheapest pets are _____. They can live long and healthy lives in a big bowl of fresh water with plants and room to swim.

   e. Don't be afraid of these rodents. Mice and white _____ (not the ones that live in the city!) make nice pets. They don't cost much, and they don't need a lot of care.

   f. Bushy-tailed and long-eared, _____ aren't expensive, but they do need moderate care and special food. No carrots!

3. What about you? Have you ever had a pet? How did you care for it?

   Example: *I have a dog. I walk it every morning before school…*

   Challenge Look at **page 185** in this book and follow the instructions.

Mammals

1. Look in your dictionary. Which animals have these forms of protection?

   horns: _____buffalo_____   _____   _____

   quills: _____

   antlers: _____   _____

   tusks: _____

   a bad smell: _____

   Name two other
   forms of protection: _____   _____

2. Look at the bar graph. Complete the sentences.

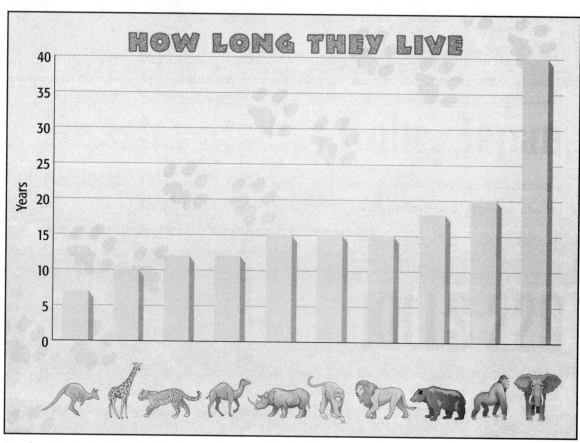

Based on information from: *The World Almanac and Book of Facts 1998.* (NJ: World Almanac Books, 1997)

   a. The black _____bear_____ lives 18 years.

   b. The _____ lives ten years.

   c. The camel lives as long as the _____.

   d. The black _____ lives five years longer than the giraffe.

   e. The _____ lives just as long as the rhinoceros and the _____.

   f. The gorilla lives 13 years longer than the _____.

   g. The _____ lives the longest.

3. Look at the pictures. Make a list of endangered* animals and the continent(s) where they live.

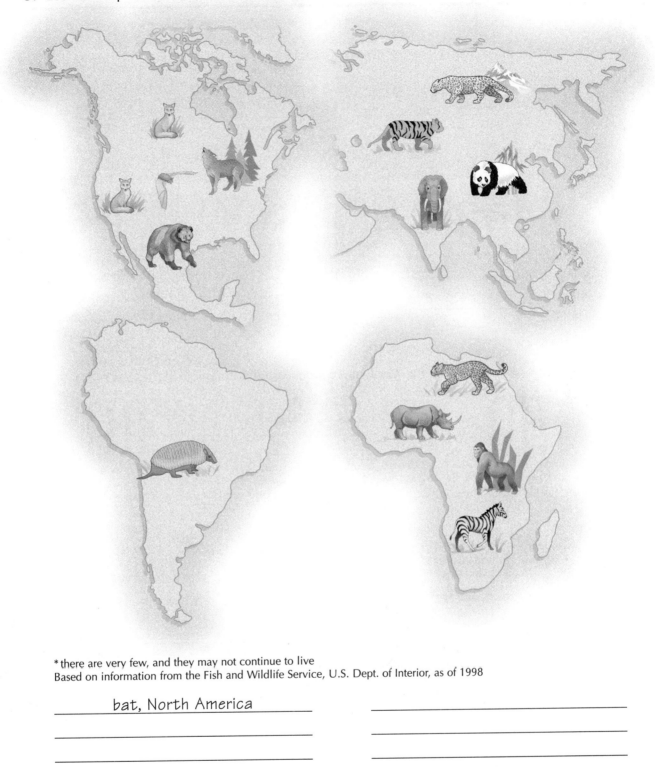

*there are very few, and they may not continue to live
Based on information from the Fish and Wildlife Service, U.S. Dept. of Interior, as of 1998

bat, North America
_____   _____
_____   _____
_____   _____
_____   _____
_____   _____
_____   _____

Challenge List reasons why some animals are endangered. You can use an encyclopedia for help.
(Look up *endangered species*.) **Example:** *People kill elephants for their tusks.*

▶ **Go to page 179 for Another Look (Unit 10).**

1. Look in your dictionary. Write the job titles.

Help Wanted	Help Wanted	Help Wanted
a. _Dentist_ to examine, clean, and repair teeth, and treat diseases of the mouth at our East Side clinic. Saturdays and evening hours. 555-3443	**c.** _____ to examine and treat patients at busy medical clinic. 555-0432	**e.** _____ to receive payment, give change and receipts to customers. Douglas Drugstore, Mineral Springs Road. 555-2243
b. _____ to make bread, pies, and cakes at our midtown restaurant. $8.67/ hr. 555-2343	**d.** _____ to prepare and sell meat at our busy counter. S&W Supermarket. **$ 25,000/yr.** Call 555-4345	**f.** _____ to plan and design public buildings at our growing firm. McKAY, BROWN & PETRILLO 555-3451

2. Look at the bar graph. Circle the correct words to complete the sentences.

How Stressful* Is the Job?

*A *stressful* job is one that can make you feel nervous and not relaxed.
Based on information from: Krantz, L.: *Jobs Rated Almanac.* (NY: John Wiley & Sons, Inc., 1995)

According to the bar graph...

a. a doctor / (firefighter) has the job with the most stress.

b. a florist / computer programmer has the job with the least stress.

c. a doctor's job is more / less stressful than a dentist's job.

d. a hairdresser has a little less job stress than a garment worker / graphic artist has.

e. the garment worker, hairdresser, and computer programmer / dentist have about the same amount of stress.

3. Look in your dictionary. Write the job titles.

Help Wanted

g. _____Caregiver_____
to watch our two preschoolers. Good storytelling skills a must! Excellent references required. $10/hr. 555-3406

h. _____
to plan menus and prepare meals at our small Mexican restaurant. Work closely with servers and restaurant manager. La Paloma. 345 Riverside Avenue

i. _____
to build walls, fireplaces, patios, etc. C&O Construction. 555-9723

j. _____
to put together parts in radio factory.
ON-THE-JOB-TRAINING
$350/wk.
call Frank Collins, 555-9922

Help Wanted

k. _____
to plan and supervise the building of roads, bridges, tunnels, and buildings.
FAX RESUME
555-3423

l. _____
to cut and arrange flowers.
THE ROSE BUD
Mon.–Sat. 10:00–6:00
555-4936

m. _____
to repair and maintain cars at small garage. Part-time, weekends.
555-7396

Help Wanted

n. _____
to help build shelves and doors in new building. $350/wk.
555-4345
Ask for Mr. Heller.

o. _____
to perform in plays for a small theatre company. TV, stage, or movie experience.
555-8299

p. _____
to plan and organize appointments for busy business executive.
H. THOMAS & SONS
555-8787

Exciting opportunities exist at our new locations:

---

4. What about you? Compare these jobs. Which do you think is more interesting? more stressful?

a. cook / baker   I think a baker's job is more interesting than a cook's job.
A cook's job is probably more stressful.

b. engineer / carpenter _____
_____

c. assembler / dockworker _____
_____

d. caregiver / administrative assistant _____
_____

e. Other: _____ / _____   _____
_____

Challenge Look at Exercise 4. Explain your choices.

137

Jobs and Occupations, H–W

1. Look in your dictionary. Cross out the word that doesn't belong. Give a reason.

a.　　　　receptionist　　　　~~model~~　　　　secretary

　　<u>A model doesn't work in an office.</u>

b.　　　　nurse　　　　veterinarian　　　　truck driver

　　_____

c.　　　　mover　　　　salesperson　　　　stock clerk

　　_____

d.　　　　welder　　　　serviceman　　　　machine operator

　　_____

e.　　　　student　　　　teacher　　　　housekeeper

　　_____

2. Read the conversations. Who's talking? Use the words in the box.

interpreter	~~Instructor~~	lawyer	messenger	musician
police officer	receptionist	repair person	reporter	student
	telemarketer	travel agent		

a. ___Instructor___ : There will be a math test on Monday.

　 _____ : Can we use our calculators?

b. _____ : Your Honour, I object! My client is not guilty!

　 _____ : Monsieur le juge, je récuse! Mon client n'est pas coupable!

c. _____ : I'm Monica Stone, from Channel 5 news. Have you made any arrests, Detective Wong?

　 _____ : We're questioning a suspect now.

d. _____ : Hello. This is Dan from T & J Tools. We're selling excellent quality hammers at a great price.

　 _____ : Thanks. But I don't use hammers when I work on TVs.

e. _____ : I have to go to Miami tomorrow. I'm giving a concert.

　 _____ : OK. Do you want a round-trip or one-way ticket?

f. _____ : I've got a package for Bob Johnson.

　 _____ : Mr. Johnson's office is the first door on your right.

3. Look at the chart. **True** or **False**?

Occupation	Hrs/Wk	males ♂	females ♀
(farmer)	60	317 900	167 705
(trappers/fishers)	45	38 085	7 605
(health services)	40	267 400	1 141 770
(construction)	40	727 300	95 045
(teacher)	37.5	368 185	637 395
(manufacturing)	40.5	1 450 845	589 000
(hospitality)	47.5	405 275	583 315
(retail/SALE)	50	873 630	907 615
($ financial)	45	175 145	346 920
(communications)	40.5	286 645	160 130

Source: Statistics Canada 1996 Census.

a. A farmer works longer hours than a nurse. _____True_____

b. A financial planner works fewer hours than a construction worker. _____

c. A teacher works as many hours as a waitress. _____

d. There are more men than women working in financial services. _____

e. There are more women than men working in retail stores. _____

f. There are more men working in communications than in health services and they work longer hours. _____

g. Almost as many women work in manufacturing as in hospitality services. _____

h. The fewest woman work as trappers and fishers. _____

4. What about you? Look at the chart in Exercise 3. Which jobs would or wouldn't you like? Why?

_____

_____

_____

_____

Challenge Look at **page 186** in this book. Complete the chart.

Job Skills

1. Look in your dictionary. Complete these job descriptions.

   a. A cashier <u>uses a cash register</u> .

   b. A chef _____ .

   c. An orderly _____ .

   d. A garment worker _____ .

   e. A secretary _____ .

   f. A server _____ .

   g. An interpreter _____ .

   h. A babysitter _____ .

2. What about you? Complete the questionnaire. Write your name and check (✔) the job skills you have.

CAN YOU...?	KIM	ALEXIS	CARLOS	DIANA	(Your Name)
use a cash register	✔				
work on a computer	✔			✔	
supervise people		✔			
speak another language	✔		✔	✔	
sell clothes		✔		✔	
repair appliances				✔	
operate heavy machinery			✔		
drive a truck		✔			
cook	✔				
do manual labour	✔		✔		
assemble parts		✔	✔		

3. Look at the chart in Exercise 2. **True** or **False**?

   a. Kim could apply for a job as a chef. ___True___

   b. Carlos could get a job as a truck driver. _____

   c. Diana could apply for a job as a secretary. _____

   d. Only Diana could apply for a job as a repair person. _____

   e. Both Kim and Alexis could get jobs as assemblers. _____

   f. Alexis could apply for a job as a salesperson, but not as a repair person. _____

   g. You could work as a cashier. _____

   h. Both Diana and you could be managers. _____

   i. You and Carlos can both work with your hands. _____

Challenge List three other job skills. Check (✔) the ones you and a classmate have.

Your Name _____   Classmate's Name _____

	Your Name	Classmate's Name
_____	☐	☐
_____	☐	☐
_____	☐	☐

1. Look in your dictionary. **Before** or **After**? Circle the correct word.

a. Dan called for information (before)/ after he went on the interview.

b. Before / After he talked to friends, he looked in the classifieds.

c. Before / After he went on the interview, he filled out an application.

d. Dan inquired about the salary before / after he talked about his experience.

2. Complete the information with the words in the box.

ask about benefits	ask about the hours	call for information	fill out an application
~~Talk to friends~~	go to the interview	inquire about the salary	look at job boards
look in the classifieds	look for help wanted signs	talk about your experience	get hired

Looking for a Job

It can take a lot of time—and work—to find a job. Here are some tips.

Tell everyone that you are looking for work. Begin close to home. Talk to friends, relatives, teachers, and
a.

classmates. Keep your eyes open. When you're walking down the street, _____ in store
b.

windows. _____ in school or in the supermarket. Get the newspaper every day and
c.

_____ . But remember — "Help Wanted" ads do not tell you the whole story. You will probably
d.

have to pick up the phone and _____ .
e.

_____ : Is the job 9:00 to 5:00? Do you have to work on weekends?
f.

Applying for a job When you apply for a job, you will probably have to _____ . This gives the
g.

employer basic information about your skills and experience. Then, when you _____ , you will
h.

have the chance to _____ in greater detail. The interviewer will ask you a lot of questions,
i.

but it's also important for you to ask questions.

_____ : What's the starting pay?
j.

_____ : What about a pension plan? Remember: Be patient and don't give up. You may
k.

have to try many different approaches before you finally _____ and get that first pay cheque!
l.

3. What about you? Think about a time you or someone you know went on a job search. Write the steps. **Example:** *First, I looked at the classifieds. Then I…*

Challenge Look at **page 186** in this book. Follow the instructions.

An Office

1. Look in your dictionary. Cross out the word that doesn't belong. Give a reason.

a. office manager ~~microcassette transcriber~~ executive assistant file clerk

A microcassette transcriber isn't a person.

b. desk swivel chair supply cabinet pencil sharpener

_____

c. rubber stamp envelope Post-it notes notepad

_____

d. paper clip glue rubber cement paper cutter

_____

e. fax machine calculator typewriter stapler

_____

2. Match the word parts. Write the numbers.

__5__	**a.** paper	**1.** pins	
_____	**b.** correction	**2.** book	
_____	**c.** postal	**3.** scale	
_____	**d.** push	**4.** pad	
_____	**e.** appointment	**5.** shredder	
_____	**f.** legal	**6.** fluid	

3. Read the notes. What do you need to do the job? Use the words from Exercise 2.

a.
Hang this notice on the cafeteria bulletin board.
Thanks.
𝓛

pushpins

c.
*This is for your eyes only!
Please read and destroy.

_____

e.
I'll be out of the office on Friday. Please take notes at the staff meeting.
—Thanks.
R.F.

_____

b.
There are some mistakes in this report. Please correct them before you make copies.

_____

d.
Please let me know when my next meeting with L. J. Inc. is.

_____

f.
Mail two copies to Anne Miles.

_____

142

4. Look at the picture and the instructions. What mistakes did the assistant make?

John—Type this report on letterhead paper. Make 3 copies, then collate and staple them. Leave them on my desk. Thanks.

R. Smith

Annual International Sales Conference

We are pleased to announce the plans for our Annual International Sales Conference. This year the conference will be held on April 20-23, in Miami, Florida, USA.

Catherine Hartman is in charge of the conference logistics. Her fax number is (212) 555-2121 and her telephone number is (212) 555-2100, ext. 321.

Catherine has prepared the attached information packet in which she has provided information about the costs of the conference as well as the weather in Miami in April and recommendations for clothing. She will send additional information about activities in which you

1

may wish to participate if you plan to be in Miami the weekend before the conference.

The conference headquarters will be at the Greatwood Hotel. We have had very good reports about this hotel from previous clients and visitors. Please fax the attached accommodations request form directly to the hotel by January 31. If you need to call the hotel, please ask for John Norton, the manager with whom we have made our arrangements.

Please book your own flights. Once you know the details, please fax the information to Catherine so she can arrange to have someone meet you at the airport.

If you have any questions about travel or accommodations, please call Catherine

2

M. SHAKTER

a. He didn't use letterhead. He used plain paper.

b. _____

c. _____

d. _____

e. _____

5. Circle the correct words to complete the instructions.

MEMO

To: Alice Rader   **From:** Marta Lopez

—The (photocopier) / mailer is broken again. Please call the repair person. You'll find the phone number
    a.
in the rotary card file / stacking tray under "r."
          b.
—Put the clients' names on the staples / labels before you file the papers on my desk.
              c.
—Check my desk calendar / pad to see when the staff meetings are next month.
        d.
—The book on my desk goes to A. Olinski at 354 Main Street. Use packing / clear tape so you can read
                                          e.
the address through it.
—Before you file the Thompson report, use the paper cutter / shredder to make it standard letter size.
                                            f.
It's too long now.
—Staple / Transcribe my notes from Tuesday's meeting. The microcassette / fax machine is on my desk.
    g.   **h.**
—Please stamp all letters to Japan "air mail." (The legal / ink pad is in the top left drawer.)
                                            i.

Challenge Look at the office supplies in your dictionary. Which items can you use for the same job?
Example: *You can use a desk calendar or an appointment book to write appointments.*

Computers

1. Look in your dictionary. Complete the definitions from a user's manual.

INPUT (entering information)

a. _____program_____: (application) A type of software that tells the computer how to do different things (for example, doing math, playing games, making pictures).

b. _____: This looks like the part of a typewriter that has letters and numbers. You type on it to enter information into the computer.

PROCESSING (inside the computer)

c. _____: (central processing unit) This is the computer's "brain."

STORAGE (keeping information to use later)

d. _____: A small, square piece of plastic for saving information.

e. _____: A narrow opening in the computer for floppy disks.

f. _____: Inside the computer, it contains a disk that holds a lot of information.

OUTPUT (seeing your work)

g. _____: This looks like a TV screen. On it, you can read the words and numbers you type or see the charts and pictures you make.

h. _____: This gives you a "hard" or paper copy of your work.

COMMUNICATIONS (talking to other computers)

i. _____: This sends information from one computer to another over telephone lines.

j. _____: This special round disc holds a lot of information including pictures and sound. You can buy encyclopedias, dictionaries, and games in this form.

OTHER TERMS

k. _____: A small computer that uses batteries. Instead of a _____, it has a trackball.

l. _____: This can "read" words and pictures from a book, newspaper, etc., into the computer without using a mouse or keyboard.

Challenge Write definitions for *power switch*, *cable*, and *port*.

144

1. Look in your dictionary. Complete these job descriptions. Write the job.
   a. Open and close the front lobby _____door_____ : _____doorman_____
   b. Supervise the bellhops: _____
   c. Register and check out _____ : _____
   d. Carry the guests' luggage on a luggage _____ : _____
   e. Clean rooms, _____ beds, and provide fresh towels: _____

2. Circle the correct words to complete this hotel brochure.

The Greatwood Hotel
Where great things happen!

Be our doorman / (guest!) For business or pleasure—everything you need...
a.
Accommodations: We have 285 comfortable halls / guest rooms (non-smoking
b.
available). Cable TV and VCR.

Food: Eat at our two restaurants and express breakfast buffet. Don't want to leave

your room? Call our 24-hour pool / room service.
c.
Recreation: Swim in our heated outdoor lobby / pool. Work out in our health club.
d.
Services and Features: Driving here? Enjoy our free housekeeping cart / valet parking.
e.
Shop at our beautiful gift shop / luggage cart. Do business in our large
f.
ballroom / meeting room. Dance to live music in our ballroom / meeting room.
g. **h.**
For more information or for reservations, call 800-555-9868

3. What about you? How important to you are these hotel features? Rank them.
   (Number 1 = most important)
   _____ ice machine   _____ valet parking   _____ gift shop   _____ pool
   _____ ballroom   _____ room service   _____ meeting room   _____ doorman

Challenge Imagine you are staying at the hotel in your dictionary. Write a postcard to a friend. Describe the hotel.

A Factory

1. Look in your dictionary. Complete the factory newsletter.

Vol. 25, No. 2
June 7, 2002

THE LAMPLIGHTER

*Sun Electric
"We light up
your life"*

From the _____front office_____
a.

T.J. Rolf, *President and* _____
b.

As we enter our 25th year of business, I want to thank

the following people for their dedication and hard work:

Ivonne Campis, _____
c.

For 15 years, Ivonne has assembled the

_____ that make our lamps. Her
d.

skill and care have contributed to the high quality of

our product.

Prem Singh, _____
e.

For 10 years, Prem has watched over the assembly line,

assuring the highest product quality. He helps create a

friendly and productive work environment.

Alice Carver, _____
f.

Alice has worked in the _____ for
g.

5 years, taking finished lamps off the conveyor belt and

putting them in boxes ready for shipment.

**Employee of
the Month!**

Pete Tresante, *shipping clerk*

Pete has punched a time clock for more than 20 years.

He has stood on the _____ carefully
h.

checking the orders that we _____.
i.

Congratulations Pete!

Jan Larson, _____
j.

Jan has been hired to _____ a new
k.

desk lamp. We will begin to _____
l.

this new product in September. Welcome Jan!

Challenge Look in your dictionary. Write short paragraphs about the order picker and the forklift
operator for the factory newsletter in Exercise 1. Use your imagination.

1. Look in your dictionary. Write the name of the safety symbol for each hazard.

    a. a bottle of pesticide   _poison_

    b. a can of gasoline   _____

    c. a bottle of cleaning fluid   _____

    d. an old car battery   _____

    e. an aerosol can of paint   _____

2. Circle the correct words to complete the safety poster.

WARNING

Protect Yourself from Head to Toe! Use Safety (Equipment) Symbols!
a.

Protect your head: A hair net / hard hat
b.
can protect you from falling objects.

Don't forget your hair. If it's long, wear

a hair net / safety visor so it won't get
c.
caught in machinery.

Protect your eyes: Always wear safety

glasses / gloves or earmuffs / goggles
d.   **e.**
to protect your eyes from flying objects.

Protect your ears: Noise can cause hearing

loss. Wear earplugs / toe guards or safety
f.
earmuffs / goggles if you work near loud machinery.
g.

Protect your hands: Always wear work

or latex gloves / vests when handling
h.
hazardous / radioactive materials.
i.

Protect your feet: Always wear safety

work shoes or back supports / boots.
j.

Avoid dangerous situations: Don't use

power tools in wet locations or near

corrosive / flammable liquids or gases.
k.
Keep a fire extinguisher / toe guard
l.
on the wall.

Remember: Be careful / careless! Better safe than sorry!
m.

3. What about you? What safety equipment do you use? When do you use it?

    Example: _I wear earplugs when I go to a loud concert._

Challenge Look at **page 186** in this book. Follow the instructions.

Farming and Ranching

1. Look in your dictionary. Write an example of....

   a. a type of livestock   _goats_

   b. a crop used for feed   _____

   c. a crop used to make clothing   _____

   d. something that grows in a vegetable garden   _____

   e. something that grows in an orchard   _____

   f. something that grows in a vineyard   _____

2. Circle the correct words to complete the letter.

Vernon, British Columbia

Dear Carlos,

My first day on the (farm) / ranch! When I got up, it was still dark. John
              a.
Johnson, the farmer / hired hand who owns the place, was already in the
           b.
corral / barn. He was harvesting / milking the cows. My job was to feed / plant
  c.   **d.**   **e.**
the chickens and other cattle / livestock. I was happy when it was time for
                   f.
breakfast. We had fresh eggs and ham along with tomatoes from the
vegetable garden / vineyard and rice / fruit from the orchard.
      g.   **h.**
    After breakfast, it was time to work in the fence / field. John says
                                i.
that in the old days horses pulled most of the farm equipment / steers. Today,
                           j.
a hired hand / tractor does the job. John and his farmworkers / ranchers
  k.   **l.**
planted rows of corn and other crops / wheat.
                   m.
It looks beautiful. They also grow alfalfa / cotton
                 n.
for animal feed. I'd like to come back when
they harvest / milk the corn in the summer.
      o.
Life on the farm is hard work, but it's
great being outside, close to nature.

See you soon,
Jeff

Challenge Would you like to spend some time on a farm or a ranch? Write a paragraph explaining your opinion.

1. Look at the construction site in your dictionary. **True** or **False**? Correct the underlined words in the false sentences.

eleven
    a. There are ~~eight~~ construction workers on the site.   ___False___

    b. One worker is climbing a <u>ladder</u>.   _____

    c. Two construction workers are lifting <u>plywood</u>.   _____

    d. The <u>backhoe</u> is orange.   _____

    e. A worker is using a <u>sledgehammer</u> near the crosswalk.   _____

2. Complete the sentences. Use the words in the boxes.

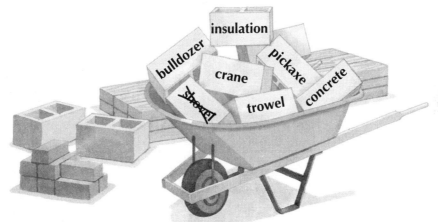

    a. You can use a _____*shovel*_____ to dig a small hole in the ground.

    b. A _____ moves earth or large rocks from one place to another.

    c. _____ keeps a house warm.

    d. A _____ can lift and place beams on high floors.

    e. A _____ and a _____ mixture are used to lay bricks.

    f. A _____ is used to dig in very hard ground.

3. What about you? Check (✓) the materials that your school and home are made of.

	SCHOOL BUILDING	HOME
bricks		
shingles		
stucco		
wood		
Other: _____		

Challenge Look for pictures of buildings in a newspaper, magazine, or in your picture dictionary. What building materials are used? **Example:** *The house on page 39 is made of brick.*

Tools and Building Supplies

1. Look in your dictionary. Cross out the word that doesn't belong. Then write the section of the hardware store.

a. <u>hardware</u>	nail	bolt	~~outlet~~	screw
b. _____	ax	plunger	pipe	fittings
c. _____	circular saw	hammer	router	electric drill
d. _____	brush	roller	spray gun	chisel
e. _____	wire stripper	drill bit	wire	extension cord
f. _____	hacksaw	flashlight	wrench	mallet

2. Complete the conversations with the correct words from the box.

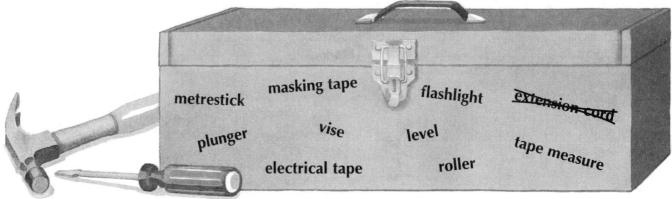

metrestick   masking tape   flashlight   ~~extension cord~~
plunger   vise   level   tape measure
electrical tape   roller

a. **Ty:** I want to plug in this electric drill, but it doesn't reach the outlet.

   Jade: No problem. Use this <u>extension cord</u>.

b. **Ian:** I've been painting for hours and I still have three more walls to do.

   Tina: Why don't you use this _____? It's faster than a paintbrush.

c. **Lily:** Oh, no. The toilet is plugged again.

   Dan: Here. Use this _____. It always works.

d. **Kim:** Do you know how long the shelf in the dining room is?

   Lian: No. Use the _____ or _____ to find out.

e. **Eva:** Help! I could use a third hand here!

   Jana: Use the _____ to hold the wood in place.

f. **Jules:** Don't get paint on the glass.

   Lyle: I won't. I put _____ around the panes before I started.

g. **Nico:** That wire doesn't look very safe.

   Iris: Don't worry. I'll put some of this _____ on before using it.

h. **Olga:** Does this shelf look straight?

   Boris: Hmm. I'm not sure. Let's use the _____. Then we'll know for certain.

i. **Enzo:** It's so dark behind here. I can't see what I'm doing!

   Pia: Give me the _____. I'll hold it for you.

3. Look at the pictures. Each situation shows a mistake. Describe the mistake and tell the people what they need to do the job right.

a. That's a Phillips screwdriver.
You need the other kind.

b. _____
_____

c. _____
_____

d. _____
_____

e. _____
_____

4. What about you? Check (✓) the tools you have used (or someone you know has used). What did you use them for?

☐ hammer _____

☐ axe _____

☐ handsaw _____

☐ screwdriver _____

☐ pliers _____

☐ wrench _____

☐ vise _____

☐ electric drill _____

☐ Other: _____ _____

Challenge Imagine you can have only three tools from the ones in Exercise 4. Which would you choose? Explain your choice.

▶ Go to page 180 for Another Look (Unit 11).

Places to Go

1. Look in your dictionary. Complete the schedule.

What's Happening

Sports

Reds v. Kings <u>baseball game</u> . 2:00, Sun.
      a.

Hunter Field _____ , $8.
        b.

Art

Clark _____ . Special exhibit of
    c.

modern painting and _____ by
          d.

American Artists. Fri. & Sat. 10–5, Sun. 1–5.

Children

Carousel Village. Home of the 50 m high

_____ _____ by the
  e.   **f.**

Candycane Theatre at 12, 1, & 2. Free with

admission to the _____ park.
        g.

At _____
   h.

Independence Day*** (PG-13) Cinema 1,

Jack** (PG-13) Cinema 2.

Call 555-9347 for reserved

_____ , $7.
 i.

General Interest

• Vilas Park _____ . Elephants,
        j.

giraffes, and many other _____ .
          k.

3:00 talk by _____ Sue Ray.
       l.

Daily 10–4. $5 adults, $2.50 children

(under age 3, free).

• Warwick _____ . More than 20
       m.

_____ selling clothes,
   n.

sunglasses, and other _____ .
         o.

10–4 Sat. Free.

• Bayside _____ . More than 20
      p.

varieties of roses, and many other flowers.

Greenhouse tours daily, 11–4. Free.

• 23rd Street _____ . Games and
       q.

rides. Weekends 11–4. Free.

• Tiverton _____ . Livestock
      r.

exhibitions, prizes. Free.

2. Look at the schedule in Exercise 1. Recommend events for these people.

    a. Jack wants to be an announcer.   <u>baseball game</u>

    b. David wants to be a gardener.   _____

    c. Julia needs some things for the house.   _____

    d. Ten-year-old Tina likes rides.   _____ or _____

3. What about you? Look at the schedule in Exercise 1. Where would you like to go? Why?

Example: *I'd like to go to the zoo because I like animals.*

_____

_____

Challenge Look in a local newspaper. List four possible places to go next weekend. Rank them in order of interest. (Number 1 = the most interesting) Explain your choices.

1. Look in your dictionary. Where can you hear…?

    a. "OK. Now, try to catch this."   _ball field_

    b. "Would you like some more chicken?"   _____

    c. "Look! They're swimming toward the bread!"   _____

    d. "Push me higher, Mommy!"   _____

    e. "Let's ride around one more time."   _____

    f. "Is that your pail and shovel?"   _____

    g. "Bring your arm all the way back when you serve the ball." _____

2. Read about the children. What should they use? Use your dictionary for help.

    a. Toby likes to jump.   _skipping rope_

    b. Jennifer is a little too young to ride a bicycle. _____

    c. Timmy is thirsty.   _____

    d. Cindi likes to climb on bars.   _____

    e. Shao-fen likes to play on things that go up and down. _____

    f. Carlos is tired and just wants to sit down and rest. _____

3. What about you? Look at the park in your dictionary. What would you do there…?

    a. alone

    Example: _I would sit on a bench and watch the children._

    _____

    b. with a friend

    _____

    c. with three of your classmates

    _____

    d. with a three-year-old child

    _____

    e. with a ten-year-old child

    _____

    f. with a 65-year-old relative

    _____

Challenge Design the ideal park. What would it have? Write a description.

Outdoor Recreation

1. Look at the top picture in your dictionary. Find and correct six more mistakes in the letter. Do not change any of the number words.

Dear Robyn,

    Here's a picture of our first camping trip. (Tony just took it). As you can see, I'm cooking outside our tent. (That's me in front of the ~~camping stove~~ *campfire*)

    Aren't the lake and mountains beautiful? Do you see the man fishing? He just caught something with his rope and fishing net. On the lake, two people are rafting, one person is boating in a small red motorboat, and three people are canoeing. Back on land, you can see people horseback riding and mountain biking. There are also three people hiking. One of them is sitting on a rock and resting. His life vest sure looks heavy! I'd prefer backpacking like those two people standing on the rocks in front of him.

    I'd better go. See you next week.

                                           Becca

---

2. Read the conversations. What are they talking about? Use your dictionary for help.

a. Ming: *Brrr.* It's getting cold out here.

    Sue: Hand me <u>those</u>, and I'll light the fire.   _____matches_____

b. Dave: *Ow.* These mosquitoes are driving me crazy.

    Eva: Put some of <u>this</u> on.   _____

c. Bob: I'm thirsty.

    Julie: I don't think there's any more water in <u>this</u>.   _____

d. Mia: This rope is too long.

    Tom: Here. You can use <u>this</u> to cut it.   _____

e. Doug: I can't sleep. The ground is really hard.

    Sarah: Why don't you put <u>this</u> under your sleeping bag?   _____

f. Luke: It's really dark out here.

    Mike: Take <u>this</u> with you so you can see where you're going.   _____

3. What about you? Would you like to go camping? Why or why not?

Example: *I'd like to go camping. I like sleeping outside.*

_____

Challenge Look in your dictionary. Imagine you are on a camping trip. List the five most important items to have. Give reasons.

1. Look in your dictionary. Complete the sentences.

   a. The man and woman are wearing _____*wet suits*_____ and scuba tanks.

   b. The boy standing in the shade is wearing a diving mask and _____.

   c. There's a red _____ hanging from the lifeguard station.

   d. A woman is putting _____ on a little girl.

   e. The little girl in the pink bathing suit is listening to a _____.

2. Circle the correct words to complete this hotel ad.

The Sand Castle/Seashell Inn
a.

YOUR NUMBER ONE CHOICE FOR FUN IN THE SUN!

Relax under a beach towel/umbrella on our white-sand beach/pier.
b.   c.

Swim among the gentle fins/waves of our beautiful blue-green
d.

ocean/scuba tank. Eat inside our fine restaurant or buy a fresh fish
e.

sandwich to put in your bucket/cooler.
f.

Sailboats/Surfboards and scuba/rock equipment available.
g.   h.

For more information or for reservations call
1-800-555-SAND
or visit our WEB site at *www.sand_castle.com*

3. What about you? What would you take to the beach? What would you buy or rent at the beach? Check (✔) the columns.

	TAKE	BUY/RENT
surfboard		
beach umbrella		
beach chair		
beach towels		
sunblock		

	TAKE	BUY/RENT
cooler		
scuba tank		
fins		
pail		
Other: _____		

Challenge Imagine you are at the beach in your dictionary. Write a postcard describing it.
Begin: *I'm sitting…*

Sports Verbs

1. Look in your dictionary at page 156. Write the sports verbs that complete the phrase: _____ *a ball*.

_____throw_____   _____   _____

_____   _____   _____

_____   _____

2. Circle the correct words to complete the article.

SKI *or* SWIM? Getting and Staying Fit for Life

There are many choices for people who want to get and stay fit. Some sports require

very little special equipment. All you really need is a good pair of shoes to ski /(walk) your
a.

way to good health. And remember: Some experts say that it is better to walk fast than

to jog / kick or run. Walking, a "low-impact" sport, causes less stress to your bones and
b.

muscles. A water sport such as skiing / swimming is another good low-impact choice.
c.

But don't dive / dribble into a pool or lake unless you know the water is deep enough.
d.

And *never* go into the water alone.

Want to exercise / serve with other people? Many neighbourhoods have gyms that
e.

you can join. There you can tackle / work out alone or with others. Bending and
f.

serving / stretching helps firm muscles and keep your body flexible.
g.

For those people who enjoy competing, there are many opportunities to race / pass in
h.

city marathons. But remember: Winning isn't everything. Even if you don't finish / start
i.

the race, feel good that you participated.

It's not really important which sport you choose. You can throw / shoot a baseball
j.

or ride / swing a bicycle. Just start slowly and be careful. (If you skate / ski , wear
k.   **l.**

a helmet and knee, wrist, and elbow pads.) Most of all, enjoy what you do and do it

regularly. In order to get and stay fit, sports should be a part of your everyday life.

3. Look in your dictionary. **True** or **False**? Correct the underlined words in the false sentences.

                               walking

    a. Two women in sweat suits are ~~running~~ in the park.   *False*

    b. Some teenage boys are <u>throwing and catching</u> a baseball.   _____

    c. Some <u>girls</u> are shooting baskets.   _____

    d. A woman is <u>bouncing</u> a tennis ball.   _____

    e. A woman is <u>jumping</u> into the swimming pool.   _____

    f. The girl with the helmet is <u>racing</u>.   _____

    g. <u>Three</u> runners are finishing the race.   _____

4. Look at the bar graph. Complete the sentences. Use the *-ing* form of the verb.

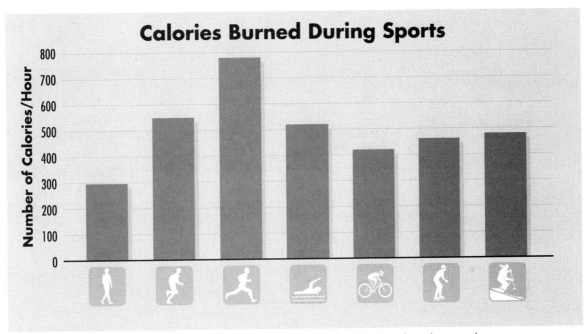

Based on information from: Sutcliffe, A. (ed.): *Numbers: How many, how far, how long, how much.*
(NY: HarperCollins, 1996)

    a. _____*Walking*_____ burns 300 calories an hour.

    b. _____ burns about 550 calories an hour.

    c. According to the chart, _____ burns the most number of calories.

    d. _____ burns the fewest number of calories.

    e. _____ burns about 40 more calories an hour than riding a bike.

    f. _____, skiing, and skating burn more calories than riding a bike but fewer calories than jogging.

5. What about you? Look at the chart in Exercise 4. Which activity would you most like to do? Why?

    Example: *I'd like to swim because I love the water.*

Challenge Write five more sentences like the ones in Exercise 4.

Team Sports

1. Look at the hockey rink in your dictionary. Complete these sentences.
   a. The referee is standing in the _face-off circle_.
   b. The _____ is in the net.
   c. The home team's score is _____.
   d. The _____ players are standing behind the blue line.

2. Look at the table below. **True** or **False**? Write a question mark (**?**) if the information isn't in the table.

MOST POPULAR SPORTS FOR CHILDREN	AGES 6-10	AGES 11-14
	% OF CHILDREN	
	14	16
	3	11
	3	. . .
	12	13
	14	10
	. . .	10
Other	27	24

. . . figures not appropriate or not applicable
Source: Statistics Canada, Catalogue no. 87-211-XPB.

   a. Almost 90% of children play baseball. _____False_____
   b. More than 10% of children aged 6-10 play hockey. _____
   c. Soccer is as popular as baseball for children aged 6-10. _____
   d. About 20% of children of all ages play basketball. _____
   e. Soccer is as popular as baseball for children aged 11-14. _____
   f. Gymnastics is the least popular sport. _____
   g. Volleyball is the most popular team sport. _____
   h. Hockey is the second most popular team sport. _____
   i. Basketball is usually played more by older children. _____
   j. More girls than boys enjoy gymnastics. _____

3. What about you? Which sports would you prefer to play? Why? Use your own paper.
   a. baseball or softball   b. basketball or volleyball   c. soccer or football
   Example: *I'd prefer to play softball. It's less dangerous than baseball.*

Challenge Look at **page 186** in this book. Complete the chart.

158

1. Look in your dictionary. Cross out the word that doesn't belong. Give a reason.

   a. billiards   ~~track and field~~   golf   _It doesn't use a ball._

   b. fencing   gymnastics   wrestling   _____

   c. archery   inline skating   skateboarding   _____

   d. biking   horse racing   weightlifting   _____

   e. bowling   martial arts   flying disc   _____

2. Look at the line graph. Circle the correct words to complete the sentences.

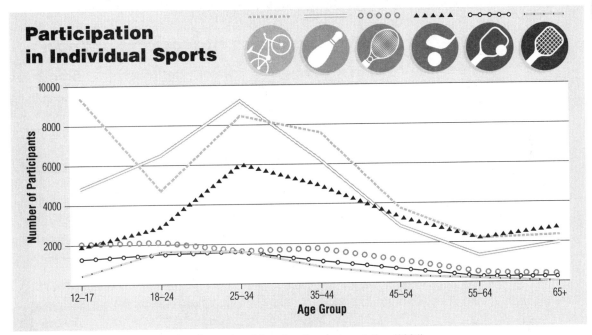

Participation in Individual Sports

Based on survey of 10,000 homes by The National Sporting Goods Association (1994)

   a. (Biking) / Bowling is the most popular sport for people 12 to 17 years old.

   b. Racquetball / Table tennis is the least favourite sport for most age groups.

   c. About the same number of people between the ages of 12 and 24 play racquetball / tennis.

   d. Golf / Table tennis is the most popular sport for people over 65.

   e. After the age of 45, golf / biking becomes more popular than bowling.

   f. Between the ages of 12 and 24 participation in biking / bowling goes down.

   g. Participation in racquetball / bowling goes down after age 34, but it goes up after age 64.

3. What about you? How has your participation in sports changed? Write sentences.
   Use your own paper.

   Example: _I started to play more soccer in high school._

Challenge   Look at the chart in Exercise 2. Give possible reasons for some of the facts.

Winter Sports and Water Sports

1. Look in your dictionary. For which sports do you need...?

   a. ice _____skating_____ _____

   b. wind _____ _____

   c. waves _____

   d. a motorboat _____

   e. mountains or hills _____ _____ _____

   f. a mask and fins _____ _____

2. Look at the chart. Write the name of the sport to complete the sentences.

1998 Winter Olympics in Nagano, Japan

Event		Gold (1st place)	Silver (2nd place)	Bronze (3rd place)
	Men	Jean-Luc Cretier France 1:50.11	Lasse Kjus Norway 1:50.51	Hannes Trinkl Austria 1:50.63
	Women	Katja Seizinger Germany 1:28.89	Pernilla Wiberg Sweden 1:29.18	Florence Masnada France 1:29.37
	Men (10 km)	Bjorn Dahlie Norway 27:24.5	Markus Gandler Austria 27:32.5	Mika Myllylae Finland 27:40.1
	Women (10 km)	Larissa Lazutina Russia 46:06.9	Olga Danilova Russia 46:13.4	Katerina Neumannova Czech Republic 46:14.2
	Men	Ilya Kulik Russia	Elvis Stojko Canada	Philippe Candeloro France
	Women	Tara Lipinski United States	Michelle Kwan United States	Lu Chen China
	Men (500 m)	Hiroyasu Shimizu Japan 1:11.35	Jeremy Wotherspoon Canada 1:11.84	Kevin Overland Canada 1:11.86
	Women (500 m)	Catriona LeMay-Doan Canada 1:16.60	Susan Auch Canada 1:16.93	Tomomi Okazaki Japan 1:17.10
	Men	Ross Rebagliati Canada 2:03.96	Thomas Prugger Italy 2:03.98	Ueli Kestenholz Switzerland 2:04.08
	Women	Karine Ruby France 2:17.34	Heidi Renoth Germany 2:19.17	Brigitte Koeck Austria 2:19.42

   a. Canada won four medals in the speed _____skating_____ event.

   b. Russia won a gold and a silver medal in women's _____.

   c. The United States won a gold and a silver medal in women's _____.

   d. Austria won the bronze medal in the men's _____ event.

   e. Thomas Prugger lost the gold medal in men's _____ by only .02 of a second.

   f. _____ is not a timed event.

_____ **Challenge** Which winter sports or water sports are best for where you live? Why?

1. Look in your dictionary. Which pieces of equipment are the customers talking about?

   a. "These are too heavy for me to lift." _____weights_____

   b. "Oh, I see them now. They're to the right of the bow." _____

   c. "There's one. Under the volleyball." _____

   d. "They look like ice skates with wheels." _____

   e. "Great! It's red and white—the same as my team's colours." _____

   f. "Well, this will really protect my head." _____

   g. "It would be fun to throw one of these around in the park. Nice colours, too." _____

   h. "Oh, there they are. Between the snowboard and the ski poles." _____

   i. "I have to wear them to protect my legs." _____

2. Look at the chart. Write comparisons with *more … than…*.

On an average day, sports players buy ...

3014   6153   8493   6619   33 973

Based on information from: Heymann, T.: *On an Average Day*. (NY: Ballantine Books, 1989)

   a. soccer balls / basketballs   _They buy more basketballs than soccer balls._

   b. golf clubs / hockey sticks   _____

   c. tennis racquets / golf clubs   _____

   d. basketballs / tennis racquets   _____

3. What about you? Look in your dictionary. What would you buy from the store? Why?

   Example: *I'd buy a bat for my niece because she wants to play baseball.*

<u>**Challenge**</u> Try to find the prices of these pieces of sports equipment. (Look at an ad, go to a sports store, or ask someone who knows.)

baseball glove _____   tennis racquet _____   Other: _____

Hobbies and Games

1. Look in your dictionary. Complete the crossword puzzle.

ACROSS ➡

1. It's not oil paint
5. It looks like a woman
7. It holds things together
8. Red, but not hearts
9. A board game
10. Black, but not spades
12. Type of paint
15. Type of game
16. You do this with needles
17. It's red, brown, yellow, and blue

DOWN ⬇

2. It has a flower on it
3. These are cubes
4. You can collect these
6. You can build these
9. It's on the easel
11. Type of figure
13. You can collect these
14. You can make one from paper

2. Cross out the word that doesn't belong. Give a reason.

a.	checkers	chess	~~crochet~~

It's not a board game.

b.	dolls	diamonds	clubs
c.	watercolour	acrylic	clay
d.	woodworking	yarn	doll making
e.	cartridge	knitting needle	paintbrush

162

3. Look at the bar graph. Circle the correct words to complete the sentences.

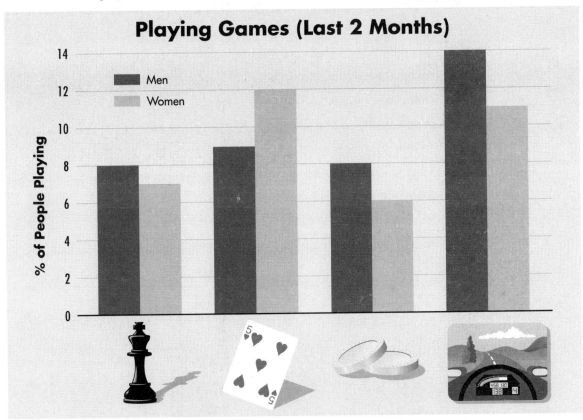

Playing Games (Last 2 Months)

% of People Playing

Men
Women

Based on information from: Weiss, D. E.: *The Great Divide: How Females and Males Really Differ.* (NY: Poseidon Press, 1991)

a. In the last two months, women played more (cards)/ chess than men did.

b. Men played more cards / video games than any other type of game.

c. The smallest difference in per cent of players was for checkers / chess .

d. The same per cent of men played checkers and cards / chess .

e. Two per cent fewer women played checkers / video games than men did.

4. Read the conversations. What are the people doing?

a. **Amy:** Six of diamonds.
   Luis: Ten of clubs.
   _____playing cards_____

b. **Li-jing:** That's nice yarn. What are you making?
   Taro: A sweater for Hachi.
   _____

c. **Tommy:** OK. Now I'll be an astronaut.
   Nicki: And I'll be a woman from Mars.
   _____

d. **Min Ho:** I found a 1963 penny.
   Young Mee: And I found an old stamp.
   _____

5. What about you? Check (✔) the things you collect.

   ☐ stamps   ☐ coins   ☐ baseball cards   ☐ figurines   ☐ Other: _____

Challenge Make a list of other things to collect. Ask your classmates for ideas.

Electronics and Photography

1. Look in your dictionary. What can you use to...?

a. wake up to music every morning .... _clock radio_

b. watch television programs on a small screen .... _____

c. keep photos neatly in one place .... _____

d. listen to music while jogging .... _____

e. record music from the radio .... _____

f. change TV channels without getting up .... _____

g. listen to music without anyone else hearing it .... _____

h. listen to a news program from a country that is far away .... _____

2. Look at the bar graph. Complete the sentences.

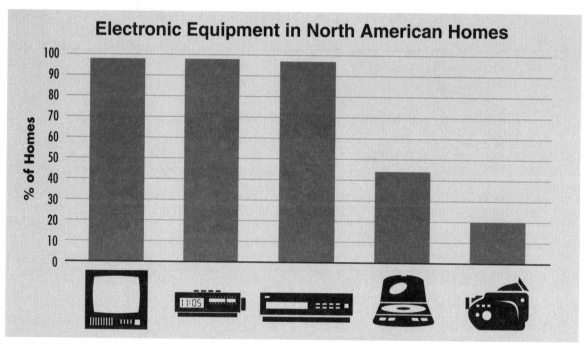

Based on information from: *The World Almanac and Book of Facts 1997.* (NJ: World Almanac Books, 1996)

a. Almost all homes in North America have a _____radio_____, a _____,
   and a _____.

b. Less than a quarter of the homes have a _____.

c. A little less than half of the homes have a _____.

d. Almost 55% more homes have a VCR than a _____.

3. What about you? Look at the electronic equipment in Exercise 2. Which is the most important to you? Why?

_____

_____

4. Complete these instructions for a VCR.

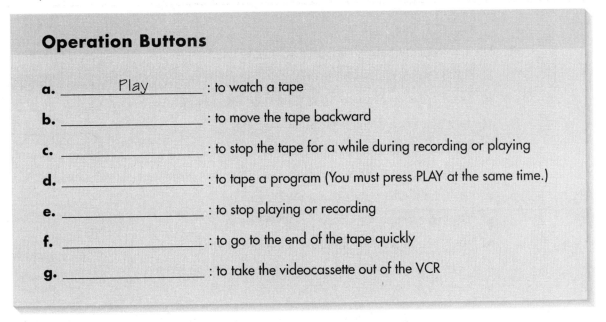

Operation Buttons

a. _____Play_____ : to watch a tape

b. _____ : to move the tape backward

c. _____ : to stop the tape for a while during recording or playing

d. _____ : to tape a program (You must press PLAY at the same time.)

e. _____ : to stop playing or recording

f. _____ : to go to the end of the tape quickly

g. _____ : to take the videocassette out of the VCR

5. What's wrong with these pictures? Circle the words to complete the sentences.

a. The (photo)/ slide is out of focus.

c. It's overexposed / underexposed.

b. She didn't use a camera case / tripod.

d. He didn't use a 35 mm camera / zoom lens.

Challenge Write instructions for using a cassette recorder, a clock radio, or another piece of electronic equipment.

Entertainment

1. Look in your dictionary. Where can you hear…?

   a. "Giddyap, Star. They're waiting for us back at the ranch."   western

   b. "And now a look at what's happening today in Europe."   _____

   c. "It's Supercat, coming to save the world!"   _____

   d. "Oops! Who put that banana peel there?"   _____

   e. "A look at the score shows Bill leading by 98 points."   _____

   f. "Bye, honey. Have a good day at the office."   _____

   g. "Sir, tell our guest on stage what you think."   _____

   h. "Don't be afraid. I come from a friendly planet."   _____

   i. "And this beautiful necklace can be yours for just $39.95."   _____

   j. "I love you and only you! Not your sister!"   _____

   k. "Pandas live in the forests of central China."   _____

   l. 🎼   _____, _____,

   or _____

2. Look at the chart. **True** or **False**? Write a question mark (?) if the information isn't there.

Based on information from: Neilson Media Research (August 24-30, 1998)

   a. The most popular kind of program is the news.   True

   b. Medical drama programs are more popular than detective shows.   _____

   c. More people watch medical drama programs than comedies.   _____

   d. More than one million people watch movies on TV.   _____

   e. Talk shows are as popular as news programs.   _____

166

3. Circle the correct words to complete these movie listings.

📺 MOVIE LISTINGS

ASTEROID ✪✪ (1997) Interesting made-for-TV mystery / (science fiction story) about an astronomer
a.
who works with the government to try to save the earth from a comet. With Michael Biehn and Annabella Sciorra. (2 hrs.) Sun 9 P.M. (Part 1) Ch 4

BIZET'S CARMEN ✪✪✪✪ (1984) Excellent film adaptation of the famous concert / opera by
b.
Georges Bizet, starring singers Julia Migenes-Johnson, Placido Domingo, and Jose Carreras. In French with English subtitles. (PG) (2½ hrs.) ART Sat 8 P.M.

HOME ALONE ✪✪✪✪ (1990) A very funny comedy / tragedy starring Macaulay Culkin about a
c.
family who accidentally goes on vacation without their eight-year-old son. Lots of laughs. (PG) (1¾ hrs.) ENS Sat 9 P.M.

JAWS ✪✪✪✪ (1975) A large shark terrorizes tourists at a local beach in this frightening horror story / romance directed by Steven Spielberg.
d.
You'll be scared out of your seat. (PG) (2 hrs.) TRE Sat 9 P.M.

THE LION KING ✪✪✪✪ (1994) Children and adults will love this full-length Disney cartoon / nature program which tells the story of
e.
baby Simba who will one day become king of the jungle. Great voices by James Earl Jones and Jeremy Irons. (G) (1½ hrs.) DIS Fri 7 P.M.

MISSION IMPOSSIBLE ✪✪✪ (1996) Tom Cruise stars in this very exciting, fast-moving action adventure story based on the popular radio / television program watched by millions
f.
of people in the 1970s. (PG-13) (1¾ hrs.) DVS Fri 9 P.M.

THE TURNING POINT ✪✪✪ (1977) Serious story of two dancers (Anne Bancroft and Shirley MacLaine) and the choices they make between family and career. Ballet / Mystery fans will love the
g.
beautiful dance scenes starring Mikhail Baryshnikov in his first film / play appearance. (PG) (2 hrs.)
h.
GEB Fri 9 P.M.

4. What about you? Look at the movie listings in Exercise 3. Which movie would you like to watch? Which movie wouldn't you like to watch? Why? Try to use the words *serious, funny, sad, boring,* and *interesting.*

_____

_____

Challenge Write two short reviews of television programs or movies. Give them a one- to four-star (★) rating.

Holidays

1. Look in your dictionary. Complete these holiday cards.

a.

I looked real hard
to find this ___card___
just to say
on this special day—
That you're always a part
of my _____.
Happy _____

b.

Resolutions are made,
Here comes the _____.
I'm more than ready,
so throw the confetti!
The time is now near
to say Happy New _____!

c.

Our maple leaf _____
we will fly
As_____
light up the night sky!
Happy_____!

d.

I hope that there
will always be—
many _____
on your tree!
Merry _____

e.

To give thanks for
the good things this year
And, not the least,
A delicious _____
Where _____ and
stuffing appear.
Happy _____!

f.

_____ burning bright
on a cool October night.
In scary costumes and a _____
for _____ treats
the children ask.
Happy _____!

2. Look at the information. Complete the sentences.

Number of Cards Sold in North America

| 28 000 000 | 40 000 000 | 1 000 000 000 | 2.3 billion |

Based on information from: Droste, K. and J. Dye, (eds.): *Gale Book of Averages*. (MI: Gale Research, Inc., 1994)

a. The _____Halloween_____ card has a picture of a jack-o'-lantern on it.

b. A billion cards are sold for _____.

c. North Americans buy the most number of cards for _____.

d. The fewest number of cards are sold for _____.

e. Twelve million more cards are sold for _____ than for Halloween.

Challenge Make a card for one of the holidays in your dictionary or for any other event.

168

1. Look in your dictionary. Complete Sue's letter. Use the past tense form of the verbs.

Dear Alicia,

Last night I went to Dave's house. When I got there, I rang the bell. As soon as Dave _____answered the door_____,
a.
people jumped up and _____. They had
b.
been hiding behind the furniture! (And I thought Dave and I were going to spend a quiet evening alone!) I was really surprised.

Dave _____ (8 of my classmates), and
c.
_____ with red, yellow, and blue balloons. He
d.
even baked a cake! It was beautiful. When it was time to eat it, Dave took a match and _____.
e.
Everyone _____ (in English!). Before
f.
I _____ (I was glad Dave only put
g.
eight in), I _____. Everyone asked what
h.
it was, but I didn't tell. After we had some cake, I
_____. And yours was there too!
i.
Thanks so much for the beautiful sweater. You
_____ the box so beautifully, too.
j.
Wish you could have been there with us.

                                                Sue

2. What about you? Describe a party that you went to. Include as many details as possible. For example, what kind of party was it? Was it a surprise? How many guests were there? Was there a cake? Did people sing songs? Were there presents? Use your own paper.

Challenge Find out about birthday celebrations in other countries. Do people…?

sing songs   have a birthday cake   make a wish

blow out candles   give wrapped presents   open presents at the party

▶ Go to page 181 for Another Look (Unit 12).

Picture Comparison

Write about the two classrooms. How are they the same? How are they different?

Example: *Both of these classes are ESL classes. One class is ESL 101, the other class is ESL 102. Both classes have six students. In class 101, half the students are women, but in 102...*

A Picture Is Worth a Thousand Words

These are photographs taken during Alexander Graham Bell's lifetime. Write about the photographs.

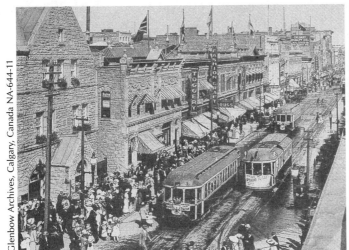

Glenbow Archives, Calgary, Canada NA-644-11

NAC/PA118224

Describe the scene in each photograph.

What is happening?

Where were the photos taken?

What are some differences between these historic photos and similar scenes today?

Vancouver Public Library

NAC C-20549/Department of Mines and Natural Resources Collection

Word Map

Complete the diagram. Use the words in the box.

bathroom	bed	bedroom	blanket	~~children's bedroom~~

china cabinet   counter   dining area   drawer   dresser   end table

faucet   food processor   ~~house~~   kitchen   lamp   living room

medicine cabinet   ~~napkin~~   ~~pillow~~   place mat   pot   ~~rubber mat~~

set of dishes   shower   ~~stereo system~~   ~~stove~~   ~~stuffed animal~~

table   toothbrush   ~~toy chest~~   wall unit

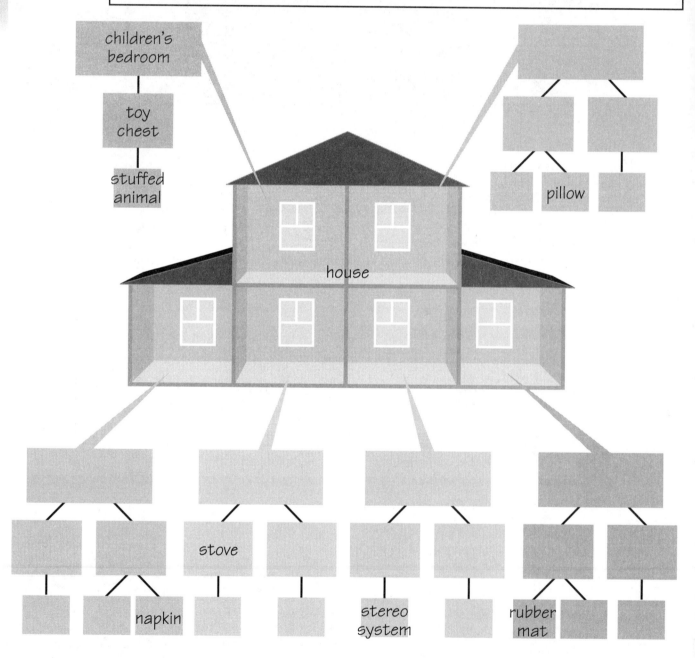

THE GOOD-EATING FOOD RAINBOW

Adapted from *Canada's Food Guide to Healthy Eating*, Health Canada 1992.

	Grain Group	Fruits and Vegetables Group	Milk Products Group	Meats and Meat Alternatives	Other Foods
Servings per Day	5-12	5-10	2-4	2-3	few

Find 24 "food" words in the puzzle. Words may go (↓↑ → ←).

X	B	S	M	A	Y	B	E	A	N	S
W	P	O	P	N	J	U	I	C	E	A
M	B	U	A	U	Z	T	H	A	M	N
I	R	P	S	T	W	T	P	R	S	D
L	E	T	T	U	C	E	R	R	A	W
K	A	F	A	R	X	R	I	O	L	I
N	D	C	A	K	E	D	C	T	A	C
U	Q	C	H	E	E	S	E	G	D	H
T	O	F	U	Y	O	G	U	R	T	A
C	A	N	D	Y	C	E	R	E	A	L

Use your own paper. Write the following titles: Grain Group, Fruits and Vegetables, Milk Products, Meats and Meat Alternatives, Other Foods. Write the words that you found in the puzzle under the appropriate title. Some foods are mixed (they contain foods from more than one group). Write these separately.

Pack It Up!

You are going away for the weekend. What clothing and accessories would you take for each place? Put at least six items in each suitcase. You can use your dictionary for help.

WEEKEND FUN IN THE SUN!

Special 2-day package at The Sunshine Inn

2 bathing suits

Nature Club Overnight Trip

Fall Weekend
Meet: Sat. Sept 9, 7:00 A.M.

Rain or shine!

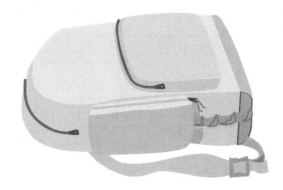

You are cordially invited
to celebrate the marriage of

HEATHER MILLER TO BRIAN JOHNSON

at the
Country Manor Hotel Ballroom
Saturday, June 29, 8:00 P.M.

R.S.V.P.

WHISTLER MOUNTAIN SKI WEEKEND

Come join us for two days of fun and relaxation.

For further information: call 1-888-555-3421

Crossword Puzzle

Complete the puzzle.

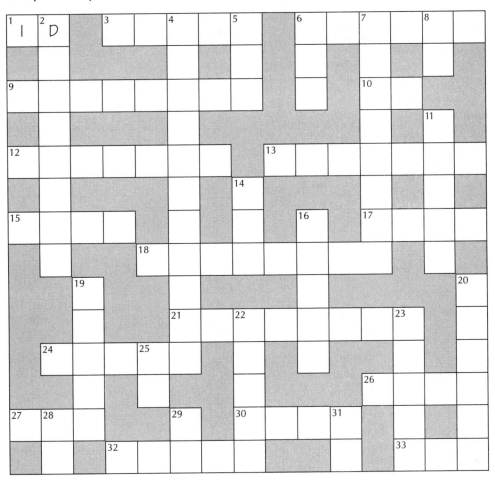

ACROSS ➡

1. Identification (short form)
3. _____ your teeth
6. A hole in a tooth
9. It holds your hair in place
10. Tuberculosis (short form)
12. Women wear it to smell good
13. You wash your hair with it
15. Your brain is inside it
17. Your throat is inside it
18. They help you walk
21. They operate on patients
24. Throw up
26. It holds gauze in place
27. It's part of the foot
30. _____-the-counter medication
32. Temperature
33. It has a lid

DOWN ⬇

2. A serious disease
4. An eye specialist
5. You do this with your eyes
6. Cardiopulmonary resuscitation (short form)
7. A, C, D, B_6, etc.
8. Listen _____ your heart
11. One of the five senses
14. You put a bandage on this
16. Part of your face
19. Break (past form)
20. You do this when you have a cold
22. You shave with this
23. You use this to find out your weight
25. Look _____ your throat
28. Put _____ sunscreen
29. Intravenous (short form)
31. Registered nurse (short form)

Things Change

Look at the maps of Middletown 50 years ago and Middletown today. What's different? What's the same? Write sentences. Use your own paper.

Example: *There was a bakery on the southeast corner of Elm and Grove. Now there's a coffee shop. There's still a…*

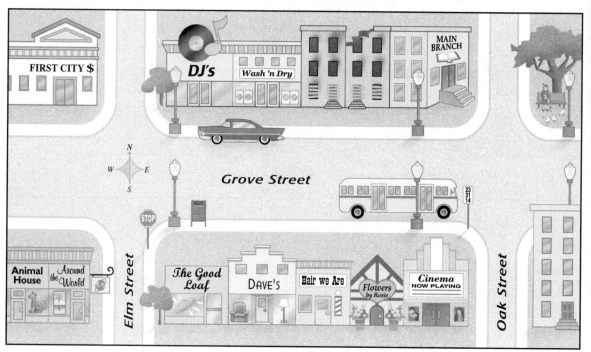

50 years ago

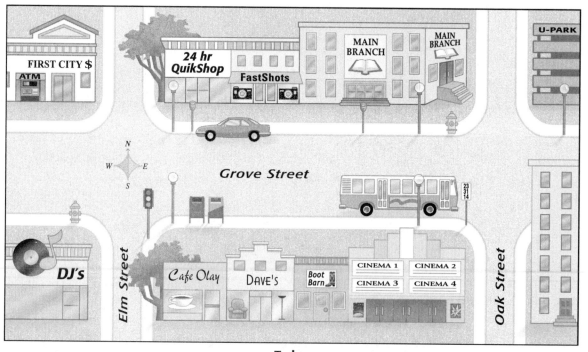

Today

What's Wrong With This Picture?

Look at the picture. Describe ten more problems. Use your own paper.

Example: *There's a plane flying under the bridge.*

Word Map

Complete the diagram. Use the words in the box.

~~addition~~   chemistry   comma   desert   **English composition**
geography   guitar   high school   ~~Confederation~~   magnet
~~math~~   mountain peak   mountain range   **Settlement**
multiplication   music   ocean   paper   paragraph
percussion   ~~physics~~   ~~piano~~   product   ~~sand dune~~   science
~~sentence~~   strings   test tube   ~~total~~   Canadian history

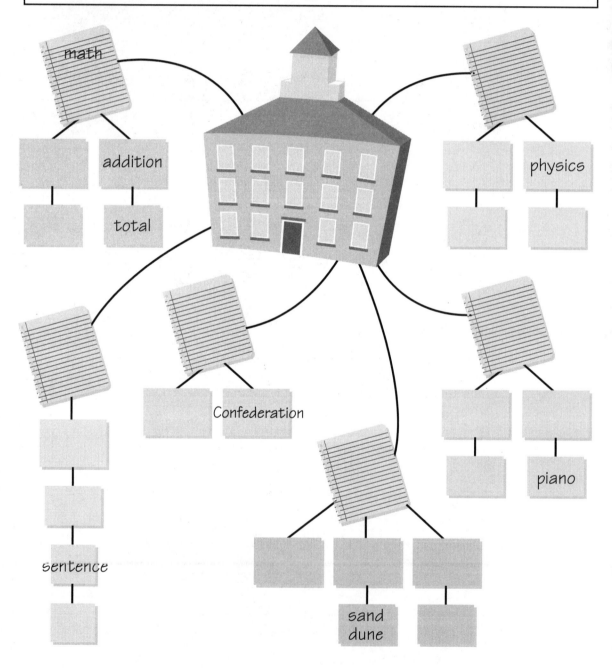

Word Search

There are 25 plant and animal words in the box. The words go → and ↓. Find and circle them.

L	I	O	N	P	A	R	O	S	E
L	C	A	T	I	R	O	O	E	L
A	D	K	O	N	A	O	C	A	E
M	O	N	K	E	Y	S	T	L	P
A	L	L	I	G	A	T	O	R	H
P	P	L	L	G	N	E	P	R	A
O	H	I	F	O	E	R	U	A	N
W	I	L	L	O	W	A	S	P	T
L	N	Y	Y	S	T	T	O	A	D
W	H	A	L	E	A	G	L	E	Y

Put the circled words into the correct categories.

FLOWERS	SEA ANIMALS	AMPHIBIANS	INSECTS
_____	_____	_____	_____
_____	_____	_____	_____

MAMMALS	SEA MAMMALS	TREES AND PLANTS	BIRDS
llama	_____	_____	_____
_____	_____	_____	_____
_____	_____	_____	_____
_____			_____

REPTILES	RODENTS
_____	_____

On the Job

Look at the pictures. Describe each photograph and answer the questions. Use your own paper.

a. Where are the people?

b. What are they doing?

c. What types of equipment are the people using?

d. What types of job skills do the people need to do these jobs?

e. How do you think the workers feel?

f. Compare the four jobs. How are they the same? How are they different?

g. Would you like to work in any of these places? Why or why not?

Crossword Puzzle

Complete the puzzle.

ACROSS ➡

2. A water sport
4. Not funny
6. A type of paint
8. It goes up and down
11. You use them to light a campfire
14. Compact disc (short form)
15. Bucket
16. _____ and touch your toes
17. You see them in a theatre
18. 35 _____ camera
19. Stand-_____ comedy
23. A bike with three wheels
25. You put a camera on it
26. Water at the beach
27. Run slowly

DOWN ⬇

1. _____ a swing
2. A winter snow sport
3. _____ Year's Day
5. _____ crafts
7. _____ skating
9. Toronto 5, Edmonton 3
10. Track and _____
12. Type of park
13. You can collect these
16. Dribble
20. Movie
21. You look at slides on it
22. Not interesting
23. You can sleep in it
24. Billiards

Challenge for page 9

How did you use the telephone last week? How many times did you…?

a. call collect _____

b. dial the wrong number _____

c. make an international call _____

d. call from a pay phone _____

e. use a phone card _____

f. call from a cellular phone _____

g. use directory assistance _____

h. use the telephone book _____

Challenge for page 10

Look at the temperatures below. Make a list of the clothing you might wear at each temperature. Look at page 66 in your dictionary for help.

a. +22°C _____ *short-sleeved shirt, cotton pants, cotton socks, sneakers*

b. −40°C _____ _____

c. 0°C _____ _____

d. +14°C _____ _____

e. +34°C _____

Challenge for page 17

Write six sentences comparing times in different cities. Use words, not numbers.

Example: *When it's five in the afternoon in Athens, it's eleven at night in Hong Kong.*

WHEN IT'S NOON EASTERN STANDARD TIME, IN … IT'S….					
Athens	7 P.M.	Hong Kong	1 A.M.*	Riyadh	8 P.M.
Baghdad	8 P.M.	Mecca	8 P.M.	St. Petersburg	8 P.M.
Bangkok	12 midnight	Mexico City	11 A.M.	San Juan	12 noon
Buenos Aires	2 P.M.	Paris	6 P.M.	Seoul	2 A.M.*
Halifax	1 P.M.	Rio de Janeiro	2 P.M.	Tokyo	2 A.M.*

* = morning of the next day

Challenge for pages 18–19

Add to the chart. Continue on your own paper if you need more space.

INTERNATIONAL HOLIDAYS		
DATE	HOLIDAY	COUNTRY
January 15	Adults Day	Japan
February 5	Constitution Day	Mexico
June 20	Flag Day	Argentina
July 14	Bastille Day	France
December 26	Boxing Day	Canada
_____	_____	_____
_____	_____	_____

Challenge for pages 24–25

Complete the sentences with the information from the chart below and your dictionary.

a. Tom, Lily and Alex belong to a family in the ___76___ per cent group.

b. Look at picture 25 in your dictionary. Carol is in the _____ per cent group.

c. In picture 26, Lisa lived with her Dad. She was in the _____ per cent group.

d. Which 11% group is not mentioned in your dictionary? _____

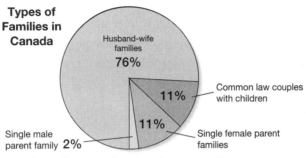

Based on Information from StatsCan—1996 Census

Challenge for pages 30–31

Imagine that you are the person in the far left of this picture. Complete the story.

When I went into the room, I felt _____. Everyone looked _____.
One person seemed _____. The first thing I did was _____. That
made me feel _____. Then I…

Challenge for page 45

What's your opinion? Write appropriate toys for each group. Use your dictionary for help.

AGE GROUP	ACTIVITIES	TOYS
Babies	looking and listening holding things	
Toddlers	throwing, rolling, and pushing objects listening to stories and songs	
Children over three	learning stories and songs drawing	

Challenge for page 57

Check the labels on the containers of four of your favourite foods. Make a chart like this one.

FOOD	SERVING SIZE	CALORIES	CALORIES FROM FAT	PROTEIN	CARBOHYDRATE
ice cream	118 mL	170	90	3g	17g

Challenge for page 100

What type of punishment should crimes get? Check (✓) the columns to complete the chart.

	PRISON	HOSPITALIZATION	COMMUNITY SERVICE*	FINES**
Assault				
Murder				
Burglary				
Vandalism				
Drunk driving				
Using illegal drugs				
Gang violence				

*Community service is work that a person does without pay. An example is cleaning a park.
**A fine is an amount of money a person has to pay for doing something wrong.

Challenge for pages 108–109

Read the ad. Write a description of the car. Do not use abbreviations.
Example: *The car is a four-door 1994 Venus XL...*

VENUS XL 4DR '94
Black w/tan leath Int, auto, A/C, AM/FM cass, pwr wndws/lks, 1400 km, $15,000. Call 555-3265

Note: int = interior, pwr = power

Challenge for page 112

ENROLMENT IN CANADIAN ELEMENTARY AND SECONDARY SCHOOLS

	CANADA¹	PUBLIC	PRIVATE	FEDERAL	SCHOOLS FOR THE VISUALLY AND HEARING IMPAIRED
1990-1991	5 141 003	4 845 308	240 968	52 285	2 442
1991-1992	5 218 237	4 915 630	245 255	55 221	2 131
1992-1993	5 284 145	4 967 848	257 605	56 416	2 276
1993-1994	5 327 826	5 002 834	265 275	57 378	2 339
1994-1995	5 362 799	5 029 114	271 974	59 383	2 328
1995-1996	5 440 334	5 095 901	277 704	64 268	2 461

1. Canada total also includes Department of National Defence schools overseas.
Source: Statistics Canada, Catalogue no. 81-229-XPB.

1. During this period, enrolment in private schools:
   a. increased   b. remained the same   c. decreased
2. Why do you think over 277 000 people chose to enrol their children in private schools?
3. Why do you think most people choose to enrol their children in public schools?
4. Enrolment in schools for the visually and hearing impaired only increased slightly. Why do you think this is so?

Challenge for page 119

Do one of the experiments below. Observe and record the results.

Experiment 1.

Equipment:
an egg,
a glass,
a water tap

egg

Procedure:
Place an egg in a glass of water.
Put the glass under a water tap.
Turn the water on. What happens
to the egg?

Observations: _____
_____
_____

Experiment 2.

Equipment:
a small glass,
a paper napkin
or paper towel,
a glass bowl,
water

crumpled paper towel   *water*

Procedure:
Crumple the paper and put it in the
bottom of the glass (it should fit tightly
and not fall out when you turn the glass
upside down).
Fill the bowl with water. Turn the glass
upside down over the bowl and put it in
the bowl. Lift the glass out. Dry the
inside of the glass. Remove the paper.
What happened to the paper?

Observations: _____
_____
_____

Based on information from: Loeschnig, L.: *Simple Chemistry Experiments with Everyday Materials.* (NY: Sterling Publishing Company, 1994)

Challenge for page 131

Find out more information about at least two animals in Exercise 4. Look in an encyclopedia or science book to make a chart like the one below. Use your own paper.

NAME	TYPE	WHAT IT EATS	HOW IT PROTECTS ITSELF
salamander	amphibian	insects and worms	produces poison

Challenge for page 133

Compare these animals. Use *than* and the words in parentheses ( ).

a. cat / kitten (big)   A cat is bigger than a kitten. _____

b. puppy / dog (young)   _____

c. mouse / rat (small)   _____

d. horse / donkey (fast)   _____

e. pig / goat (fat)   _____

f. rooster / hen (colourful)   _____

Challenge for pages 138–139

Look at employment ads in the newspaper. Make a chart. You may have to do some math!

JOB	HR / WK	$ / YR

Challenge for page 141

What do you think are the best ways of finding a job? Add to the list. Rank the ways. (Number 1 = the best) Explain your choices to your classmates.

WAYS TO FIND A JOB

_____ parents, friends, neighbours   _____ employment agencies

_____ school/college placement services   _____ employment service offices

_____ classified ads   _____ the Internet

_____ _____   _____ _____

Challenge for page 147

Look at the worker. Write about the safety hazards. What should the worker do to protect herself?

Example: *She's wearing sandals. She should wear safety boots.*

Challenge for page 158

Interview five or more people. Which sports do they like to play? Which sports do they like to watch? Complete the chart.

Number of people who like to…							
	BASKETBALL	BASEBALL	SOFTBALL	FOOTBALL	SOCCER	HOCKEY	VOLLEYBALL	CURLING
Play								
Watch								

ANSWER KEY

UNIT 1

Pages 2 and 3 A Classroom

Exercise 1
a. False, talking
b. False, listening
c. True
d. False, erasing
e. False, opening
f. True

Exercise 2
(Students will supply their own names, date, and class.)
a. Open
b. Listen
c. point
d. Close
e. write
f. notebook
g. pencil
h. erase
i. Stand up
j. Look at
k. screen
l. Talk to

Exercise 3
a. 1 bookcase
b. 0 bulletin boards
c. 3 cassette players
d. 1 chalkboard
e. 4 chalkboard erasers
f. 0 clocks
g. 0 computers
h. 2 maps
i. 3 markers
j. 0 overhead projectors
k. 2 pencil sharpeners
l. 6 desks, 17 chairs*, 11 books

or 18 if students count 6 desks, 3 chairs each

Exercise 4
There's one bookcase. There aren't any/are no bulletin boards. There are three cassette players. There's one chalkboard. There are four chalkboard erasers. There aren't any clocks. There aren't any computers. There are two maps. There are three markers. There aren't any overhead projectors. There are two pencil sharpeners.

Page 4 Personal Information

Exercise 1
a. 16   b. 18   c. 15   d. 4   e. 5   f. 11

Exercise 2
Items circled:
1. 12 June
3. Ann Brown
4. (area code)
7. Stoodent
9. City

Challenge
(Answers may vary slightly.)
In number 3, she signed her name, she didn't print her name. (Since she signed her name, she wrote her first name last and her last name first.)

In number 4, she didn't write her area code.
In number 7, she didn't spell *student* right.
In number 9, she didn't write the city.

Page 5 School

Exercise 1
a. principal
b. counsellor
c. clerk
d. teacher/instructor

Exercise 2
a. library
b. cafeteria
c. auditorium
d. field
e. main office
f. gym

Exercise 3
a. track
b. classroom
c. washroom
d. bleachers
New word: school

Pages 6 and 7 Studying

Exercise 1
a. False, repeating
b. True
c. False, passing out
d. True
e. False, marking
f. False, matching

Exercise 2
1. Circle
   a. What
   b. Where
   c. How many
2. Cross out
   a. hello
   b. coach
   c. greet
3. Write/Put, order

answer	copy	draw	share
ask	dictate	help	spell
collect	discuss	say	talk

Exercise 3
a. read
b. copy
c. collect
d. pass out
e. draw
f. repeat
g. talk
h. brainstorm
i. help
j. discuss
k. share

Page 8 Everyday Conversation

Exercise 1
a. Did you say *Tuan?*
b. Beth, this is Mary.
c. Excuse me.
d. Good night.
e. How are you?

Exercise 2
a. 7   b. 4   c. 8   d. 6   e. 2   f. 3
g. 1   h. 5

Page 9 The Telephone

Exercise 1
a. phone card
b. cellular phone
c. answering machine
d. cordless phone
e. pager

Exercise 2
a. emergency
b. 911
c. directory assistance
d. phone book
e. long-distance
f. operator
g. wrong number
h. hang up
i. dial
j. pay phone
k. 0
l. international
m. local

Page 10 Weather

Exercise 1

a. sunny/clear   d. cold air   g. raining
b. freezing rain   e. thunderstorm   h. windy
c. cloudy   f. snowing

Exercise 2

Possible answers:

It's raining and cool in St. John's with temperatures in the teens.

It's very cold with freezing rain in Goose Bay. Temperatures will be below 10°.

It's warm in Montréal with temperatures around 25°.

It's sunny/clear and very cold in Whitehorse with temperatures below 0°.

It's cloudy and warm in Québec City with temperatures in the 20s.

There are thunderstorms in Thunder Bay and it's warm, with temperatures in the low 20s.

It's raining and cool in Charlottetown with temperatures below 10°.

It's cloudy and cold in Churchill with temperatures just above freezing.

It's sunny/clear and hot in Ottawa with temperatures in the 20s.

It's snowing and very cold in Yellowknife with temperatures well below freezing.

Challenge (page 182)

a. short-sleeved shirt, cotton pants, cotton socks, sneakers
b. parka, mittens, toque, scarf, long underwear
c. coat, earmuffs, gloves, scarf
d. jacket, cap or hat, long pants
e. shorts or skirt, T-shirt or light blouse, sandals, straw hat, sunglasses

Page 11 Describing Things

Exercise 1

a. empty, full   d. messy, neat
b. noisy, quiet   e. ugly, beautiful
c. heavy, light   f. easy, difficult, hard

Exercise 2

Possible answers:

a. Classroom A has a little clock, but the clock in Classroom B is big.
b. The teacher's desk in Classroom A is neat, but the teacher's desk in Classroom B is messy.
c. The chair/seat in Classroom A is hard, but the chair/seat in Classroom B is soft.
d. The problem on the board in Classroom A is easy, but the problem on the board in Classroom B is hard/difficult.
e. The (math) book in Classroom A is thin, but the (math) book in Classroom B is thick.
f. The student's test grade in classroom A is bad, but the student's test grade in classroom B is good.
g. The computer in Classroom A is expensive, but the computer in Classroom B is cheap.

Page 12 Colours

Exercise 1

a. orange   b. purple   c. brown
d. grey and black

Exercise 2

a. blue   f. white   k. orange and black
b. red   g. green
c. green   h. yellow
d. pink   i. black
e. purple   j. red and green

Page 13 Prepositions

Exercise 1

a. above   b. next to, left   c. on   d. under

Exercise 2

Items checked:

cassettes   map
pencils   workbooks
chalkboard erasers   overhead projector
notebook paper

Exercise 3

Possible answers:

The cassette player is next to the overhead projector, on the right. It's not to the left of it.

The alphabet chart is in back of the number chart. It isn't in front of it.

The chalk is above the overhead projector. It isn't above the pencils.

The rulers are in the red box. They aren't in the blue box.

The clock is above the bookcase. It isn't on the bookcase.

Pages 14 and 15
Numbers and Measurement

Exercise 1
a. 7   b. 7   c. 50   d. 1/2

Exercise 2
Items circled:

1c. ten   3c. 5
2d. six   4b. 1 000 000 000
3a. 1

Per cent grade: 75

Exercise 3
(Answers may vary slightly.)

Question 1c. The next number is eight, not ten.

Question 2d. The Roman numeral IV is four, not six.

Question 3a. The number 12 is a cardinal number, not an ordinal number.

Question 3c. 2nd is an ordinal number, not a cardinal number.

Question 4b. One million has 6 zeroes, not 9 zeroes./One million is 1 000 000, not 1 000 000 000.

Exercise 4
c.

Exercise 5
b.

Exercise 6
a. fifth   d. first   g. ninth
b. fourth   e. sixth   h. third
c. second   f. seventh   i. eighth

Pages 16 and 17   Time

Exercise 1
a. 6:30, six-thirty/half past six
b. 7:00, seven o'clock
c. 5:30, five-thirty/half past five
d. 10:30, ten-thirty/half past ten

Exercise 2
a. 7:15 a.m., 45 minutes
b. 8:00 a.m., 1 minute
c. 8:10 a.m., 50 minutes
d. 12:15 p.m., 1 hour
e. 7:00 p.m., 2 hours 15 minutes
f. 11:10 p.m., 30 minutes/a half hour

Exercise 3
a. minutes   f. o'clock
b. after   g. a quarter after
c. o'clock   h. to
d. minutes   i. twelve
e. -thirty   j. half past

Exercise 5
a. 1:30 p.m.   c. 5:30 p.m.
b. 10:00 p.m.   d. 11:00 a.m.

Exercise 6
a. standard   f. later
b. time zones   g. earlier
c. Pacific   h. daylight saving
d. Atlantic   i. standard
e. Atlantic

Pages 18 and 19   The Calendar

Exercise 1
a. December   b. June

Exercise 2
(Answers may vary slightly.)
April 1: Science, Language Lab
April 2: English
April 3: To Edmonton
April 4: Daylight Saving Time
April 5 – April 9: No classes
April 9: Return to Vancouver
April 10: Gym
April 11: Tom
April 12: English
April 13: Science, Science Lab
April 14: English
April 15: Science, Computer Lab
April 16: English
April 17: Gym
April 18: *(no entry)*
April 19: English
April 20: Science, Science Lab
April 21: English
April 22: Science, Language Lab
April 23: English
April 24: Dania arrives, Gym
April 25: Cake sale
April 26: English
April 27: Science, Science Lab
April 28: English
April 29: Science, Language Lab
April 30, English

Exercise 4
a. spring   c. winter
b. spring   d. summer

Exercise 5
a. winter   e. winter   i. spring
b. winter   f. fall
c. summer   g. spring
d. fall   h. spring

Exercise 6
Winter:
January 1, New Year's Day
December 25, Christmas
December 26, Boxing Day

Spring:
March or April, Easter
Friday before Easter, Good Friday
May 24, Victoria Day

Summer:
July 1, Canada Day
First Monday in September, Labour Day

Fall:
Second Monday in October, Thanksgiving Day

Exercise 7
February, March or April, June, August

Page 20 Money

Exercise 1
a. a five-dollar bill, one toonie, and a nickel
b. two quarters, a dime, and four pennies
c. a loonie, a quarter, a dime, and two pennies
d. three one-hundred dollar bills, a fifty-dollar bill, a twenty-dollar bill, and a ten-dollar bill

Exercise 2

NAME OF THE MONEY	VALUE	COLOUR OF THE MONEY	PERSON ON THE MONEY	ANIMAL OR BIRD ON THE MONEY
hundred dollar bill	$100	dark brown	Robert Borden (former Prime Minister)	Canada Goose
fifty dollar bill	$50	pink	W.L. Mackenzie King (former Prime Minister)	Snowy Owl
twenty dollar bill	$20	green	Queen Elizabeth	Loons
ten dollar bill	$10	purple	Sir John A. Macdonald	Osprey
five dollar bill	$5	blue	Sir Wilfrid Laurier	Kingfisher
two dollar coin (toonie)	$2	silver and bronze	Queen Elizabeth	Polar Bears
one dollar coin (loonie)	$1	bronze	Queen Elizabeth	Loon
quarter	0.25¢	silver	Queen Elizabeth	Elk
dime	0.10¢	silver	Queen Elizabeth	Bluenose ship
nickel	0.05¢	silver	Queen Elizabeth	Beaver
penny (cent)	0.01¢	copper	Queen Elizabeth	Maple leaf

Challenge
a. sixty-seven dollars and twenty-five cents
   or
   sixty-seven twenty-five
b. one hundred and thirty-four dollars and eighty-nine cents
   or
   one-thirty-four eighty-nine
c. one dollar and fifty cents
   or
   one fifty

Page 21 Shopping

Exercise 1

2 sweater	
@ 9.99	19.98
tax @ 7%	1.40
Amount due	21.38
Amount tendered	100.00
Change	78.62

Exercise 2
a. regular   e. paid for   i. price
b. receipt   f. receipt   j. bar code
c. keep   g. price tag   k. total
d. return   h. price tag

UNIT 2

Page 22 Age and Physical Description

Exercise 1
Possible answers:
a. He is average weight.
b. She is of average height.
c. He is physically challenged.
d. He is a senior citizen.
e. She is quite tall.
f. He is slim/thin.

Page 23 Describing Hair

Exercise 1
a. the woman in picture C
b. the woman in picture D
c. the woman in picture A
d. the woman in picture B

Exercise 2
a. grey   f. Perm
b. colour   g. blow dryer
c. long   h. beard/moustache
d. Cut   i. moustache/beard
e. wavy

Exercise 3
long → short
curly → straight
blond → black
shoulder-length → long

Pages 24 and 25   Family

Exercise 1
a. Lily   b. Sara   c. Emily   d. Alice

Exercise 2
a. mother-in-law   b. father-in-law
c. husband   d. brother-in-law   e. sister-in-law
f. son   g. daughter   h. nephew   i. niece

Exercise 3
a. cousin   d. brother   g. grandmother
b. Uncle   e. parents
c. Aunt   f. niece

Exercise 5
a. True   b. True   c. False   d. True

Exercise 6
a. divorced   f. stepfather
b. married   g. stepfather
c. single father   h. stepmother
d. remarried   i. half sister
e. married

Challenge (page 183)
a. 76%   b. 11%   c. 2%   d. Common law couples
with children

Pages 26 and 27   Daily Routines

Exercise 1

Time	Mai	David
6:00 a.m.	get up	wake up
6:30 a.m.	take a shower	get dressed
7:00 a.m.	make lunch	eat breakfast
8:00 a.m.	take the bus to school	drive to work
10:00 a.m.	school	work
6:00 p.m.	cook dinner	come home/ get home
6:30 p.m.	have dinner	have dinner
10:30 p.m.	go to bed	go to bed

Exercise 2
Words underlined:
David gets up before Mai.
Mai takes the kids to school.
David stays home.
Mai does homework./ Mai does homework.
David reads the paper./ David reads the paper.
They go to sleep at 10:30./ They go to sleep at 10:30.

Exercise 3
Possible answers:
a. David doesn't get up before Mai. He gets up after her.
b. Mai doesn't take the kids to school. David takes the kids/them to school.
c. David doesn't stay home. He works/goes to work.
d. Mai doesn't do homework. Her daughter does homework./Mai reads the paper.
e. David doesn't read the paper. He relaxes./Mai reads the paper.
f. They don't go to sleep at 10:30. They go to bed at 10:30./They go to sleep at 11:00.

Exercise 4
a. What time do you get up?
b. When do you eat breakfast?
c. When do you leave the house?
d. What time do you come home?
e. When do you go to bed?

Pages 28 and 29   Life Events

Exercise 1
a. 5   b. 19   c. 24   d. 33   e. 35   f. 46
g. 60   h. 72

Exercise 2
a. was born   f. went   k. married
b. moved   g. got   l. invented
c. lived   h. was   m. included
d. died   i. rented   n. continued
e. immigrated   j. formed   o. died

Exercise 3
a. False   b. True   c. False   d. ?   e. True

Exercise 4
Items checked:
passport, marriage licence, American Citizenship Papers

Exercise 5

Year	Event
1847	was born
1862	moved to England
1870	immigrated to Canada
1871	became a teacher of the deaf
1876	invented the telephone
1877	formed Bell Telephone Co.
1877	got married
1885	moved back to Canada
1922	died in Baddeck, Nova Scotia

Pages 30 and 31   Feelings

Exercise 1
a. uncomfortable   d. well
b. cold   e. sad
c. calm   f. hungry

Exercise 2
a. homesick   c. disgusted   e. full
b. in pain   d. relieved

Exercise 3
a. scared   e. embarrassed   i. lonely
b. calm   f. proud   j. in love
c. sleepy   g. happy
d. surprised   h. confused

Pages 32 and 33   A Graduation

Exercise 1
a. guest speaker
b. photographer
c. valedictorian/graduate

Exercise 2
a. podium   h. speech
b. class   i. audience
c. graduates   j. applauded
d. gowns   k. cried
e. stage   l. guest speaker
f. diplomas   m. graduated
g. valedictorian   n. took

Exercise 3
a. caterer   b. DJ (disc jockey)   c. guests

Exercise 4
Possible answers:
There are ten guests on Brian's dance floor. There are eight guests on Ana's dance floor.

There are people/guests dancing at Brian's party. There aren't any people dancing at Ana's party.

There is no caterer at Brian's party. There's a caterer at Ana's party.

There are two gifts on the buffet table at Brian's party. There are six gifts on the dance floor at Ana's party.

A man is making a toast at Brian's party. A woman is making a toast at Ana's party.

The DJ is laughing at Brian's party. The DJ isn't laughing at Ana's party.

Two graduates/women are hugging at Brian's party. Two graduates/women are kissing at Ana's party.

UNIT 3

Page 34   Places to live

Exercise 1
a. university residence   c. ranch
b. shelter   d. townhouse

Exercise 2
a. farm   e. house
b. apartment   f. suburbs
c. city   g. nursing home
d. country

Page 35   Finding a Home

Exercise 1
a. making an offer   c. taking ownership
b. arranging the furniture   d. getting a loan

Exercise 2
a. look for   f. make an offer
b. sign a lease   g. get a loan
c. buy a house   h. take ownership
d. Realtor   i. unpack
e. look for   j. mortgage

Pages 36 and 37   Apartments

Exercise 1
a. in the elevator
b. in the swimming pool
c. near the mailboxes/in the lobby
d. at/on the roof garden
e. in the garage
f. in the laundry room

Exercise 2
a. vacancy sign   g. garage
b. security   h. parking space
c. Intercom   i. Laundry room
d. air conditioners   j. Playground
e. balconies   k. Rec room
f. roof garden   l. manager

Exercise 3
a. neighbours   f. smoke detector
b. intercom   g. elevator
c. peephole   h. stairs
d. door chain   i. doorknob
e. deadbolt   j. fire escape

Page 38 A House

Exercise 1
c.

Exercise 2
(Answers may vary slightly.)

10 Pine Street's chimney is on the right, but 12's is on the left.

10 Pine Street has an eavestrough, but 12 doesn't have an eavestrough.

10 Pine Street has a good fence, but 12's fence is broken.

10 Pine Street's front walk is straight, but 12's is crooked.

10 Pine Street's driveway is clean/neat, but 12's is dirty/messy.

10 Pine Street's doorbell is to the right of the front door, 12's is to the left of the front door.

10 Pine Street's garage is to the left of the house, 12's is to the right of the house.

10 Pine Street has a porch light, but 12 doesn't.

10 Pine Street has a storm door in front of the front door, but 12 has a screen door in front of the front door.

10 Pine Street has four windows in front, but 12 has five windows.

10 Pine Street has a mailbox on the fence, but 12 has a mailbox near the front door.

10 Pine Street has one step, but 12 has two steps.

Page 39 A Yard

Exercise 1
a. barbecue
b. rake or leaf blower
c. hammock
d. wheelbarrow
e. sprinkler
f. hedge clippers
g. watering can/sprinkler
h. shovel

Exercise 2
a. bushes
b. trees
c. hedge
d. flowers
e. lawn

Page 40 A Kitchen

Exercise 1
a. kettle   b. dish drainer   c. paper towels
d. oven drawer

Exercise 2
a. False   b. True   c. False   d. True   e. True
f. False

Page 41 A Dining Area

Exercise 1
Possible answers:

5 placemats	1 teapot	4 napkins
3 coffee cups	1 sugar bowl	4 forks
3 glasses	1 creamer	1 tablecloth
5 plates	1 salt shaker	
1 tray	1 pepper shaker	

Exercise 2
a. tablecloth
b. ceiling fan
c. vase
d. serving dish
e. tray
f. creamer
g. candles

Page 42 A Living Room

Exercise 1
a. False, stereo system
b. True
c. True
d. False, coffee table
e. False, sofa/couch

Exercise 2
a. coffee table
b. bookcase
c. love seat
d. love seat
e. the same size as
f. bookcase

Page 43 A Bathroom

Exercise 1
a. hamper
b. scale
c. toilet paper
d. towel rack
e. drain
f. (mini)blinds

Exercise 2
a. bathtub
b. hot water
c. faucets/taps
d. shower head
e. rubber mat
f. bath mat
g. soap dish
h. sink
i. medicine cabinet
j. wastebasket
k. toilet

Page 44 A Bedroom

Exercise 1
a. False, pillow
b. False, night table
c. True
d. False, photograph
e. True

Exercise 2

Possible answers:

The bed frame is broken.
There is no headboard./The headboard is missing.
There is no chair./The chair is missing.
There is no lampshade./The lampshade is missing.
There is no night table./The night table is missing.
The dresser/bureau is missing a drawer.
There aren't enough outlets./There is only one outlet.
The window shade is broken.

Exercise 3

Possible answers:

sheets	bedspread	curtains
blanket	mirror	rug
pillow	clock radio	throw pillows
pillowcases	photographs	

Page 45 A Children's Bedroom

Exercise 1

a. sleeping, puzzle
b. safety, blocks
c. storage, picture book
d. playing, diaper pail
e. playing, comforter

Exercise 2

a. crib
b. comforter
c. change table
d. diaper pail
e. chest of drawers
f. mobile
g. wallpaper
h. stuffed animals
i. night light

Page 46 Housework

Exercise 1

a. cleaning
b. scrubbing
c. drying
d. mopping

Exercise 2

a. desk
b. dresser
c. vacuumed
d. dishes
e. sheets
f. the bed
g. take out
h. dishes

Page 47 Cleaning Supplies

Exercise 1

a. mop
b. gloves
c. bags
d. towel
e. bin
f. brush
g. cleaner
h. polish

Exercise 2

a. dust mop
b. garbage bags
c. vacuum cleaner
d. dish towel
e. rubber gloves
f. recycling bin
g. furniture polish
h. scrub brush

Exercise 3

(Reasons may vary.)

a. glass cleaner; You don't use it to clean the floor.
b. bucket; You don't use it to wash the dishes.
c. feather duster; You don't use it to wash the floor.

Pages 48 and 49
Household Problems and Repairs

Exercise 1

a. the plumber
c. the locksmith
b. the roofer
d. the repair person

Exercise 2

a. The door on our kitchen cabinet is broken.
b. *(Order may vary.)*
The pipe is frozen/leaking, the sink is (plugged and) overflowing, and the toilet is (plugged and) overflowing.
c. The bathroom window is broken.
d. The water heater is broken/isn't working.
e. There's a mouse in the cabin.

Exercise 3

a. True b. False c. True d. ? e. False f. ?
g. False h. ? i. True j. False

UNIT 4

Page 50 Fruit

Exercise 1

a. lemons
b. grapes
c. not ripe
d. over ripe

Exercise 2

a. watermelon
b. cherries
c. apricots
d. grapefruit
e. avocados
f. strawberries
g. limes

Exercise 3

a. ? b. True c. ? d. False e. ?
f. ? g. True h. False i. ? j. True
k. ?

Page 51 Vegetables

Exercise 1

Root vegetables:

radishes	turnips	yams
carrots	beets	

Leaf vegetables:

artichokes	spinach	cabbage
lettuce	parsley	

Vegetables with seeds:

chili peppers	eggplants	tomatoes
zucchini	cucumbers	peas
corn	green peppers	
squash	string beans	

Exercise 2

a. four potatoes
b. three carrots
c. two turnips
d. three tomatoes

e. three onions
f. garlic
g. two

Page 52 Meat and Poultry

Exercise 1

a. poultry, bacon
b. pork, tripe

c. lamb, wing
d. beef, gizzard

Exercise 2

a. sausage
b. lamb
c. beef roast

d. Bacon
e. Tripe
f. breast

g. ground beef
h. liver

Page 53 Deli and Seafood

Exercise 1

a. False, potato salad
b. True
c. True
d. False, mozzarella

e. True
f. False, halibut steaks
g. False, fresh
h. True

Exercise 2

a. $17.60
b. $17.50

c. $18.00
d. $12.50

e. $21.00
f. $29.04

Pages 54 and 55 The Supermarket

Exercise 1

a. canned goods, sugar
b. produce (section), rolls
c. dairy (section), ice cream
d. beverages, sour cream
e. baked goods, rice
f. snack foods, butter
g. meat and poultry (section), cheese
h. baking products, spaghetti
i. paper products, pet food

Exercise 2

a. cookies
b. cart
c. basket
d. coffee
e. beans
f. margarine
g. produce
h. vegetables
i. line

j. checkouts
k. manager
l. cash register
m. cashier
n. bottle return
o. bagger
p. paper/plastic
q. plastic/paper

Page 56
Containers and Packaged Foods

Exercise 1

a. bottles
b. jars
c. boxes
d. cartons
e. cans

f. bags
g. containers
h. rolls
i. packages
j. tubes

Exercise 2

Yes:

a bottle of oil
2 cans of tuna
a carton of milk

3 containers of yogurt
a jar of jam
a carton of eggs

No:

2 loaves of bread
a bag of string beans
2 boxes of rice

2 rolls of toilet paper
a tube of toothpaste
2 packages of spaghetti

Page 57 Weights and Measures

Exercise 1

a. 3 tablespoons
b. 1 litre
c. 500 millilitres

d. 1 tablespoon
e. 1 kilogram
f. 250 millilitres

Exercise 2

a. a cup of beans
b. 26
c. 948 mL

d. 24g
e. 30g
f. 9%

g. 12.5
h. 64%

Page 58 Food Preparation

Exercise 1

a. bake
b. barbecue
c. beat
d. boil
e. broil

f. chop/cut up
g. fry
h. grate
i. grill
j. mix

k. peel
l. sauté
m. simmer
n. steam

Exercise 2

a. Grease
b. Add

c. Mix
d. Pour

e. Slice
f. Bake

Page 59 Kitchen Utensils

Exercise 1

a. False, counter
b. True
c. False, lettuce
d. True

e. True
f. False, roast beef
g. False, cookies
h. True

Exercise 2

a. Whisk
b. Colander
c. Ladle
d. Paring
e. Lids

f. Plastic storage containers
g. Pot holders
h. Wooden spoons
i. Double boiler
j. pans

Page 60 Fast Food

Exercise 1
a. booth   b. counter   c. booth

Exercise 2
a. False   b. True   c. False   d. ?   e. True
f. False   g. ?

Exercise 3
a. 3   b. 2   c. 4   d. 1

Page 61 A Coffee Shop Menu

Exercise 1
a. desserts, mashed potatoes   d. lunch, sausage
b. breakfast, garlic bread   e. dinner, bacon
c. beverages, syrup

Exercise 2
a. soup   g. Pudding
b. a chef's salad   h. pancakes
c. coffee   i. syrup
d. roast chicken   j. sausage
e. rice pilaf   k. tea
f. coffee

Exercise 3
a. scrambled eggs, toast, and a cup of tea
b. a grilled cheese sandwich, chef's salad, and a cup of tea
c. steak, baked potato, pie, and a cup of coffee

Pages 62 and 63 A Restaurant

Exercise 1
a. hostess   d. server/waitress
b. server/waiter   e. busperson
c. patron/diner   f. dishwasher

Exercise 2
a. dining room   h. server   o. carried
b. diners   i. ordered   p. tray
c. seated   j. took   q. kitchen
d. bread basket   k. plates   r. cup
e. busperson   l. bowls   s. paid
f. pour   m. steak knife   t. left
g. menu   n. cleared

Exercise 3
a. place setting   g. soup spoon
b. dinner plate   h. fork
c. napkin   i. water glass
d. salad fork   j. wine glasses
e. dinner fork   k. bread-and-butter plate
f. knife   l. knife

UNIT 5

Pages 64 and 65 Clothing I

Exercise 1
a. The man in the sweatshirt and sweatpants.
b. The woman in the skirt and blouse.
c. The man in the three-piece suit.
d. The girl in the jumper.
e. The man in the uniform.
f. The boy/man in the jeans and shirt.
g. The woman in the maternity dress.
h. The boy in the overalls.
i. The man in the coveralls.

Exercise 2
a. suit   f. suit   k. cardigan
b. shirt   g. blouse   l. dress
c. sports coat   h. T-shirt   m. Slacks
d. shirt   i. skirt   n. jeans
e. turtleneck   j. blouse

Page 66 Clothing II

Exercise 1
a. raining, toque
b. cold/windy, cover-up
c. hot/warm/sunny/clear, parka
d. snowing, baseball cap

Exercise 2
parka → jacket
earmuffs → gloves
straw hat → cap/hat

Exercise 3
Possible answers:
a. It's sunny out there, but Abdulla is dressed for the weather in swimming trunks, a windbreaker, and a baseball cap. Those sunglasses protect him from the summer sun.
b. It's cold/snowing out there, but Polly is dressed for the weather in dark tights, a white vest, a turtleneck/sweater, and boots. Those white mittens and ski hat protect her from the winter snow.
c. It's rainy/raining out there, but Julio is dressed for the weather in a raincoat and black boots. That big black umbrella protects him from the spring rain.

Page 67 Clothing III

Exercise 1
bike shorts   (bikini) panties
pyjamas   underpants
slippers   knee-highs
boxer shorts   kneesocks
briefs   stockings
socks   pantyhose

Exercise 2
a. Bobby
   two sleepers
   two undershirts
   three pairs of socks
b. Inga
   one pair of bike shorts
   one tank top
   two bras
   two pairs of underpants
   two pairs of knee socks
   one nightshirt
c. Amanda
   one full slip
   two pairs of (bikini) panties
   two bras
   one pair of knee-highs
   two pairs of pantyhose
   one bathrobe
d. Julio
   one pair of long underwear
   one athletic supporter/jockstrap
   one pair of boxer shorts

Pages 68 and 69   Shoes and Accessories

Exercise 1
a. change purse   e. tote bag
b. (wrist)watch   f. locket
c. handkerchief   g. wallet
d. pin

Exercise 2
a. tie   e. ring
b. belt   f. earrings
c. buckle   g. shoulderbag/
d. track shoes   handbag/purse

Exercise 3
The Neck Stop
The Bag House/Accessories East
E.R. Jewellers
The Bag House/Accessories East
E.R. Jewellers
Foot Smart

Exercise 4
a. shoes   e. heel
b. toe   f. loafers
c. high heels   g. shoelaces
d. pumps   h. track shoes

Pages 70 and 71   Describing Clothes

Exercise 1
a. sweater styles, casual   d. types of material, plain
b. patterns, nylon   e. problems, sleeveless
c. sizes, too small

Exercise 2
a. linen   c. silk   e. wool
b. leather   d. cotton   f. nylon

Exercise 3
a. short   g. tight   m. striped
b. baggy   h. low   n. paisley
c. long   i. longer   o. solid
d. heavy   j. tighter   p. formal
e. long-sleeved k. fancy
f. longer   l. long

Page 72   Doing the Laundry

Exercise 1
a. True   b. False   c. False   d. True   e. False

Exercise 2
a. detergent   h. lint trap
b. washer   i. Load
c. Sort   j. wrinkled
d. Washer   k. dryer sheets
e. bleach   l. Dryer
f. washer   m. dry
g. fabric softener

Page 73   Sewing and Alterations

Exercise 1
a. safety pin   e. tape measure
b. (pair of) scissors f. zipper
c. pin cushion   g. hook and eye/button
d. seam ripper   h. thimble

Exercise 2
a. buttonhole   e. pocket
b. collar   f. Take in
c. waistband   g. hem
d. Shorten

UNIT 6

Pages 74 and 75   The Body

Exercise 1
a. 4   b. 2   c. 5   d. 6   e. 1   f. 3

Exercise 2
a. palms   i. nose   q. pelvis
b. eyes   j. lips   r. buttocks
c. hands   k. tongue   s. heels
d. face   l. mouth   t. hands
e. thumbs   m. abdomen   u. back
f. ears   n. ankles   v. wrist
g. finger   o. thighs   w. forehead
h. eyelashes   p. chest

Exercise 3
1. brain   5. liver   9. bladder
2. skin   6. gallbladder 10. intestines
3. heart   7. stomach   11. pancreas
4. lung   8. kidney   12. muscles

Pages 76 and 77 Personal Hygiene

Exercise 1
a. drying her hair
b. taking a shower
c. gargling
d. putting on sunscreen
e. rinsing her hair
f. shaving
g. combing her hair

Exercise 2
a. 3, emery board
b. 1, nail polish remover
c. 4, nail polish
d. 2, nail clipper

Exercise 3
a. hair clips
b. soap
c. moisturizer
d. foundation
e. eye shadow
f. an eyeliner
g. mascara
h. eyebrow pencil
i. blush
j. lipstick
k. face

Exercise 4

Answer to question: A HOT BATH

Page 78 Symptoms and Injuries

Exercise 1
a. toothache
b. fever/temperature
c. stomachache
d. blister
e. chills
f. bloody nose/sneeze

Exercise 2
a. sunburn
b. sprained
c. insect bites
d. vomit
e. sore throat
f. bruise
g. nasal congestion
h. cough

Page 79
Illnesses and Medical Conditions

Exercise 1
a. asthma
b. chicken pox
c. cold
d. diabetes
e. ear infection
f. flu
g. heart disease
h. HIV (human immunodeficiency virus)
i. measles
j. mumps
k. strep throat
l. TB (tuberculosis)

Challenge
Possible answer:
High blood pressure is a medical condition. It is not contagious. There are usually no symptoms unless the condition is severe. Severe symptoms are headache, drowsiness, confusion, numbness and tingling in the hands and feet, coughing blood, and severe shortness of breath/difficulty breathing.

Pages 80 and 81 Health Care

Exercise 1
a. False, exercising
b. True
c. False, an injection
d. True
e. False, optometrist
f. True

Exercise 2
a. cough syrup
b. ointment
c. capsules
d. ointment
e. capsules
f. cough syrup
g. ointment
h. capsules
i. capsules
j. cough syrup

Exercise 3
a. casts
b. sling
c. wheelchair
d. get bed rest
e. casts
f. braces
g. walker
h. crutches
i. physiotherapist
j. a heating pad
k. pain relievers
l. take medicine
m. Acupuncture
n. prescription medication
o. cane

Page 82 Medical Emergencies

Exercise 1
a. swallowed poison
b. got frostbite
c. got an electric shock
d. broke a bone
e. burned himself
f. is unconscious
g. is choking/choked

Exercise 2
a. injured
b. fell
c. drowned
d. burned themselves
e. bled
f. overdosed on drugs
g. had an allergic reaction

Page 83 First Aid

Exercise 1
a. gauze
b. tweezers
c. splint
d. sterile pad/gauze
e. tape
f. antibacterial ointment/hydrogen peroxide
g. adhesive bandage
h. hydrogen peroxide
i. elastic bandage
j. antihistamine cream
k. ice pack
l. stitches
m. medical alert bracelet

Exercise 2
a. Heimlich manoeuvre
b. artificial respiration
c. CPR

Page 84 Clinics

Exercise 1
a. eye chart
b. scale
c. medical information form
d. blood pressure gauge
e. syringe
f. thermometer
g. stethoscope

Exercise 2
a. tartar
b. dentist
c. hygienist
d. cavities
e. braces
f. patients
g. orthodontist
h. fillings

Page 85 Medical and Dental Exams

Exercise 1
a. looking in his throat
b. making an appointment
c. examining his eyes
d. taking his temperature
e. cleaning his teeth
f. drilling a tooth
g. giving a shot of anaesthetic

Exercise 2
a. check your blood pressure
b. listen to your heart
c. examine your eyes
d. look in your throat
e. draw blood
f. take an X-ray

Pages 86 and 87 A Hospital

Exercise 1
a. False, dress
b. True
c. True
d. False, lab
e. True
f. False, flowers
g. False, medication tray/medicine
h. True
i. False, paramedics
j. True

Exercise 2
a. operating
b. gurney
c. operating table
d. surgeon
e. caps
f. gloves
g. anaesthetist
h. vital signs
i. IV (intravenous drip)

Exercise 3
a. registered nurse
b. registered nursing assistant
c. intravenous drip

Exercise 4
a. radiologist
b. cardiologist
c. opthalmologist
d. pediatrician
e. psychiatrist
f. obstetrician/ gynecologist
g. general practitioner
h. anaesthetist
i. internist

Challenge
Possible answers:
An orthopedist is a bone doctor. An oncologist is a cancer specialist. A podiatrist is a foot doctor. A dermatologist is a skin doctor. A neurologist specializes in diseases of the nervous system.

UNIT 7

Pages 88 and 89 City Streets

Exercise 1
a. coffee shop, Main and Elm
b. bakery, Main and Pine
c. barber shop, Main
d. high-rise building, Second
e. bank, First and Elm
f. grocery store, First and Pine
g. gas station, Pine between First and Second
h. furniture store, Main and Elm
i. car dealership, First
j. hardware store, Main
k. hotel, First; *or* motel, Pine and Second

Exercise 2

a. skyscraper	f. City Hall
b. office buildings	g. hotel
c. Hospital	h. park
d. Post Office	i. school
e. Library	

Pages 90 and 91 An Intersection

Exercise 1

a. fast food restaurant	d. convenience store
b. drugstore/pharmacy	e. photo shop
c. dry cleaners	f. donut shop

Exercise 2

a. drive-thru window
b. copy centre/print shop
c. Laundromat
d. newsstand/convenience store/drugstore/pharmacy

Exercise 3

Words underlined:

motorcycle	streetlight
car	parking meter
nail salon	buses
mailbox	drive-thru window
in the crosswalk	

Exercise 4

Words changed in the article:

motorcycle → bicycle
car → cart
nail salon → donut shop
mailbox → fire hydrant
in the crosswalk → at the bus stop
streetlight → traffic light
parking meter → street sign
buses → garbage trucks
drive-thru window → pay phone

Pages 92 and 93 A Mall

Exercise 1

Items checked:

Buy a birthday card, card shop
Look at CD players, electronic store
Rent movies, video store
Plan a vacation, travel agency
Get new eyeglasses, optician
Buy flowers, florist
Buy a dictionary, bookstore
Buy a dog, pet store
Buy chocolates, candy store

Exercise 2

a. ice cream stand	e. shoe store
b. hair salon	f. jewellery store
c. music store	g. food court
d. escalator	h. information booth

Exercise 3

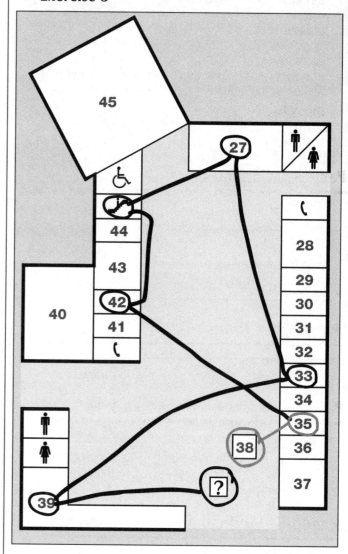

Pages 94 and 95 A Childcare Centre

Exercise 1

a. stroller	d. rocking chair
b. parent	e. on a change table
c. in the cubbies	

Exercise 2

a. feed	i. feed him
b. bottle	j. playpen
c. nurse	k. wipes
d. drop him off	l. disposable diapers
e. rock him	m. change her diapers
f. read him a story	n. dress
g. pick her up	o. tie
h. takes a nap	

Exercise 3
(Reasons may vary slightly.)
a. baby backpack; Babies don't sit on a backpack.
b. pacifier; Babies don't wear a pacifier.
c. disinfectant; Babies don't eat disinfectant.
d. diaper pail; Babies don't play with a diaper pail.
e. teething ring; Babies don't sit in a teething ring.

Exercise 4
a. high chair, bib
b. playpen
c. car safety seat
d. baby backpack/baby carrier

Page 96   Canada Post

Exercise 1
a. stamp
b. letter carrier
c. postmark
d. package

Exercise 2
a. Letter
b. Postage rate
c. Postcard
d. delivers
e. send
f. sender's
g. address
h. packages

Challenge
a. $.95/95¢
b. $.55/55¢
c. $4.46
d. $.95/95¢

Page 97   A Bank

Exercise 1
a. teller
b. security guard
c. safety deposit box, vault
d. PIN

Exercise 2
a. chequing account
b. savings account
c. bank card
d. deposit
e. deposit slip
f. balance
g. withdrew
h. transferred

Page 98   A Library

Exercise 1
a. atlas, encyclopedia
b. card catalogue
c. library card
d. checkout desk

Exercise 2
a. videocassettes
b. newspaper
c. periodical
d. magazines
e. microfilm
f. microfilm reader
g. CD/compact disc
h. encyclopedia
i. title
j. online catalogue

Page 99   The Legal System

Exercise 1
a. the suspect
b. the witness
c. the court reporter
d. the defendant
e. the convict
f. the bailiff

Exercise 2
a. went to prison
b. released
c. hire a lawyer
d. appeared in court
e. judge
f. stood trial
g. Crown counsel
h. jury
i. sentenced
j. jail

Page 100   Crime

Exercise 1
Crimes against people:
gang violence   assault
mugging   murder

Crimes against property:
vandalism   burglary

Substance abuse crimes:
drunk driving   illegal drugs

Exercise 2
a. assaults
b. burglaries
c. burglaries/assaults
d. murders
e. assaults
f. vandalism

Page 101   Public Safety

Exercise 1
a. Lock your doors.
b. Don't drink and drive.
c. Don't open your door to strangers.
d. Hold your purse close to your body.
e. Protect your wallet.
f. Walk with a friend.
g. Stay on well-lit streets.
h. Report crimes to the police.

Exercise 2
a. He isn't staying on well-lit streets.
b. He isn't walking with a friend.
c. He isn't protecting his wallet.

Pages 102 and 103
Emergencies and Natural Disasters

Exercise 1
a. volcanic eruption
b. tidal wave/hurricane
c. car accident
d. lost child
e. tornado

Exercise 2
a. earthquake
b. Airplane Crash
c. fire, firefighters
d. Explosion, search and rescue team
e. Hurricane
f. Blizzard
g. drought

UNIT 8

Page 104 Public Transportation

Exercise 1
a. transit pass, subway
b. schedule, bus stop
c. transfer, bus
d. meter, taxi/cab

Exercise 2
a. bus
b. fare
c. schedule
d. bus stop
e. subway
f. token
g. conductor
h. train station
i. ticket
j. train
k. platform
l. taxi stand
m. tracks
n. driver
o. ferry
p. meters

Page 105 Prepositions of Motion

Exercise 1
a. around the corner
b. off the highway
c. into the taxi
d. down/up the stairs

Exercise 2
a. go under
b. out of
c. across
d. onto
e. over

Page 106 Cars and Trucks

Exercise 1
a. tow truck
b. compact
c. tractor trailer/semi
d. RV
e. convertible
f. full-size car

Exercise 2
a. sport utility vehicle
b. sports car
c. minivan
d. subcompact
e. subcompact
f. full-size and sport utility vehicle

Page 107 Directions and Traffic Signs

Exercise 1
a. Elm and First
b. Pine and Second
c. Main and Oak
d. Main and Elm

Exercise 2
1. b   2. b   3. c   4. c   5. c   6. a
7. a

Pages 108 and 109
Parts of a Car and Car Maintenance

Exercise 1
a. 4   b. 2   c. 2   d. 1   e. 3   f. 1
g. 2   h. 1

Exercise 2
a. gas gauge
b. front seat
c. radio
d. air conditioning
e. glove compartment
f. rearview mirror
g. accelerator
h. temperature gauge
i. licence plate
j. stick shift

Exercise 3
a. steering wheel
b. tires
c. brake pedal
d. Turn signals
e. Brake lights
f. horn
g. Headlights
h. windshield
i. windshield wipers
j. speedometer
k. air bags
l. dashboard
m Seat belts
n. locks
o. gas
p. engine
q. radiator
r. oil
s. muffler

Challenge (page 184)
(Answers will vary.)
The car is a four-door 1994 Venus XL. It's black with tan leather seats. It has an automatic transmission, air conditioning, an AM/FM radio cassette player/tape deck, and power windows and locks. The car has 1400 kilometres on it, and it costs $14,000.

Page 110 An Airport

Exercise 1
a. passenger, carousel
b. airline representative, gate
c. customs officer, declaration form
d. flight attendant, oxygen mask

Exercise 2
a. the airline terminal
b. departure monitor
c. check-in counter
d. airline representative
e. gate
f. boarding area
g. overhead compartment
h. flight attendant
i. oxygen mask
j. seat belt
k. a declaration form
l. baggage claim area
m. carousel
n. customs

Page 111 A Plane Trip

Exercise 1
a. after   b. before   c. before

Exercise 2
a. True   b. False   c. False   d. False   e. True
f. ?   g. ?   h. True   i. False   j. True
k. False   l. False   m. True   n. ?   o. True
p. ?

UNIT 9

Page 112 Types of Schools

Exercise 1
a. high school
b. vocational school/ trade school
c. adult school
d. preschool

Exercise 2
a. High School, public
b. Adult School, public
c. Preschool, private
d. Vocational School/Trade School, private
e. College/University, private
f. Elementary, public
g. Middle School/Junior High School, Catholic/ Separate School

Exercise 3
a. a   b. d   c. b   d. c   e. f   f. e

Page 113 English Composition

Exercise 1
a. Oct. 1   b. Sept. 27   c. Oct. 3

Exercise 2
a. True   b. ?   c. True   d. False   e. False
f. True   g. False   h. False   i. True   j. False
k. True   l. ?

Page 114 Government and Citizenship in Canada

Exercise 1
a. Federal
b. Members of Parliament
c. Prime Minister
d. Members of Provincial Parliament
e. Provinical
f. Territorial
g. Premier
h. Municipal
i. Councillor
j. Mayor
k. representatives
l. election

Exercise 2
a. 18
b. permanent
c. basic
d. English or French
e. three
f. responsibilities

Pages 115 and 116 Canadian History Timeline

Exercise 1
Possible answers:

a. Jacques Cartier's voyages	1534-1531
b. Battle of Plains of Abraham	1759
War of 1812	1812
World War I	1914-1918
World War II	1939-1945
c. Confederation	1867
Canada's Centennial	1967
New Canadian Flag	1965
d. First settlement at Port Royal	1604
Colony of British Columbia established	1866
e. Free Trade Agreement	1989
NAFTA	1994
f. Red River Rebellion	1869
North-West Rebellion	1885

Exercise 2
1. b   2. a   3. b   4. a
5. c   5. a   7. b   8. a

Exercise 3
a. Confederation, (1867)
b. internment of the Japanese, (1942)
c. right to vote, (1918)
d. The Great Depression (1929-1934)
e. maple leaf flag, (1965)
f. Constitution, (1982)

Page 117 Geography

Exercise 1
a. False, rain forest
b. True
c. False, An island
d. True
e. False, meadow
f. False, sand dune
g. True

Exercise 2
a. waterfall
b. ocean
c. mountain peak
d. river
e. desert
f. island
g. lake

Page 118 Mathematics

Exercise 1

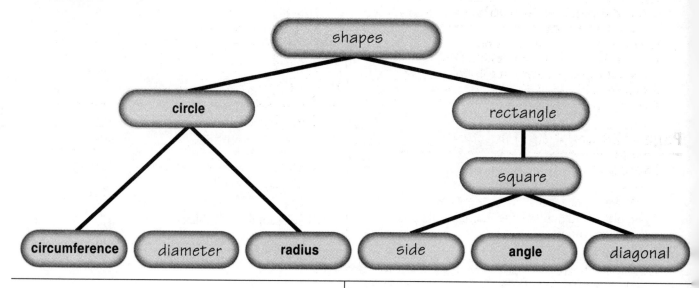

Exercise 2
a. square
b. A triangle
c. longer
d. straight
e. parallel
f. Perpendicular
g. geometry
h. cube

Exercise 3
a. cube
b. four
c. division
d. solid
e. pyramid
f. difference

Page 119 Science

Exercise 1
a. Physics   b. Chemistry   c. Biology

Exercise 2
a. crucible tongs
b. graduated cylinder
c. Bunsen burner
d. balance
e. funnel
f. forceps

Exercise 3
(Order may vary.)
beaker, Bunsen burner, test tube, dropper, slide

Challenge
Experiment 1: The egg rises.
Experiment 2: The paper stays dry.

Page 120 Music

Exercise 1
a. brass, bass
b. percussion, clarinet
c. strings, organ
d. woodwinds, xylophone

Exercise 2
a. violins
b. clarinet
c. other instruments
d. strings
e. bassoon
f. trombone
g. clarinet

Page 121   More School Subjects

Exercise 1
a. Computer Science
b. English as a Second Language
c. Foreign Language
d. Theatre Arts
e. Phys. Ed. (Physical Education)
f. Family Studies
g. Industrial Arts/Shop
h. Art
i. Economics
j. Law
k. Business Education
l. Choir

Pages 122 and 123
North America and Central America

Exercise 1
a. Canada, Alaska
b. States, Baja California
c. Louisiana
d. Countries, Ontario
e. Atlantic Provinces
f. Regions, Prairie Provinces
g. Southern Uplands
h. Islands, Costa Rica

Exercise 2
a. southwest
b. Honduras, Costa Rica
c. Haiti
d. Prince Edward Island
e. Chihuahua
f. Pacific
g. Atlantic Ocean
h. Hawaii
i. Yucatán Peninsula
j. Cuba

Exercise 3
a. False, north
b. True
c. False, south
d. True
e. False, east
f. True
g. True
h. True

Challenge
Possible answers include:
Corn is grown in many places. (Baja California South, Chihuahua, Coahuila, Sinaloa, Nuevo Leon, Guerrero, Oaxaca)
Coconuts grow in Quintana Roo.
Glass products are made in Coahuila.
Cattle is/Cows are raised in Chihuahua.
Sheep are raised in Baja California Sur.
Pigs are raised in Sinaloa.

Pages 124 and 125 The World

Exercise 1
a. seven
b. Africa
c. Europe
d. bigger
e. Asia
f. six
g. Russia
h. six
i. bigger
j. Turkey

Exercise 2
a. Angola is bigger than Uganda.
b. Italy is warmer than Finland.
c. Laos is smaller than Thailand.
d. Argentina is wider than Chile.
e. Antarctica is colder than Australia.
f. The Red Sea is narrower/more narrow than the Arabian Sea.
g. *(Answers will vary.)*

Exercise 3
Possible answers include:

Africa:
Chad, Niger, Mali, Central African Republic, Burkina Faso, Zambia, Zimbabwe, Botswana

Europe:
Czech Republic, Slovakia, Hungary, Romania, Switzerland, Belarus, Moldova, Luxembourg, Liechtenstein, Austria, Serbia

South America:
Paraguay, Bolivia

Asia:
Mongolia, Bhutan, Nepal, Afghanistan, Tajikistan

Exercise 4
a. Mexico, (North) Pacific
b. Madagascar, Indian
c. Austria, Italy
d. China, Thailand
e. Liberia, Sierra Leone
f. Ecuador, Pacific Ocean/Galápagos Islands
g. Latvia, Ukraine
h. Afghanistan, Iran

Page 126 Energy and the Environment

Exercise 1
a. Solar
b. natural gas
c. wind
d. Hydroelectric power
e. radiation
f. Old batteries
g. Acid rain
h. recycle

Exercise 2
Items checked:
a. energy, water
b. water pollution
c. energy, air pollution
d. energy, trees
e. energy
f. water
g. energy, air pollution
h. hazardous waste
i. energy
j. pesticide poisoning

Page 127 The Universe

Exercise 1
a. Mars
b. Venus
c. Earth
d. Saturn
e. Pluto
f. Jupiter
g. Uranus
h. Neptune
i. Mercury

Exercise 2
a. planets
b. telescope
c. astronomer
d. asteroids
e. Constellations
f. galaxy
g. new moon

UNIT 10

Page 128 Trees and Plants

Exercise 1
Colourful flowers:
dogwood, magnolia, cactus

Berries:
poison sumac, holly, poison oak

Needles:
spruce, pine

Leaves that can give you a rash:
poison oak, poison sumac, poison ivy

Exercise 2
a. plants
b. Sitka spruce
c. trunk
d. roots
e. trunk
f. leaves
g. maple
h. pine
i. cones
j. trunk
k. palm
l. leaves
m. branches
n. magnolia
o. oak

Page 129 Flowers

Exercise 1
a. 2 irises
b. 4 tulips
c. 3 daffodils
d. 1 white lily
e. 2 chrysanthemums
f. 2 orchids

Exercise 2
a. Lilies, crocuses
b. Marigolds, violets, gardenias
c. Gardenias
d. carnations
e. roses

Pages 130 and 131
Marine Life, Amphibians, and Reptiles

Exercise 1
a. 3   b. 5   c. 2   d. 6   e. 4   f. 1

Exercise 2
a. jellyfish   e. dolphin
b. sea anemone   f. octopus
c. ray   g. shark
d. swordfish   h. snail

Exercise 3
a. flounder   g. turtle's
b. squid   h. urchin
c. octopus   i. dolphins
d. amphibians   j. whales
e. frogs   k. sea lions
f. rattlesnake

Exercise 4
a. O   d. R   g. D
b. L   e. E   h. I
c. O   f. C   j. C
Unscrambled letters: crocodile

Page 132 Birds, Insects, and Arachnids

Exercise 1
Birds: feathers, claws, two legs, a beak
Both: wings
Insects and Arachnids: six or eight legs

Exercise 2
a. honeybee   i. woodpecker
b. goose   j. penguin
c. tick   k. mosquito
d. robin   l. cricket
e. ladybug   m. blue jay
f. owl   n. fly
g. butterfly   o. peacock
h. hummingbird

Page 133
Domestic Animals and Rodents

Exercise 1
a. kitten, puppy   e. groundhog
b. hen, rooster, parakeet   f. goat, cow, sheep
c. goldfish   g. hen
d. chipmunk   h. donkey, horse

Exercise 2
a. Dogs   c. parakeets   e. rats
b. Cats   d. goldfish   f. rabbits

Challenge (page 185)
a. A cat is bigger than a kitten.
b. A puppy is younger than a dog.
c. A mouse is smaller than a rat.
d. A horse is faster than a donkey.
e. A pig is fatter than a goat.
f. A rooster is more colourful than a hen.

Pages 134 and 135 Mammals

Exercise 1
horns: buffalo/bison, rhinoceros, antelope
quills: porcupine
antlers: deer, moose
tusks: elephant
a bad smell: skunk
Other forms of protection: (possible answers) hoof, tail, claws, teeth, colour, poison

Exercise 2
a. bear   e. monkey/lion,
b. giraffe   lion/monkey
c. leopard   f. kangaroo
d. rhinoceros   g. elephant

Exercise 3
bat, North America   elephant, Asia
bear, North America   leopard, Asia and Africa
wolf, North America   panda, Asia
fox, North America   gorilla Africa
armadillo, South America   rhinoceros, Africa
tiger, Asia   zebra, Africa

UNIT 11

Pages 136 and 137
Jobs and Occupations, A–H

Exercise 1
a. Dentist   c. Doctor   e. Cashier
b. Baker   d. Butcher   f. Architect

Exercise 2
a. firefighter   d. garment worker
b. florist   e. computer programmer
c. more

Exercise 3
g. Caregiver/Babysitter   l. Florist
h. Cook   m. Auto Mechanic
i. Bricklayer   n. Carpenter
j. Assembler   o. Actor
k. Engineer   p. Administrative Assistant

Pages 138 and 139
Jobs and Occupations, H–W

Exercise 1
(Reasons may vary.)
a. model; A model doesn't work in an office.
b. truck driver; A truck driver doesn't work in a clinic/doesn't have a health-care job.
c. mover; A mover doesn't work in a store.
d. serviceman; A serviceman doesn't use tools/ doesn't wear a mask. A serviceman works for the government.
e. housekeeper; A housekeeper doesn't work in a classroom/school.

Exercise 2
a. Instructor, Student
b. Lawyer, Interpreter
c. Reporter, Police officer
d. Telemarketer, Repair person
e. Musician, Travel agent
f. Messenger, Receptionist

Exercise 3
a. True b. False c. False d. False e. True
f. True g. True h. True

Page 140 Job Skills

Exercise 1
a. uses a cash register
b. cooks
c. assists medical patients
d. sews clothes
e. types/works on a computer
f. waits on customers
g. speaks another language
h. takes care of children

Exercise 3
a. True b. False c. True d. True e. False
f. True g.–i. *(Answers will vary.)*

Page 141 Job Search

Exercise 1
a. before b. After c. Before d. after

Exercise 2
a. Talk to friends
b. Look for help wanted signs
c. Look at job boards
d. look in the classifieds
e. call for information
f. Ask about the hours
g. fill out an application
h. go to the interview
i. talk about your experience
j. Inquire about the salary
k. Ask about benefits
l. get hired

Pages 142 and 143 An Office

Exercise 1
(Reasons may vary.)
a. microcassette transcriber; A microcassette transcriber isn't a person.
b. pencil sharpener; A pencil sharpener isn't furniture.
c. rubber stamp; A rubber stamp isn't paper.
d. paper cutter; A paper cutter doesn't hold things together.
e. stapler; A stapler doesn't have numbers/a keyboard. A stapler doesn't need an outlet.

Exercise 2
a. 5 b. 6 c. 3 d. 1 e. 2 f. 4

Exercise 3
a. pushpins
b. correction fluid
c. paper shredder
d. appointment book
e. legal pad
f. postal scale

Exercise 4
(Answers may vary slightly.)
a. He didn't use letterhead. He used plain paper.
b. He didn't make three copies. He made two copies.
c. He didn't collate the copies/pages.
d. He didn't staple the pages. He used paper clips.
e. He didn't leave them on R. Smith's desk. He left them on M. Shakter's desk.

Exercise 5
a. photocopier
b. rotary card file
c. labels
d. calendar
e. clear
f. cutter
g. Transcribe
h. microcassette
i. ink

Page 144 Computers

Exercise 1
a. program
b. keyboard
c. CPU
d. disk/floppy
e. disk drive
f. hard disk drive
g. monitor
h. printer
i. modem
j. CD ROM
k. laptop, mouse
l. scanner

Challenge
Possible answers:
power switch: the part that turns the computer on and off
cable: a plastic or rubber tube that has wires
port: part of the computer where you can connect another piece of equipment in it

Page 145 A Hotel

Exercise 1
a. door, doorman
b. bell captain
c. guests, desk clerk
d. cart, bellhop
e. make, housekeeper

Exercise 2

a. guest
b. guest rooms
c. room service
d. pool
e. valet parking
f. gift shop
g. meeting room
h. ballroom

Page 146   A Factory

Exercise 1

a. front office
b. factory owner
c. factory worker
d. parts
e. line supervisor
f. packer
g. warehouse
h. loading dock
i. ship
j. designer
k. design
l. manufacture

Page 147   Job Safety

Exercise 1

a. poison
b. flammable
c. poison
d. corrosive
e. explosive

Exercise 2

a. Equipment
b. hard hat
c. hair net
d. glasses
e. goggles
f. earplugs
g. earmuffs
h. gloves
i. hazardous
j. boots
k. flammable
l. fire extinguisher
m. careful

Challenge (page 186)

Possible answers:
She's wearing sandals. She should wear safety boots.
She has long hair. She should wear a hair net.
She should wear ear plugs or safety earmuffs.
The floor is wet. She should mop the floor.
She shouldn't use power tools near flammable material/liquids.

Page 148   Farming and Ranching

Exercise 1

Possible answers:
a. goats, cows
b. corn, alfalfa
c. cotton
d. lettuce, tomatoes, cabbage
e. oranges
f. grapes

Exercise 2

a. farm
b. farmer
c. barn
d. milking
e. feed
f. livestock
g. vegetable garden
h. fruit
i. field
j. farm equipment
k. tractor
l. farmworkers
m. crops
n. alfalfa
o. harvest

Page 149   Construction

Exercise 1

a. False, eleven
b. True
c. False, an I beam/a girder
d. True
e. False, jackhammer/pneumatic drill

Exercise 2

a. shovel
b. bulldozer
c. Insulation
d. crane
e. trowel, concrete
f. pickaxe

Pages 150 and 151
Tools and Building Supplies

Exercise 1

a. hardware, outlet
b. plumbing, axe
c. power tools, hammer
d. paint, chisel
e. electrical, drill bit
f. hand tools, flashlight

Exercise 2

a. extension cord
b. roller
c. plunger
d. tape measure/metrestick *or* metrestick/tape measure
e. vise
f. masking tape
g. electrical tape
h. level
i. flashlight

Exercise 3

(Answers may vary slightly.)
a. That's a Phillips screwdriver. You need the other kind.
b. That's a screwdriver. You need a hammer.
c. There are four bolts and four washers, but only three nuts. You need one more nut.
d. That's a pair of pliers. You need a pipe wrench.
e. You need to remove the old paint with a scraper before you paint the wall.

UNIT 12

Page 152   Places to Go

Exercise 1

a. baseball game
b. Stadium
c. Art Gallery
d. sculpture
e. roller coaster
f. Puppet show
g. amusement
h. the Movies
i. seats
j. Zoo
k. animals
l. zookeeper
m. Flea Market
n. booths
o. merchandise
p. Botanical Gardens
q. Carnival
r. Fair

Exercise 2
a. baseball game
b. botanical gardens
c. flea market
d. amusement park/carnival *or*
   carnival/amusement park

Page 153 The Park and Playground

Exercise 1
a. ball field
b. picnic table
c. duck pond
d. swings
e. bike path
f. sandbox
g. tennis court

Exercise 2
a. skipping rope
b. tricycle
c. water fountain
d. climbing apparatus
e. seesaw/swings
f. bench

Page 154 Outdoor Recreation

Exercise 1
camping stove → campfire
rope → fishing rod
rafting → canoeing
canoeing → rafting
hiking → backpacking
life vest → backpack
backpacking → hiking

Exercise 2
a. matches
b. insect repellent
c. canteen
d. multi-use knife
e. foam pad
f. lantern

Page 155 The Beach

Exercise 1
a. wet suits
b. fins
c. lifesaving device
d. sunscreen/sunblock
e. seashell

Exercise 2
a. Sand Castle
b. umbrella
c. beach
d. waves
e. ocean
f. cooler
g. Sailboats
h. scuba

Pages 156 and 157 Sports Verbs

Exercise 1
throw   hit   dribble/bounce
catch   pass   kick
pitch   shoot

Exercise 2
a. walk
b. jog
c. swimming
d. dive
e. exercise
f. work out
g. stretching
h. race
i. finish
j. throw
k. ride
l. skate

Exercise 3
a. False, walking
b. True
c. True
d. False, serving
e. False, diving
f. False, skating
g. True

Exercise 4
a. Walking
b. Jogging
c. running
d. Walking
e. Skating
f. Swimming

Page 158 Team Sports

Exercise 1
a. face off circle
c. o
b. goalie
d. defence

Exercise 2
a. False   b. True   c. True   d. False   e. False
f. True   g. False h. True   i. True   j. ?

Page 159 Individual Sports

Exercise 1
Possible answers:
a. track and field; It doesn't use a ball.
b. gymnastics; It doesn't need two people.
c. archery; It doesn't need wheels.
d. weightlifting; You don't ride.
e. martial arts; You don't throw something.

Exercise 2
a. Biking
b. Racquetball
c. tennis
d. Golf
e. golf
f. biking
g. bowling

Page 160
Winter Sports and Water Sports

Exercise 1
a. skating, figure skating
b. sailing, sailboarding
c. surfing
d. waterskiing
e. downhill skiing, sledding, snowboarding
f. snorkelling, scuba diving

Exercise 2
a. speed skating
b. cross-country skiing
c. figure skating
d. downhill skiing
e. snowboarding
f. Figure skating

Page 161 Sports Equipment

Exercise 1
a. weights
b. arrows
c. bowling ball
d. inline skates
e. uniform
f. football helmet/
   catcher's mask
g. flying discs
h. skis
i. shin guards

Exercise 2

a. They buy more basketballs than soccer balls.
b. They buy more golf clubs than hockey sticks.
c. They buy more golf clubs than tennis racquets.
d. They buy more basketballs than tennis racquets.

Pages 162 and 163   Hobbies and Games

Exercise 1

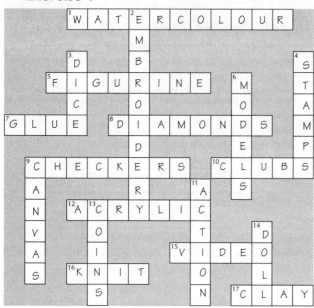

Exercise 2

(Reasons may vary.)
a. crochet; It's not a board game.
b. dolls; They aren't cards./They aren't on cards.
c. clay; It's not paint.
d. yarn; It's not a hobby/craft.
e. cartridge; It's not a tool.

Exercise 3

a. cards   c. chess   e. checkers
b. video games   d. chess

Exercise 4

a. playing cards c. pretending
b. knitting   d. collecting things

Pages 164 and 165
Electronics and Photography

Exercise 1

a. clock radio
b. portable TV
c. photo album
d. personal radio-cassette player with headphones
e. portable radio-cassette player/cassette recorder/
   personal radio-cassette player
f. remote control
g. headphones
h. shortwave radio

Exercise 2

a. radio, TV (television), VCR (videocassette recorder)
b. camcorder
c. CD player
d. CD player

Exercise 4

a. play   e. stop (and eject)
b. rewind   f. fast forward
c. pause   g. (stop and) eject
d. record

Exercise 5

a. photo   c. overexposed
b. tripod   d. zoom lens

Pages 166 and 167   Entertainment

Exercise 1

a. western   g. talk show
b. news   h. science fiction story
c. cartoon   i. shopping program
d. comedy   j. soap opera
e. game show/quiz show   k. nature program
f. sitcom   l. concert, ballet, or opera
   (situation comedy)

Exercise 2

a. True   b. False   c. False   d. True   e. ?

Exercise 3

a. science fiction story   e. cartoon
b. opera   f. television
c. comedy   g. Ballet
d. horror story   h. film

Page 168   Holidays

Exercise 1

a. card, heart, Valentine's Day
b. parade, Year
c. flag, fireworks, Canada Day
d. ornaments, Christmas
e. feast, turkey, Thanksgiving
f. Jack-o'-lantern, mask, candy, Halloween

Exercise 2

a. Halloween   d. Halloween
b. Valentine's Day   e. Thanksgiving
c. Christmas

Page 169   A Party

Exercise 1

a. answered the door
b. shouted "surprise!"
c. invited the guests
d. decorated the house
e. lit the candles
f. sang "Happy Birthday"
g. blew out the candles
h. made a wish
i. opened the presents
j. wrapped

Page 170 Another Look (Unit 1)

Possible answers include:

Both of these classes are ESL classes. One class is ESL 101, the other class is ESL 102.

Both classes have six students. In class 101, half the students are women, but in 102, two thirds of the students are women.

Class 101 is a winter class, and it's cold. The date is January 20. Class 102 is a spring class, and it's hot. The date is May 4.

Both classes have the same teacher. The board in class 101 says Ms. Mary Lyons; the board in 102 says Mary Lyons.

Class 101 meets three days a week: Monday, Wednesday, and Friday. Class 102 meets two days a week: Tuesday and Thursday. Class 101 is an hour. Class 102 is an hour and a half. The clocks in both classes say 6:05.

There's an easy sentence on the board in class 101. There's a more difficult/harder sentence on the board in class 102.

The teacher is standing in front of the classroom in 101. She is sitting with the students in 102.

In 101 the teacher's desk is closer to the students. It is very neat. In 102 the teacher's desk is against the wall. It's messy.

One of the students in 101 has a beeper. The same student in 102 has a cellular phone.

Page 171 Another Look (Unit 2)

Answers will vary.

Page 172 Another Look (Unit 3)

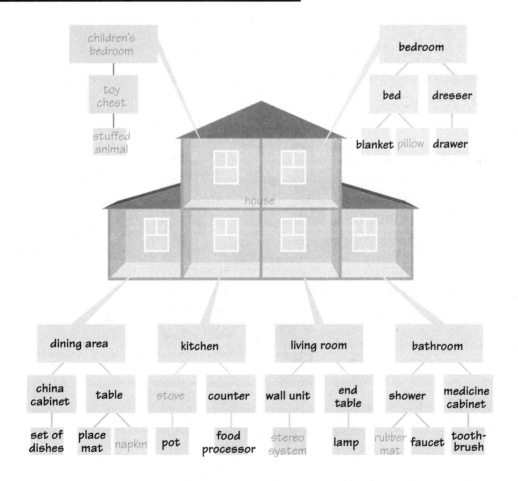

```
X  B  S  M  A  Y  B  E  A  N  S
W  P  O  P  N  J  U  I  C  E  A
M  B  U  A  U  Z  T  H  A  M  N
I  R  P  S  T  W  T  P  R  S  D
L  E  T  T  U  C  E  R  R  A  W
K  A  F  A  R  X  R  I  O  L  I
N  D  C  A  K  E  D  C  T  A  C
U  Q  C  H  E  E  S  E  G  D  H
T  O  F  U  Y  O  G  U  R  T  A
C  A  N  D  Y  C  E  R  E  A  L
```

Grain Group	Fruits and Vegetables	Milk Products	Meats and Meat Alternatives	Other	Mixed Foods
cereal	lettuce	milk	turkey	candy	soup
bread	carrot	yogurt	nut	butter	salad
rice	juice	cheese	tofu	pop	sandwich
pasta	yams		ham	cake	
			beans		
			tuna		

Page 174 Another Look (Unit 5)

Answers will vary.

```
 I  D     F  L  O  S  S        C  A  V  I  T  Y
    I        P     E           P     I     O
 B  A  R  R  E  T  T  E        R     T  B
    B        O                 A        T
 P  E  R  F  U  M  E     S  H  A  M  P  O  O
    T        E     C           I     U
 H  E  A  D     T  U     C     N  E  C  K
    S        C  R  U  T  C  H  E  S     H
       B     I        E                 S
       R     S  U  R  G  E  O  N     S  N
    V  O  M  I  T     A     K        C  E
       K     N        Z           T  A  P  E
 T  O  E     I     O  V  E  R     L        Z
    N     F  E  V  E  R        N     E  Y  E
```

Page 176 Another Look (Unit 7)

Possible answers:

There was a bakery on the southeast corner of Elm and Grove. Now there's a coffee shop.

There's still a furniture store on Grove.

There was a florist and barber shop on Grove. Now there's a shoe store.

There was a small movie theatre on the southwest corner of Grove and Oak. Now there's a large movie theatre there.

There's still a bus stop in front of the movie theatre.

There's still a library on the northwest corner of Oak and Grove, but the library is bigger now.

There was a park on the northeast corner of Oak and Grove. Now there's a parking garage.

There was a five-storey apartment building on the southeast corner of Oak and Grove. Now there's a seven-storey apartment building.

Fifty years ago there was a fire on Grove Street. Now there is a fire hydrant in front of the library.

There was a Laundromat on Grove Street. Now there's a photo shop.

There was a music store on the northeast corner of Elm and Grove. Now there's a convenience store there. There are now parking meters on the north side of Grove. The music store is now on the southwest corner of Elm and Grove, and there is a fire hydrant in front of it. Fifty years ago there were a pet store and a travel agent on that corner.

There was a stop sign on the southeast corner of Elm and Grove. Now there's a traffic light there.

There was a mailbox on the southeast corner of Elm and Grove. Now there are two mailboxes there.

There was a bank on the northwest corner of Elm and Grove. The bank is sill there, but now it has a bank machine.

Page 177 Another Look (Unit 8)

(Answers may vary slightly.)
There's a bus on a train track.
The taxi cab is missing a wheel.
There's a plane flying under the bridge.
The station wagon doesn't have doors.
A car is turning left onto a street that has a no left turn sign.
The car is turning left, but its right turn signal is on.
The car's licence plate is on wrong/upside down.
There's a car parked at a bus stop.
There's a child safety seat under the car's hood.
There's an air traffic control tower on the street corner.
A plane is taking off from/landing on a building.

Page 178 (Unit 9) Another Look

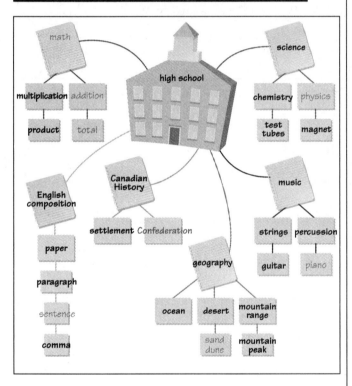

Page 179 Another Look (Unit 10)

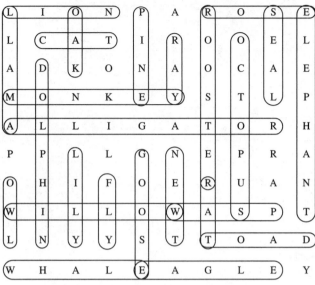

Flowers: lily, rose
Sea Animals: ray, octopus
Amphibians: toad, newt
Insects: fly, wasp
Mammals: llama, lion, monkey, elephant, cat
Sea Mammals: whale, seal, dolphin
Trees and Plants: willow, oak, pine
Birds: owl, goose, rooster, eagle
Reptiles: alligator
Rodents: rat

Page 180 Another Look (Unit 11)

Top Left Picture
a. a (cheese) factory/an assembly line
b. working on an assembly line
c. conveyor belt
d. be able to assemble

Top Right Picture
a. a farm
b. feeding cows
c. bucket/pail
d. be able to do manual labour

Bottom Left Picture
a. an office
b. using computers, having meetings, reading reports
c. computers, telephones
d. be able to type, be able to work on a computer

Bottom Right Picture
a. a construction site
b. lifting wood/lumber, using tools
c. (power) saw; hammers
d. be able to do manual labour, be able to use a hammer
(Answers to questions e.-g. will vary.)

¹P		²S	U	R	F	I	N	G		⁴S	A	D	⁵D
U		L					E					⁶O	⁷I	L
⁸S	E	E	S	A	W		W			⁹S		C	
H		D				¹⁰F		¹¹M	¹²A	T	C	H	E	¹³S
	¹⁴C	D		¹⁵P	A	I	L		M		O			T
		I			E				U		R			A
¹⁶B	E	N	D		¹⁷P	L	A	Y	S		E		¹⁸M	M
O		G			D				E					P
¹⁹U	P		²⁰F		²¹S		M		²²B				S
N		²³T	R	I	C	Y	C	L	E		O		²⁴P
C		E		L		R		N		R		O
E		N		M		E		²⁵T	R	I	P	O	D
		T				E				N		L
			²⁶O	C	E	A	N		²⁷J	O	G